Intercultural Language Teaching and Learning

Intercultural Language Teaching and Learning

Anthony J. Liddicoat and Angela Scarino

This research-based survey of teaching and learning practice in intercultural language education explores the full spectrum of methodological issues. Its focus on the intercultural aspects of language teaching and learning is vitally relevant to our increasingly integrated world, reflecting the current consensus that learning languages plays a crucial role in developing our understanding of the rich diversity of human cultures. The text offers trainee and practicing teachers, as well as researchers and graduate students, a ready point of access to the wealth of insight and experience accumulated by the authors over a decade of research. Underpinned by the material generated throughout years of collaboration with working teachers, the work features detailed documentation of teaching practice spanning a multitude of languages.

Progressing from a discussion of core theoretical concepts in language, culture, and learning, the book provides detailed assessment of numerous factors related to teaching languages, including classroom interactions, technologies, program evaluation, language assessment, and professional development. It provides a much-needed practical resource for teachers preparing to develop language programs in which intercultural understanding has a central role to play. Eschewing prescriptive notions of "method," the authors advocate a responsive pedagogy that is open to the particularities of context and adapts to the diverse requirements of language learners.

WILEY-
BLACKWELL

Anthony J. Liddicoat is Professor in Applied Linguistics at the Research Centre for Languages and Cultures in the School of Communication, International Studies and Languages at the University of South Australia.

Angela Scarino is Associate Professor in Applied Linguistics and Director of the Research Centre for Languages and Cultures in the School of Communication, International Studies and Languages at the University of South Australia.

WILEY-
BLACKWELL

Intercultural Language Teaching and Learning

Anthony J. Liddicoat and Angela Scarino

A John Wiley & Sons, Ltd., Publication

This edition first published 2013
© 2013 Anthony J. Liddicoat and Angela Scarino

Blackwell Publishing was acquired by John Wiley & Sons in February 2007. Blackwell's publishing program has been merged with Wiley's global Scientific, Technical, and Medical business to form Wiley-Blackwell.

Registered Office
John Wiley & Sons, Ltd, The Atrium, Southern Gate, Chichester, West Sussex, PO19 8SQ, UK

Editorial Offices
350 Main Street, Malden, MA 02148-5020, USA
9600 Garsington Road, Oxford, OX4 2DQ, UK
The Atrium, Southern Gate, Chichester, West Sussex, PO19 8SQ, UK

For details of our global editorial offices, for customer services, and for information about how to apply for permission to reuse the copyright material in this book please see our website at www.wiley.com/wiley-blackwell.

The right of Anthony J. Liddicoat and Angela Scarino to be identified as the authors of this work has been asserted in accordance with the UK Copyright, Designs and Patents Act 1988.

Library of Congress Cataloging-in-Publication Data

Liddicoat, Anthony, 1962– author.
  Intercultural Language Teaching and Learning / Anthony J. Liddicoat and Angela Scarino.
    pages cm
  ISBN 978-1-4051-9810-3 (cloth)
1. Language and languages–Study and teaching.   2. Intercultural communication–Study and teaching.
3. Language and culture–Study and teaching.   4. Multicultural education.   5. Communicative competence.
I. Scarino, Angela, author.
  P53.45.L53 2013
  418.0071–dc23
                                        2012045274

A catalogue record for this book is available from the British Library.

Cover image: © Nicholas Eveleigh / Alamy
Cover design by Nicki Averill Design

Set in 11/13pt Dante by SPi Publisher Services, Pondicherry, India

1   2013

Contents

Acknowledgments

The authors and publisher gratefully acknowledge the permission granted to reproduce the copyright material in this book: Pearson Education Australia for the material from *Ecco Uno!* on p. 87 and *Katzensprung 1* on p. 88; Cengage Australia for the material from *Tapis Volant 2* on p. 90; Owen Franken for permission to publish the photographs from *Tapis Volant 2* on p. 90; Plantu for the cartoon on p. 92; Rod Ellis for permission to publish the table on p. 34; Robert O'Dowd for the table on p. 113; the Australian Government for permission to reproduce material from *Language Teaching and Learning: A Guide*; and Stephanie Andrews, Melissa Gould-Drakeley, Marnie Foster, Catherine Moore, Jill Bignell, and their students for permission to publish examples of their work.

Every effort has been made to trace copyright holders and to obtain their permission for the use of copyright material. The publisher apologizes for any errors or omissions in the above list and would be grateful if notified of any corrections that should be incorporated in future reprints or editions of this book.

1

Introduction

Language, Culture, and Language Education

The study of an additional language has long been understood as a way of coming to understand another culture and its people. As a goal of language teaching, understanding others has been prominent in educational rationales in different ways, but has often been in the background of educational practice. As the processes of globalization, increased mobility, and technological development have come to shape ways of living and communicating, there has been a growing recognition of the fundamental importance of integrating intercultural capabilities into language teaching and learning. One of the challenges facing this integration has been to move from recognition of the need for an intercultural focus in language education to the development of practice. Early in the development of intercultural language teaching and learning, Zarate (1986) argued that the teaching and learning of culture in language education had been problematic because sufficient attention had not been given to considering what is to be taught and how. One important theme to emerge early in consideration of what and how to teach was the need to integrate language and culture in an interculturally oriented view of language education (e.g. Byram, 1991). This theme in turn has led to a rethinking of what is involved in the teaching of a second or foreign language.

Kramsch (2008) argues that in the teaching of any language the focus is not only on teaching a linguistic code but also on teaching meaning. The focus on meaning involves important shifts in understanding the fundamental concerns of language teaching and learning, which do not replace traditional foci, but add broadly to them. In particular it means engaging with broader ways of understanding the fundamental concepts involved in the theory and practice of language education: language, culture, and learning, and the relationships between them. To teach meaning is to actively engage with the processes involved in making and interpreting meaning. These go well beyond processes of comprehension of

Intercultural Language Teaching and Learning, First Edition. Anthony J. Liddicoat and Angela Scarino.
© 2013 Anthony J. Liddicoat and Angela Scarino. Published 2013 by Blackwell Publishing Ltd.

forms and structures, to consider meanings as subjective and intersubjective, growing out of not only the language in which meaning is communicated but also from the memories, emotions, perceptions, experiences, and life worlds of those who participate in the communication. Moreover, teaching meaning involves recognizing that as part of learning any additional language the learner inevitably brings more than one language and culture to the processes of meaning-making and interpretation. That is, there are inherent intercultural processes in language learning in which meanings are made and interpreted across and between languages and cultures and in which the linguistic and cultural repertoires of each individual exist in complex interrelationships. Languages and cultures in language learning are not independent of each other. Phipps and Gonzalez (2004) argue that: "The student of a language other than their own can be given an extraordinary opportunity to enter the languaging of others, to understand the complexity of the experience of others to enrich their own. *To enter other cultures is to re-enter one's own*" (p. 3; emphasis in original). That is, language learning, because languages and cultures are always in complex interrelationship, is both an act of learning about the other and about the self and of the relationships which exist between self and other.

In this book, we present a view of language education that is a complex engagement with linguistic and cultural diversity through the possibilities that a focus on meaning affords the processes of teaching and learning. We see language teaching as an art that is developed over time and which remains in a constant state of development. It is a thoughtful, mindful activity that is not reducible to prescriptions for practice. For us then, it is important to think beyond an understanding of teaching practice as *method* to consider how the complexity of lived experiences of linguistic and cultural diversity shape both the focus of language teaching and learning and the processes through which it happens in classrooms – what we call a *perspective*. To frame this idea it is useful to consider the concept of method and how it has been understood in language teaching.

The Concept of Method

"Method" has been a well-established construct in language education and has a long history as an organizing concept in the field. In fact, the recent history of language teaching can be understood as a series of innovations in method, and a number of established named methods have come to be recognized (e.g. Grammar–Translation Method, Audiolingual Method, Communicative Language Teaching). The distinctions between methods and the comparative advantages of different methods have become a key element in debates around language teaching.

In one of the earliest formulations of method, Anthony (1963) makes a basic hierarchical distinction in his model of language teaching between approaches, methods, and techniques. For Anthony, an approach is an overarching category involving a set of assumptions dealing with the nature of language teaching and learning and focuses on describing the nature of the material to be taught and learned. Methods are a middle-level construct that outlines the "orderly presentation of language material" (p. 65), given a particular approach. A technique is the most local level: techniques are the particular activities or strategies adopted in the classroom to accomplish a particular learning goal. In Anthony's model, methods were viewed as procedural accounts of teaching and learning through which broader, philosophical accounts of languages teaching and learning could be enacted in classrooms. It is a point of intersection between theory and practice.

In distinguishing levels of organization in language education, Anthony did not elaborate the nature of method as a construct, as Richards and Rodgers (1986) have noted. Beginning with Anthony's model, Richards and Rodgers argue that an approach is theoretical in its orientation and becomes a method, in Anthony's sense, through a process of design that maps theory onto practice to create an instructional system. That is, method relates to instruction and is a systematized way of implementing language teaching and learning in classrooms. This system comprises objectives for learning, principles for selecting and organizing content, preferred learning tasks and activities, and roles for teachers, learners, and materials. In their model, Richards and Rodgers propose three tiers, labeled approach, design, and procedures, which essentially replicate Anthony's model and uses "method" to refer to a superordinate category that encapsulates all three levels. In this case, method becomes a tight fusing of broader philosophy and classroom practice.

Richards and Rodgers' model effectively removes some of the inherent diversity Anthony articulated in his understanding of method. For Anthony, approach was the prime organizing mechanism for language teaching, with any approach effectively generating multiple methods that could translate the theoretical positions of the approach into practice. For Richards and Rodgers, however, methods are not a collection of diverse ways of enacting theoretical understandings – they are unities of thought and practice that organize how languages are taught and learned. Most conventional discussions of method emphasize the unity of method as the superordinate category, and method itself has come to be seen as a statement of orthodox practice to be adopted in order to achieve effective language learning.

Critiques of Method

Although the idea of method has been powerful in understanding, describing, and evaluating teaching practice, it has not been without criticism. In particular, in spite of research on method in language teaching, the idea of method itself has often been accepted as either self-evident or as little more than a convenient heuristic for talking about ways of doing language teaching and learning. The lack of attention to the idea of method led Clarke (1983, p. 109) to maintain that "the term 'method' is a label without substance." He noted that "method is so vague that it means just about anything that anyone wants it to mean, with the result that, in fact, it means nothing" (p. 111). In many cases, the term has been used in quite different ways and some fluidity is found in the meanings attributed to the term.

The critique of method, however, has not simply focused on the vagueness of the term, but also on its utility for understanding how language teaching and learning actually happen. Stern (1983) has suggested that there is a "fundamental weakness" in the concept of method and that the complexities of language teaching could not be reduced to methods alone. He argued that the focus on the comparative benefits of methods had become "unproductive and misguided" (p. 251) and that more sophisticated ways are needed to understand the nature of language teaching and learning in practice. We can see in work on methods a desire to establish unified parameters for language teaching practice, usually based on claims of effectiveness or efficiency, which constitute methods as homogeneous bodies of practice. In reality, teaching practice is highly diverse and variable and is influenced by the complexities of context (Liddicoat, 2004b). This means that the idea of method is insufficient to capture the necessary variability in practice that is responsive to local needs and conditions. In fact, Pennycook (1989) has argued that the debate around method has not led to a developing understanding of how languages can be taught, but rather has limited what can be known about language teaching.

The way in which methods have been presented as unified bodies of practice has led to methods often being understood statements of orthodox practice in language education. As Pennycook has claimed, "the Method concept is ultimately prescriptive rather than descriptive: Rather than analysing what is happening in language classrooms, it is a prescription for classroom behaviour" (1989, p. 611). Thus, there is a powerful discourse around methods as statements of what teachers should or must do, with the result that changes in practice in language teaching and learning have often been understood as processes of transmitting new orthodoxies. The method concept has therefore been a force for promoting homogeneity in practice and has often constructed diversity of practices as deviations from accepted norms. Moreover, the idea of method has privileged the role of the method developer over the role of the teacher as a decision-maker in the practice of teaching, subordinating practice to theory (Clarke and Silberstein, 1988). The prescriptive view of method has reproduced a view of methods as templates that constrain the options for practice. This view effectively constrains what can be done in language classrooms and limits the ways in which teachers and learners can engage with language and culture.

Moving beyond Methods

One response to the constraining effects of methods is that teachers have come to use them eclectically in language teaching, selecting from various recommendations for different purposes from the range available (e.g. Fanselow, 1987; Hammerley, 1991; Rivers, 1981). Thus, advocates of eclecticism resolve the problem of the prescriptivity of methods by challenging the prescriptivity and favoring teacher selection. Such views, however, remain located within a method paradigm and continue to imply a conceptual unity in methods themselves. Eclecticism does not address the prescriptivism of methods, nor does it address critique of methods themselves, rather, it locates practice in a problematic relationship with theory. If methods are considered theoretically coherent and defensible, then eclecticism runs the risk of being seen to work outside or even in contradiction to theory, and the gap between theory and practice is reinforced. In fact, even sympathetic treatments of eclecticism in teaching typically contrast eclectic approaches with "scientific" approaches. Freeman and Richards (1993) contrast theory-based teaching and "art/craft" teaching, with the former systematic and principled and the latter more *ad hoc* and intuitive. Diller (1975) contrasts eclecticism with reason, noting a transformation in language teaching in which a "temporary phase of eclecticism is giving way to a reasoned choice of methods and techniques" (p. 65).

By leaving methods intact, eclecticism may attempt to deal with the limitations that methods can impose on practice but risk diverse practice being considered in some way less rigorous or inferior when compared to methods-based practice. Other ways of dealing with method have tried to address the utility of methods as ways of describing language-teaching practice. Prabhu (1990) contrasts arguments for eclecticism – that different methods apply to different contexts or that methods are only partial truths – with an argument against the notion of a best method. He maintains that the pursuit of an objectively best method is misplaced and unrealistic because methods omit much that is important in teaching. Rather than defining good teaching as the implementation of a good method, Prabhu argues that it is necessary "to think of good teaching as an activity in which there is a sense of involvement by the teacher" (p. 171). That is, the engagement of the teacher in the act of teaching is fundamental to good teaching. A prescriptive method implemented routinely or mechanistically will not constitute good teaching because the method does not embody the teacher or the learner. Rather than focusing on methods as templates for teaching, he argues that the focus should be on more subjective aspects of teachers' understanding of their work: "There is a factor more basic than the choice between methods, namely, teachers' subjective understanding of the teaching they do. Teachers need to operate with some practical conceptualisation of how their teaching leads to the desired learning – with a notion of causation that has a measure of credibility" (p. 172). Prabhu calls this subjective understanding teachers' sense of plausibility and argues that the important issue for good teaching is whether the sense of plausibility is demonstrably active and alive, not whether it is based on some particular method. In effect, this decouples the idea of the use of a method as an instructional system from good language teaching and opens up greater complexity for understanding what constitutes teaching. Prabhu sees the sense of plausibility not as an entrenched body of subjective knowledge, but as an open capacity to evolve in the process of teaching; and he maintains that openness to investigate practice, to change and to draw on experiences, is fundamental to teachers' professional learning. At the same time, teaching practice must be accepted as inherently open to diversity both between teachers and for individual teachers at different times.

Kumaravadivelu (1994, 2003) contends that language teaching now faces a post-method condition, that is, language education has moved beyond method as a basic organizer of practice. He argues that the post-method condition gives more recognition to the role of the teacher in the act of teaching and constructs the relationship between theory and practice as closer and multivalent. In particular, there is a recognition that practice needs to be location-specific and student- and classroom-oriented rather than imposed from outside. This idea gives the teachers the ability and the responsibility of drawing on their experience as language learners and language users in constructing learner experiences.

In the post-method condition, methods can no longer be framed as the core way in which practice is organized or developed and so the elaboration of new methods is not a valid response to any desire to change practice in language teaching and learning. Rather, taking language education into new directions necessitates articulating theories of language, culture, and learning in ways that generate new possibilities for teachers to develop and theorize their own practices of teaching and learning. The focus is not, however, one which proposes an eclectic view of teaching. If eclecticism is understood simply as selection between available possibilities, it runs the risk of becoming a random assortment of techniques assembled unsystematically and uncritically. Rather, what is needed for post-methods language teaching is what Kumaravadivelu (1994) calls "principled pragmatism." Principled pragmatism encompasses both practice and theory in an integrated and mutually reinforcing way. It recognizes diversity in pragmatism but bases this diversity on a clear articulation of the nature, purpose, and context of teaching and learning. In this way, selections of aspects of practice are guided by a rationale for practice that allows possibilities to be evaluated critically. The alternate to methods, therefore, is not simply eclecticism but rather a principled and professional selection to address teaching and learning needs.

Cochran-Smith and Lytle (1999) propose the idea of *stance* as a way of understanding how teachers adopt principled positions in their teaching. Stance emphasizes the idea that, in teaching, teachers are positioned in particular ways, intellectually and in practice, in relation to what and how they teach:

> In our work, we offer the term ... *stance* to describe the positions teachers and others who work together ... take toward knowledge and its relationships to practice. We use the metaphor of stance to suggest both orientational and positional ideas, to carry allusions to the physical placing of the body as well as the intellectual activities and perspectives over time. In this sense, the metaphor is intended to capture the ways we stand, the ways we see, and the lenses we see through. Teaching is a complex activity that occurs within webs of social, historical, cultural and political significance. (pp. 288–289)

The stance that teachers adopt in relation to their teaching provides a framing in which choices about practice are shaped and in which theory and practice are brought into relationship. In all teaching, teachers, and also their learners, adopt a stance in the sense of a set of valued positions about what is to be taught and learned and how this is to be done.

We understand intercultural language teaching and learning as an *intercultural perspective*, that is, as the self-awareness of the language teacher as a participant in linguistic and cultural diversity; it is therefore not simply a way of teaching, but a way of understanding lived experiences of language and culture as the framing for teaching. For us, an intercultural perspective can be understood as the lens through which the nature, purpose, and activity of language teaching and learning are viewed, and the focus which students develop through their language learning. The intercultural in language learning is then a way of viewing the nature of language, culture, and learning as they come together in the acquisition of a new language. The starting point for such a perspective is the view that language learning is fundamentally engagement in intercultural communication and that the addition of a new language to a person's linguistic repertoire positions that person differently in relation to the world in which they live. Language learning from an intercultural perspective is therefore an exploration of the intercultural, used as a lens for understanding language teaching and learning as both theory and practice.

We use the ideas of stance and perspective to highlight that this book does not intend to provide a "method" or prescriptions for teaching and learning languages. What we present in this book is an attempt to explore what is involved when considering language education from an intercultural perspective. In three key senses, it is not a method. First, it is not a method because it does not seek to formulate practice in particular ways, but rather to open up thinking about theory and processes of language teaching and learning in ways that can inform more elaborated understandings of both theory and practice. The act of teaching and learning is intricate and cannot be reduced to methodological prescriptions. Furthermore, the role of teachers is not one of simply receiving prescriptions from others that are subsequently "implemented" in their context. In addition, it is not a method because it sees language teaching as a fundamentally ecological activity in which those aspects of practice that are normally classed as method cannot be dissociated from the rest of the ecology. Language education is a synthesis of theory and practice, of teaching and learning, of pedagogy, resources, assessment, and evaluation. We see teaching, therefore, as a holistic process that is not reducible to compartmentalized categories such as approach, method, and technique. Finally, what we present is not a method because we understand teaching as dialogic relationships between theory and practice, between teaching and learning, and between teacher and student. Such dialogue is an opening to the complexities of teaching and what is taught. Teachers come to teaching with their own dynamic framework of knowledge and understanding, which encompasses both their own and their students' personal, social, cultural, and linguistic make-up, as well as the experiences, beliefs, ethical values, motivations, and commitments that are part of their own identity as a teacher. This framework is continuously evolving, based on teachers' distinctive worlds of experience and reflection on that experience (Scarino, 2005a). It provides the frame of reference through which, in their day-to-day teaching, teachers create learning experiences for students and through which they interpret and make meaning of their students' learning. It is through this framing that they appraise the value of their own teaching and new ideas with which they might wish to experiment to further develop or change their ways of teaching.

To teach from an intercultural perspective is a framing of the ways teachers understand the diversity of languages and cultures, their lives within this diversity and its relationship to their work as teachers. It also means teaching in such a way that the focus of learning is the development of an intercultural perspective by learners as their own experience of linguistic and cultural diversity. The enactment of an intercultural perspective occurs at each point within the ecology of teaching and learning and the articulation of an intercultural perspective is both a global and local feature of that ecology. This means that language teaching and learning from an intercultural perspective is an activity in which principles and theoretical positions affect practice at every level. In this way, such teaching is both personal, drawing on the dispositions of individual teachers and students, and coherent, integrating dispositions across the whole process of teaching and learning.

About this Book

This book aims to investigate language teaching and learning in a way that is broadly applicable to a diversity of languages, contexts, and levels of learning. We endeavor to articulate important principles of intercultural teaching and learning, recognizing that their enactment is realized in different ways in different contexts. We argue for a reconsideration of the fundamental principles that can guide language teaching and learning, and examine the consequences of such a reconsideration through the whole of the ecology of language education. In addressing language teaching and learning, this book focuses primarily on foreign language teaching, both because it is the context with which we are most familiar, and because foreign language teaching presents particular challenges for intercultural learning. This is because learners are often isolated from the communities they are studying and their experience of linguistic and cultural diversity as it relates to their language learning is necessarily mediated primarily through the classroom. While we wish to maintain a broad focus, selecting necessarily involves a focus on particular languages. In selecting examples, we have drawn from a range of different languages and cultures the general principles that can be adopted into the teaching of any language and culture, rather than focusing on the specific details of a particular language and its associated cultures.

The book is divided into two parts. Chapters 2 to 4 explore what is meant by the idea of an intercultural perspective in language teaching and learning, and the remaining chapters work through how an intercultural perspective affects aspects of practice. In Chapter 2, we explore understandings of language and culture as they apply to the contemporary context of language teaching. We examine the evolving understanding of the nature of language and culture and their interrelationship and the consequences that this has for how languages are taught. We develop a view of language as a complex, contextualized phenomenon that cannot be understood in terms of the linguistic code alone, but which must also include an understanding of language as a form of making and interpreting meaning. We examine different ways in which the idea of culture has been understood in language education and argue for an understanding of culture as a dynamic process within which meanings are created, exchanged, and interpreted. We also examine ways of understanding the intercultural and develop a view of the intercultural that emphasizes it as mediation between cultures, as personal engagement with diversity, and as played out most especially in language education through interpersonal exchanges of meaning.

In Chapter 3 we discuss the understandings of learning that underpin an intercultural perspective on language teaching and learning. The chapter considers briefly some aspects of the history of second language acquisition (SLA), leading to a discussion of the central debate that emerged in the field in the mid-1990s about the nature of SLA and second language learning. This is the debate between two families of theories, those that are traditional and cognitively based and those that are more recent and socioculturally oriented. We consider key understandings relevant to the two families of theories. We also discuss Sfard's (1998) two metaphors of learning – acquisition and participation – and her argument for complementarity and therefore sufficiency. Arguing against the sufficiency of these two metaphors, we discuss the need to expand further views of learning within an intercultural perspective, to capture the process of moving between diverse linguistic and cultural systems and to acknowledge the essentially interpretive nature of learning to communicate across languages.

The issues of language culture and learning are drawn together in Chapter 4, which frames our understanding of the intercultural as it applies in language education. In this chapter we argue that the intercultural is a dynamic engagement with the relationships between language, culture, and learning. It involves recognition of the cultural constructedness of perception and interpretation as a starting point for making, communicating, and interpreting meanings about and across languages and cultures. In particular, we argue that interculturally oriented language teaching and learning places the learners themselves at the focus of intercultural engagement. This requires a recognition of the identities that language learners have in their encounters with a new language and culture and the ways the teaching and learning context positions learners in relation to these identities. We then articulate a number of principles that we believe to be fundamental for engaging language learners in a reflexive approach to making and interpreting meanings, and some of the ways in which these principles can be enacted pedagogically.

In the remaining chapters we consider more directly some of the main aspects of practice in teaching and learning languages from an intercultural perspective. Here we break down the ecology of language teaching and learning into some of its major components. The aim is not to fragment teaching and learning but rather to show how an intercultural perspective is articulated in different parts of the broad ecology. In considering these components we have included aspects of teaching practice that may sometimes be considered as lying outside direct control of teachers (e.g. planning and evaluation) because we believe that these activities are fundamental components of the work of all teachers, and because we believe that an intercultural stance permeates all aspects of the ecology of teaching and learning.

In Chapter 5 we argue that teaching and learning languages within an intercultural perspective requires an expansion of the construct of "task" to highlight the nature of interaction as interchange, that is, as the interpretation, creation, and exchange of meaning, and to acknowledge that for learners these interactions constitute lived experience along a trajectory. These experiences contribute to the development of communication as well as to the development of an evolving understanding of what communication entails and ultimately to the learners' development of self-awareness as communicators. We use a series of examples to illustrate ways in which teachers of diverse languages construct such learning experiences.

Chapter 6 turns to an exploration of how the interactions and experiences described in Chapter 5 can be resourced within a language program. A language-learning resource does not exist in isolation but needs to connect with other resources to form a coherent whole, and resources are not simply texts and materials, but learners themselves can become the resource. We then examine the selection, adaptation, and creation of resources and the ways in which resources are used for diverse purposes, such as discovery, scaffolding, and reflection, and the ways in which teachers use resources for multiple purposes. The chapter examines the nature and role of authentic resources for intercultural language teaching and learning, arguing that resources need to be personalized to make them meaningful in learners' own terms and to enhance possibilities for connecting with diverse linguistic and cultural practices in constructive ways. Chapter 7 develops the discussion of resources by considering technology as integral to intercultural language teaching and learning because it provides the best source of contemporary material for languages education and allows for participation in the target language and its communities. The power of technology is to make other cultures present to learners in diverse, complex, and immediate ways, and to allow for and require intercultural engagement.

In Chapter 8 we turn to the issue of assessment. We contextualize assessment in relation to the tension between traditional and alternate assessment paradigms, its institutional character, and the need for a reconceptualization of the assessment process. We then consider four processes of assessment – conceptualizing, eliciting, judging, and validating – and we identify features of assessment that are required to assess language learning as an intercultural endeavor. We use a series of examples to illustrate ways in which language teachers are experimenting with assessment of language within this perspective. We conclude by discussing some complexities that remain to be addressed in this area.

In Chapter 9 we consider how a program of interculturally oriented language teaching and learning can be planned as a developmental experience of learning over time. We consider ways of understanding the content of a program of learning in which language, culture, and learning are integrated and interrelated. We argue that the framing of planning needs to be conceptual, as it is through concepts that integration can be achieved and interactions and reflections can be organized. We see the progression through a program of learning as a holistic process of developing complexity as learners engage in processes of interpreting the languages and cultures that are at play in their learning context. This development requires consideration be given to planning the experiences through which learners develop this complexity, and the connections between these experiences, which in turn enable the elaboration of understanding and interpretation.

In Chapter 10 we consider evaluation as an integral aspect of the ecology of language learning within an intercultural perspective. We discuss the nature and purpose of program evaluation, research paradigms that shape the process, and the process of evaluation itself. In so doing we highlight the way in which the view of language learning as intercultural shapes both the frame of reference for evaluation and the processes involved. We then consider the relationship between evaluation and professional learning for teachers. We conclude by considering language learning as action and interpretive understanding across languages and cultures.

2

Languages, Cultures, and the Intercultural

In order to understand how languages can be taught from an intercultural perspective it is important to first understand the main concepts within this perspective. Intercultural language teaching is fundamentally concerned with particular understandings of "language" and "culture" and the ways in which these relate to each other. This chapter will review these key ideas to provide a basis for understanding the practices and pedagogies that are associated with an intercultural perspective in language education.

Understanding Language

Language is all-pervasive in human life and everyone knows intuitively what language is and how it works. However, any attempt to define language risks being reductive, as language is a complex and multifaceted phenomenon. The theories of language that a teacher holds affect the process and practice of language teaching and what is understood as process in language development and the assessment of achievement. Although language is very much central to the work of language teachers, little attention is paid to clarifying exactly what is meant by language for the purposes of teaching. In fact, "language" for language teachers is often rendered unproblematic through the act of naming a particular language. A teacher teaches French, German, or Japanese and language means little more than the abstract entity so named. The simple process of naming, however, is not the same as conceptualizing what language is nor does it clarify what the named entity actually is. The process of naming often masks what is meant by "language" under an easily understood label. In fact, such a view of language is ultimately recursive and self-referential: the English (French, German, Japanese) language is the language spoken by speakers of English (French, German, Japanese). But as Makoni and Pennycook (2005)

Intercultural Language Teaching and Learning, First Edition. Anthony J. Liddicoat and Angela Scarino.
© 2013 Anthony J. Liddicoat and Angela Scarino. Published 2013 by Blackwell Publishing Ltd.

point out, such named languages are constructions created for political and ideological purposes. They are not simply labels of some preexisting, self-apparent entity.

Language as a structural system

A key element of the creation of named languages has been the formalization of a set of linguistic and usually literate norms (Liddicoat, 2005a). One dialect or variety of the language is chosen to serve as the basis for the standard language, reducing the amount of variation in the language to create a more regular and uniform linguistic structure. This standardized, regularized variety becomes *the* language and education focuses on the dissemination of this language to both native speakers and to new learners. The prescriptive tradition in linguistics and in language teaching has silenced linguistic variation. Language has been idealized as a set of structures that are acquired through education. This process creates a prestige variety of the language, often spoken only by a small elite group and used as a gate-keeping device. Control of the prestige variety gives access to power; lack of control of the variety excludes from power. It is in this sense that Bourdieu (1982) argues that language varieties are imbued with symbolic power and education reproduces and reinforces this power. Standardized written languages develop an authority which is not usually enjoyed by nonstandardized and unwritten forms of language and they become prescriptions for "good" language use (McGroarty, 1996). Deviations from the prescribed linguistic standard have been regarded as defective language use and have been judged negatively as lack of education or laziness instead of as a natural and significant part of a language ecology.

Language education has been closely attached to the prescriptive tradition, and language teaching has frequently been understood as the teaching of a prescriptively correct form of the language (Odlin, 1994). In other words, pedagogical grammar has been equated with prescriptive grammar (Liddicoat and Curnow, 2003). Language education has adopted a view of language that privileges a prescriptive, standardized, written code enshrined in authoritative grammars, dictionaries, and style guides (Liddicoat, 2005a). This is language as a set of agreed meanings assembled according to a set of rules. This approach treats language as a structural system – as grammar and vocabulary. In reality, such a view of language is often more concerned with grammar than with vocabulary (Fasold, 1992). Much of modern linguistics has been fundamentally preoccupied with language as a structural system and some approaches to linguistics, especially generative linguistics, have privileged grammar to such a point that vocabulary and language use have been excluded from focus almost entirely. In his theory of language, Chomsky (1981) states a very strong version of the view of the primacy of grammar, arguing that language is simply a derivative of grammar. An understanding of language only as a structural system is, however, a narrow one. Viewed as a structural system, language is fixed and finite, and the complexities of language use are ignored. Under the influence of the prescriptive tradition of authoritative grammars and the grammar-oriented focus of modern linguistics, language teaching methods have often adopted, consciously or unconsciously, an understanding of language as a structural system, with grammar the principal focus. A structural view of language has been the underlying theory of language for many approaches to language teaching and learning, most notably in the grammar–translation approach.

Language as a communicative system

Beyond the structural views of language, language is usually understood as a communicative system. This is a move from viewing language as forms to understanding its purposes. For Saussure (1916), language was the science of speech communication, and Davies (2005), for example, defines language as "the main human communication system" (p. 69). This view of languages as a communication system is not undisputed and Chomsky and his colleagues (Fitch, Hauser, and Chomsky, 2005; Hauser, Chomsky, and Fitch, 2002) have argued that communication itself is incidental to grammar as an organizing principle. If language is to be understood as a communication system, then it is important to understand what is meant in this case by communication. Linguistics, however, has tended not to give much attention to what it means by communication and its definitions have tended to remain underdeveloped (Curnow, 2009; Haugh and Liddicoat, 2009). Second language acquisition and language education have tended also to have underdeveloped understandings of the nature of communication (Eisenchlas, 2009). In fact, communication-oriented views of language may not differ much from structural views. For Saussure (1916), for example, communication was a simple process in which an active speaker encodes a message for a passive listener – an unproblematic exchange of meaning through language. The act of communication consisted of using combinations of linguistic structures to express the speaker's thought, produced by a psychophysical mechanism; that is, communication was the use of grammar to express thought. Harris (2003) has argued that Saussure's conceptualization of language as the science of speech communication relies on untenable assumptions about communication itself. In particular, he claims that Saussure adopted a "telementation" model of communication, a "theory which explains communication as the transference of thoughts from one person's mind to another person's mind" (p. 25), and that mainstream linguistics, and we would argue much contemporary language education, is implicitly committed to such a model.

Language as social practice

It is apparent that the view of communication as the straightforward transfer of thoughts from one mind to another is limited. Communication is not simply a transmission of information, it is a creative, cultural act in its own right through which social groups constitute themselves (Carey, 1989). Moreover, it is a complex performance of identity in which the individual communicates not only information, but also a social persona that exists in the act of communication (Sacks, 1975). Such complexities of communication have often been ignored in the theories of language that underlie language education, even those that have privileged communication. Communicative language teaching, for example, has typically reduced communication to the exchange of comprehensible and comprehended messages, and has left aside issues of voice, identity, co-construction between participants, and the enactment of self through language (Kern and Liddicoat, 2008). What is needed is a more interactionally grounded view of communication, where communication involves "participants' contingent, emergent and joint accomplishment" of meaning (Kasper, 2006).

The understanding of language that is part of our perspective also affects what happens in the classroom and the ways in which learners begin to understand the relationship between their own languages and the languages of their learning. Languages education, we argue, has been constrained and restricted by the definitions of language it has held and enacted and a broader view of language is required which expands beyond ideas of linguistic structure. Structurally focused theories have turned language learning into an intellectual exercise of recalling rules or an exercise of reproducing language according to rules in which form has predominated over meaning and rendered meaning incidental. Language learning models a theory of language in which the relationship between two languages is simply a matter of code replacement, where the only difference is in words and structures. Communication-focused theories that see language as communication but which have a simplistic theory of communication have marginalized the learner as a meaning-maker in the very act of communication, often trivializing what is communicated and communicable in the language classroom. Within such theories language comes to be viewed as skills, as "technical adjuncts" that remove the intellectual and educative possibilities from languages education (Phipps and Gonzales, 2004). Although the ideas of structural system and communication as meaning exchange that we have discussed so far have a place in a theory of language, for language learning the theory we envisage needs to expand beyond these ideas.

To understand language education as an intercultural endeavor, it is necessary to begin with an enlarged theory of language, seeing language as "open, dynamic, energetic, constantly evolving and personal" (Shohamy, 2007a, p. 5) and as encompassing the rich complexities of communication. This means that language variability is not something to be reduced through education, but rather it is a resource that education needs to develop in order to foster an experience of the world with which the language learning needs to engage. Shohamy (2007a) argues that it is the variability within language that makes language creative and a living expression of self. She further argues that it is therefore inappropriate to require that any language user should assimilate to a particular norm – language should be a vehicle for the expression of the self, not a constraint on self-expression. The self is fundamental to language use: each choice an individual makes from the language repertoire is a portrayal of personality (Shohamy, 2007a). The learner cannot simply be seen as a learner, as deficient in their command of language (Kern and Liddicoat, 2008). Learners are from the beginning of their learning users of language, in fact users of languages, through which they present themselves and construct and explore their worlds. Language is not a thing to be studied but a way of seeing, understanding, and communicating about the world and each language user uses his or her language(s) differently to do this.

Although we have argued that language is personal, it is also communal. Individuals use language for social purposes within social contexts. Language use is a process of adaptation, negotiation, and accommodation (Shohamy, 2007a). Knowing a language therefore means more than knowing a linguistic system or communicating information, it means engaging in social practices using that system in order to participate in the social life. Such practices exist wherever two individuals communicate across their own personal versions of their language, however, when such communication happens across languages or in contexts where multiple languages are at play, there are different needs and possibilities for adaptations, negotiations, and accommodations (Kramsch, 1999). Just as language use is an engagement in and with social practices, so too is language learning (Kramsch, 1994). Language is something that people enact in their daily lives and something they use to express, create, and interpret meanings and to establish and maintain social and interpersonal relationships. It is an involvement in processes of meaning-making and interpretation with and for others.

If language is viewed as a social practice of meaning-making and interpretation, then it is not enough for language learners just to know grammar and vocabulary. They also need to know how the language is used to create and represent meanings and how to communicate with others and to engage with the communication of others. This requires the development of awareness of the nature of language and its impact on the world (Svalberg, 2007). If language learning focuses on the interpretation and creation of meaning, language is learned as a system of personal engagement with a new world, where learners necessarily engage with diversity at a personal level.

Within a professional stance that understands language as a social practice, we need to ensure that students are provided with opportunities to go beyond what they already know and to learn to engage with unplanned and unpredictable aspects of language. Learning language as a complex, personal communication system involves ongoing investigation of language as a dynamic system and of the ways that it works to create and convey meanings. This involves learners in analysis and in talking analytically about language. Kramsch (1993a, p. 264) notes that: "talk about talk is what the classroom does best and yet this potential source of knowledge has not been sufficiently tapped, even in communicatively oriented classrooms." The emphasis on ongoing investigation and analysis assumes that learners are involved in learning that promotes exploration and discovery rather than being passive recipients of knowledge as it is transmitted to them by others. These learners need to learn the capabilities that will give them independence as users and analyzers of language (Scarino and Liddicoat, 2009; Svalberg, 2007).

The interpretive dimension of language resonates with Gadamer's (1976) view of language in philosophical hermeneutics as the theory and methodology of interpretation. For Gadamer, language is fundamentally a social, cultural, and historical phenomenon. Words do not simply represent objects and phenomena in the world; their meanings are established through consensus that comes from their use. Gadamer states that "language is the fundamental mode of operation of our being-in-the world and the all-embracing form of the constitution of the world" (p. 3). Language is not simply a tool for describing the world; it is an integral part of acting and being in the world; it is an essential condition of social life and constitutive of the human world. Gadamer explains:

> Language is by no means simply an instrument, a tool. For it is in the nature of the tool that we master its use, which is to say we take it in hand and lay it aside when it has done its service. That is not the same as when we take the words of a language, lying ready in the mouth, and with their use let them sink back into the general store of words over which we dispose. Such an analogy is false because we never find ourselves as consciousness over against the world. … Rather in all our knowledge of ourselves and in all knowledge of the world we are always already encompassed by the language that is our own. … In truth, we are always already at home in language, just as much as we are in the world. (pp. 62–63)

Language can never be discarded as we might discard a tool. It resides with us and we reside with it. It mediates our relationship with reality. Gadamer highlights that we are always "at home" in our own language (and culture) and as such language cannot be made an object of investigation, separate from the knower and user of that language. He seeks to understand the phenomenon of language while acknowledging the impossibility of moving outside of language itself. For Gadamer, life experience can be interpreted and expressed only through language. The desire to use language is part of the desire people have to make sense of and understand being in the world. This understanding, however, is always tentative and provisional, so that language is our ongoing project. At the same time, this does not mean that being is coextensive with people's capacity to express, because language has the capacity to both reveal and conceal. The task of hermeneutics is to render this process of revealing and concealing.

Language encompasses our history. The history that provides the horizon of our world is present in the language we use. As Gadamer explains, "language is not only an object in our hands, it is the reservoir of tradition and the medium in and through which we exist and perceive our world" (1976, p. 29). Language is part of the ongoing building of history where new understanding leads to an adjustment of the original understanding, and this cycle of understanding and adjustment of one's understanding is an ongoing process. The limits of our understanding coincide with the limits of our language.

The overall project in using language is understanding and self-understanding. Understanding is shaped by our prejudices (in the sense of prejudgments) or fore-understandings. Instead of seeing these fore-understandings as a problem, for Gadamer it is the framework of fore-understandings that enables interpretation and understanding. Language is integral to understanding and interpreting. For Gadamer this understanding and interpreting is not the product of individual reflection, but an intersubjective process that entails a fusion of different horizons. Thus for Gadamer: "Understanding and interpretation are ultimately the same thing ... *language is the universal medium in which understanding occurs. Understanding occurs in interpreting.* All understanding is interpretation, and all interpretation takes place in the medium of a language that allows the object to come into words and yet is at the same time the interpreter's own language" (2004, p. 390; emphasis in original). In other words, understanding and interpretation are not ready-made and available. They are constructed in and through language in dialogue or conversation and this language is one's own language. The new understanding and interpretation is mediated through the language of the interpreter, which is conditioned always by prejudices of his/her historical existence. Gadamer emphasizes that the interpreter can never achieve a full interpretation since he/she is limited by his/her historical circumstances and by his/her language and is inextricably involved in the interpretive conversation.

Concluding comments

Understanding language as social practice does not mean replacing views of language as a structural system or as the communication of messages, as these are elements of the social practice of language use. Instead, the idea of language practice can be seen as an overarching view of languages in which structural system and communication are given meaning and relationship to lived experience. This means that the views of language presented here are not seen as alternates but as an integrated whole. Language is understood as social

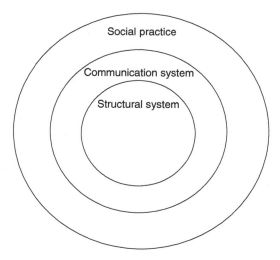

Figure 2.1 Layers of language.

practice that integrates other understandings of language, the relationships of language to other aspects of human sociality, such as culture. Language therefore can be understood in terms of a number of layers as represented in Figure 2.1. The conceptualization of language for teaching and learning is integrated: linguistic structures provide elements for a communication system that, in turn, becomes the resource through which social practices are created and accomplished. Language teaching and learning therefore needs to engage within the entire spectrum of possibilities for language and each layer of language affords opportunities for intercultural learning.

Understanding Culture

Defining culture is complex and rather than attempt a broad survey of ideas about culture, in this section we will consider some issues in understanding culture for language teaching and learning. Culture has always been considered relevant for language education, however, the ways in which culture has been handled have often been limited. Some of the ways that language education has conceptualized culture have been called into question but debates about the nature of culture in other disciplines, notably anthropology and sociology have contributed ways to resolve some of these problems, and there is a need in language teaching and learning to develop more nuanced understandings of the nature of culture and the ways in which cultures can be investigated in the language classroom. This section will examine some of the ways in which culture has been understood in language teaching and learning – as national attributes and societal norms – and then it will examine some elements of the debate around understandings of culture – as symbolic systems and as practices – in order to consider ways that the study of cultures can influence an intercultural perspective in language teaching and learning.

Cultures as national attributes

One way of understanding culture has been to see it as the particular attributes of a national group. This view of culture is analogous to the idea of naming languages: cultures are understood as being bounded by geographic borders and are constituted by the inhabitants of those borders in an undifferentiated way. It is a view of culture that sees culture as existing only as a singular phenomenon for any group and such cultures are typically labeled in terms of national affiliations: American culture, British culture, French culture, Japanese culture, etc. Such national cultures may be expanded by recognizing cultural subgroups within the territory of the overarching national group – the culture of ethnic minorities, of social classes, or other recognizable groupings. Such a view of culture is an essentializing one that reduces culture to recognizable, often stereotypicalized, representations of national attributes. Identifying a culture as a national culture does not make reference to what culture is, but rather where culture is found: American culture resides in the essentialized attributes located in the territory of the United States, French culture in France, etc. Culture is an unproblematic and unproblematized construct that can be reduced to a label derived from political geography.

The idea of national culture underlies many ways of understanding the nature of culture itself and constrains what is considered as a cultural group and what is considered as the culture of any particular group. Privileging the nation as the normal site for cultures renders invisible the existence of cultural groups within the nation, except where they are understood as being in some way not properly integrated into the national culture. Thus, ethnic cultures may be identified as recognizable departures from the national culture, but which are nonetheless present in the nation. Other possible ways of understanding cultural groupings (gender groupings, age groupings, social groupings, etc.) are filtered out of the view of culture in the essentializing process of identifying the national culture. Similarly, the internal diversity of any culture is filtered out of representations of national culture, producing a monolithic, undifferentiated understanding of what constitutes a culture. Such cultures are inevitably static and are presented as a finished product, removing the possibilities for contestation and creation as a feature of social life. This view has predominated in many approaches to the teaching of culture in language education (Abdallah-Pretceille, 2003; Holliday, 2010) and is manifested in textbooks in the form of cultural notes that present images of recognized cultural attributes of nations as cultural content. It also persists in many understandings of the domain of culture learning as being high culture or area studies.

Understanding culture as high culture, that is, as the valued artifacts of a particular national group, such as art, literature, music, etc., of a particular nation or ethnic group has had a long tradition. Frequently, in folk usages of the term culture, it is exactly this that is meant. This view has predominated in educational contexts where culture has become a focus of teaching, and notably in modern language teaching. Thus, a course on English language and culture may include texts by Shakespeare, Dickens, Hardy, and other traditionally valued authors of the English tradition, while courses on French language and culture would include Molière, Corneille, Racine, and so on. In such contexts, the text produced is seen as an instantiation of the culture of the nation in which the text is produced, often in isolation from other circumstances of the text's production or the author's identity. One attempt to counter the association of high culture with nation has been to present students with assemblages of texts, or other artifacts, produced in a particular language in different countries. In such an approach, English culture would include texts from the United Kingdom, America, and other English-speaking countries, or a course in French culture would include texts from France, Canada, Francophone Africa, and so on. This is a view of culture that does not see culture as coextensive with nation but rather as coextensive with language, often replicating earlier processes of linguistic and cultural colonization.

Within this view, cultural competence is understood as control of an established canon of literature, which can be measured in terms of the breadth of reading and knowledge about the literature. This paradigm also seems to be associated with a view of the nature of language learning that had minimal expectations of using the language for communication with native speakers. The relationship between language and culture in this paradigm may be quite tenuous. Culture is seen as residing primarily in the text itself, which is supported through the language of the text. The primacy of the text over the language leads to a view in which much of the valued cultural knowledge can be obtained from the text, even in translation, with knowledge of the original language serving to give a deeper appreciation of the text and the artistry of the text. Kramsch (1995a) argues that much of this approach to teaching began by focusing on an idea of a universal culture transmitted through classical languages, to which all educated Europeans should have access, rather than on individual cultures of individual languages. She argues that the move from universal culture to national culture came about in a context in which language itself lost its perceived cultural value and became seen as a tool for later accessing national literatures, as embodiments of unique cultural knowledge.

An alternate framing of culture as national culture can been seen in the view of culture in area studies. This view of culture treats cultural learning as learning about the history, geography, and institutions of country of the target language. Cultural competence comes to be viewed as a body of knowledge about the country. Area knowledge provides the background for understanding language and society. However, this paradigm implicitly seems to understand contact with another culture as a matter of observation, in which the learner knows about the country but remains external to it. In such a view, the relationship between language and culture remains tenuous, and language is used primarily for naming events, institutions, people, and places.

Cultures as societal norms

This paradigm became very strong in the 1980s as a result of work by anthropologists such as Gumperz (1982a, 1982b) and Hymes (1974, 1986). This approach seeks to describe cultures in terms of the practices and values that typify them. In this approach, cultures are seen as favoring "direct" or "indirect" ways of speaking, as organizing texts in particular valued ways (however, see Wierzbicka (1985, 1986, 1991) for a critique of this approach). Within this paradigm cultural competence is defined as knowing about what people from a given cultural group are likely to do and understanding the cultural values placed upon certain ways of acting or upon certain beliefs. This view of cultural competence is a problem for language learning, because it leaves the learner primarily within his/her own cultural paradigm, observing and interpreting the words and actions of an interlocutor from another cultural paradigm. One further criticism that can be made of this paradigm is that it tends to present cultures as relatively static and homogeneous (Liddicoat, 2002). This in turn leads to a possibility of stereotyping the target culture, especially in contexts in which culture learning and language learning are widely separated and the possibilities for interactions between speakers are limited.

Cultures as symbolic systems

Language education has tended to consider culture in terms of areas of focus in learning – that is, it has identified where culture is located rather than considering what culture is. The result is that the construct has remained vague and poorly operationalized in both theory and practice. It is therefore useful to consider ways of understanding the nature of culture. One important perspective in the literature about culture is the idea that cultures represent systems of symbols that allow participants to construct meaning (Geertz, 1973, 1983). Culture as practices is accomplished and realized by members of a cultural group in their daily lives and interactions and involves recognition of the meaningfulness of practices in context. From this perspective, cultures can be understood as a system of shared meanings that make collective sense of experience, which allows for experience to be communicated and interpreted as being meaningful. The focus of participation in cultures as symbolic systems is on acts of interpretation – that is, the use of symbols is seen as an element of meaning-making.

Cultures then are the lens through which people mutually create and interpret meanings and the frame that allows the communication of meanings that go beyond the literal denotations of the words being used. This means that in the context of language learning culture goes beyond its manifestation as behaviors, texts, artifacts, and information and examines the ways in which these things are accomplished discursively and interactionally within a context of use. Culture learning, therefore, becomes a way to develop the interpretive resources needed to understand cultural practices rather than exposure to information about a culture. Such a view of cultures necessarily sees action as context-sensitive, negotiated, and highly variable, but also as structured in that symbols come to have meaning as part of a system of interrelated possibilities.

Cultures as practices

The views of culture discussed so far have often incorporated the idea that cultures are logical, coherent, uniform, and static. For Bayart (2002) such an understanding of culture, which is termed *culturalism*, commits three errors: it maintains that culture is a corpus of timeless and stable representations, that boundaries between cultures are clear-cut, and that culture is endorsed by coherent political orientations. Such a view of culture therefore misrepresents as uniform things that are frequently challenged and contested. An alternate way of understanding culture is in terms of practices: "a practical activity shot through with wilful actions, power relations, struggle, contradiction and change" (Sewell, 1999, p. 44). In a view of culture as practices, culture is dialogic: it is a discursive rearticulation of embodied actions between individuals in particular contexts located in time and space (Bhabha, 1994). Cultures are therefore dynamic and emergent – they are created through the actions of individuals and in particular through the ways in which they use language. This means that meanings are not simply shared, coherent constructions about experience but rather can be fragmented, contradictory, and contested within the practices of a social group because they are constituted in moments of interaction. Culture in such a view is not a coherent whole but a situated process of dealing with the problems of social life. Cultures thus are open to elements that are diverse and contradictory, and different interpretations may be made of the same events by individuals who may be considered to be from the same culture.

One way of understanding culture as practices is to view cultures as tool kits of "symbols, stories, rituals, and world-views, which people may use in varying configurations to solve different kinds of problem" (Swidler, 1986, p. 273). In participating in life, individuals select from possibilities to construct a line of action. Cultures are the resources that individuals draw on to construct sustained courses of action and to develop new courses of action in response to changed circumstances – they do not determine practice, they allow for it to happen. Practices themselves are not preconditions of membership of cultural groups as they do not exist as coherent bodies of knowledge and values which are transmitted by groups, rather they are deployed in participation in groups and every individual has access to more practices than will be required to participate in any particular group. All individuals are therefore able to participate in multiple cultures deploying practices in context-sensitive ways to construct action in different social groups. This means that cultural identities are fluid and constructed from the multiple group memberships of individuals. Cultural identities therefore are not coherent or fixed in terms of national or other affiliations, rather they grow out of participation in interaction with groups of others. Becoming a participant in a culture means knowing how to select and deploy those practices that will accomplish one's purposes in participation and evaluating the suitability of one's repertoire of practices to achieve the sorts of actions one wishes to engage in. To become a competent member of a social group, an individual needs to know what practices are potentially usable to achieve goals in a particular context and the likely consequences of using any of the practices that exist within an individual's particular repertoire.

Culture for language teaching and learning

In reality, the approaches to culture discussed above do not represent alternates. A solid approach to culture in language education should integrate a range of different understandings of culture. The understandings of culture described above are ways of focusing on culture that are relevant to teaching and learning. In reality, they are not mutually exclusive. For example, the teaching of literature does not necessarily need to approach literature as the "high culture" of the educated elite; it can be used as a way into understanding cultural practices. The issue is more one of emphasis than of content. Many problems with models of teaching cultural knowledge lie in limited perspectives that lead to a narrow view of culture with limited usefulness for ongoing learning or for communication. In approaching language education from an intercultural perspective, it is important that the view of culture be broad but also that it be seen as directly centered in the lived experiences of people. In particular, the dichotomy that exists in anthropology between culture as symbol system and culture as practices becomes particularly problematic in language teaching and learning because it can create an artificial divide between meaning and action. Rather, as Sewell (1999, p. 47) argues, symbols and practices are better understood as complementary: "to engage in cultural practice means utilizing existing cultural symbols to accomplish some end." Moreover, symbolic systems exist only in the practices which instantiate, challenge, or change them. In fact, we would argue it is in the interrelationships between the various ways of understanding culture discussed above that the intercultural can most readily be investigated in the teaching and learning of languages, and the intersections of practices and meanings is a significant point of engagement in cultures.

There are consequences of such an integrated understanding of culture for the ways in which cultures are taught and learned. To understand culture for language learning in a way that unites symbolic systems and practices across a range of contexts, it is necessary to go beyond a view of culture as a body of knowledge that people have about a particular society. One problem for the integration of culture into language education has been that many of the early models on which culture learning has been based present culture as unvarying and composed of discrete, concrete facts that can be taught and learned as factual information (Brooks, 1975; Lafayette, 1978; Nostrand, 1974). This approach to culture is a problem for language teaching because it omits key elements of cultural knowledge that are important for intercultural communication, which is in essence what second language use entails (Paige *et al.*, 1999). This body of knowledge can be seen in various ways: as knowledge about cultural artifacts or works of art, as knowledge about places and institutions, as knowledge about events and symbols, or as knowledge about ways of living. Culture is therefore reduced to information about others and is taught as if it were a set of the learnable rules that can be mastered by students. Language teaching that emphasizes the dissemination of elements of cultural information places limitations on the learning of culture (Crawford-Lange and Lange, 1984; Liddicoat, 2002). The main reason identified for this limitation is the representation of culture as a closed, final, and fixed phenomenon, and therefore the teaching imparts no learning that can help learners to understand and participate in cultures as they change in different times, places, and contexts. Moreover, such an approach ignores the range of cultural possibilities that exist within a society, to focus instead on a perceived cultural norm for some dominant group (e.g. middle class, adult, male), which may establish stereotypes of the culture (Crawford-Lange and Lange, 1984). A view of culture as information ignores the fact that culture is not a monolithic body of information held in the same way by all members of a national group (Duranti, 1997). Instead, it is distributed in different ways across a group, is differently valued by its members, and is more like a series of family resemblances in Wittgenstein's (1953) terms than an identifiable, consistent whole.

Culture is not simply a body of knowledge but a framework in which people live their lives, communicate and interpret shared meanings, and select possible actions to achieve goals. Seen in this way, it becomes fundamentally necessary to engage with the variability inherent in any culture. This involves a movement away from the idea of a national culture to recognition that culture varies with time, place, and social category, and for age, gender, religion, ethnicity, and sexuality (Norton, 2000). Different people participate in different groups and have multiple memberships within their cultural group, each of which can and does affect the presentation of the self within the cultural context (Tajfel and Turner, 1986). The variability is not limited to membership of subcultures but extends to the ways in which the individual participates within his/her cultures. People can resist, subvert, or challenge the cultural practices to which they are exposed in both their first culture and in additional cultures they acquire. Moreover, individual members enact the culture differently and pay different levels of attention to the cultural norms that operate in their society; interactions within a cultural context have the potential to reshape the culture (Paige *et al.*, 1999). Culture in this sense is dynamic, evolving, and not easily summarized for teaching; it is the complexity of culture with which the learner must engage (Liddicoat, 2002).

Although there will be some place for cultural facts in a language curriculum, it is more important to study culture as a process in which learners engage rather than as a closed set of information that he/she will be required to recall (Liddicoat, 2002). Viewing culture as a dynamic set of practices rather than as a body of shared information engages the idea of individual identity as a more central concept in understanding culture. Culture is a framework in which the individual achieves his/her sense of identity based on the way a cultural group understands the choices made by members, which become a resource for the presentation of the self. Jayasuriya (1990) suggests that to understand the relationship between culture and individual behavior one needs to think of culture as only a blueprint for action, as "the manifest culture revealed in individual behavior is selective, and not necessarily representative of a historical cultural tradition in its abstract form" (p. 14). Individuals select from this cultural blueprint in order to act appropriately, but not reductively, in different social contexts within the same culture. This notion of selective cultural behavior recognizes that although individuals' use of language is to a certain extent "bound" by their native cultural blueprint, they are also capable of creating a personal unique expression. This reflects Sacks' (1984) notion of "doing being ordinary": who we are is an interactionally accomplished product, not an inherent quality and the culture provides a reference point for this interactional accomplishment. Such a view encourages us to consider the individual as a semiotic system, that is, as a set of meaningful choices about the presentation of self. Culture provides a context in which this semiotic is to be read and choices will be understood differently in different cultural contexts (Kramsch, 1995a, 1995c). This means that, for the second language user, "doing being ordinary" involves presenting the self within a different framework of conventions for reading the individual. Language learning provides a challenge for identity in two key ways. It raises first the question, "Who am I when I speak this language?" and second "How am I me when I speak this language?"

A view of culture as practices indicates that culture is complex and that individuals' relationships with culture are complex. Adding a language and culture to an individual's repertoire expands the complexity, generates new possibilities, and creates a need for mediation between languages and cultures and the identities that they frame. This means that language learning involves the development of an intercultural competence that facilitates such meditation. Intercultural competence involves at least the following:

- accepting that one's practices are influenced by the cultures in which one participates and so are those of one's interlocutors;
- accepting that there is no one right way to do things;

- valuing one's own culture and other cultures;
- using language to explore culture;
- finding personal ways of engaging in intercultural interaction;
- using one's existing knowledge of cultures as a resource for learning about new cultures;
- finding a personal intercultural style and identity.

Intercultural competence means being aware that cultures are relative. That is, being aware that there is no one "normal" way of doing things, but that all behaviors are culturally variable. Applied to a particular language it also involves knowing some of the common cultural conventions used by speakers of the language (Liddicoat, 2000). The emphasis here is on *some*. Given the volume, variability, and potential for change of the cultural conventions, it is impossible to learn them all and certainly well beyond the scope of any classroom acquisition. Because a learner can only ever acquire some of the cultural conventions, an important part of intercultural competence is having strategies for learning more about culture during the process of interaction in a cultural context (Liddicoat, 2002).

To learn about culture, it is necessary to engage with its linguistic and nonlinguistic practices and to gain insights into the way of living in a particular cultural context (Kramsch, 1993a; Liddicoat, 1997a). It is important that the scope of culture learning moves beyond awareness, understanding, and sympathy, and begins to address the ways in which culture learning will be practiced by learners. Carr (1999) argues that learners need to become "interculturally competent players as well as sensitive observers" and the role of culture learning is to provide a framework for productive dialogue between old and new understandings. In a dynamic view of culture, cultural competence is seen, therefore, as intercultural performance and reflection on performance. It is the ability to negotiate meaning across cultural boundaries and to establish one's own identity as a user of another language (Kramsch, 1993b). Cultural knowledge is, therefore, not limited in its use to a particular task or exercise, but instead it is a more general knowing that underlies how language is used and how things are said and done in a cultural context. As such, it very closely resembles other types of language knowledge.

Language education, because its focus is on language, will inevitably privilege language as the entry point to cultures. This is not to say that language and culture are coextensive but rather that areas of study structure ways of engagement with knowledge. The aim of intercultural language teaching and learning is not to displace language as the core focus of language education but to ensure that language is integrated with culture in conceptualizing language learning. A core belief in new approaches to the teaching of culture is that language does not function independently from the context in which it is used (Byram, 1988; Kramsch, 1993a). Language is always used to communicate something beyond itself and is at the same time affected by the context in which it is found. The cultural context therefore affects the ways in which language is shaped by participants in a particular interaction, at a particular time, and in a particular setting. People who share the same general set of cultural practices share an understanding of the meanings that are associated with language as it is used for communication, and their language use is shaped by these shared understandings. Successful communication happens because of a shared understanding of context, regardless of how well individual participants know each other

(Heath, 1986). As a process of developing intercultural understanding, learners need to be able to decenter from their own culture (Byram, 1989a; Kramsch, 1993a). In language learning, this decentering takes two forms: decentering from one's own language and culture in communicating with others and decentering in the processes of teaching and learning. This can happen only as the result of a deliberate process of teaching that brings to the students the sorts of exposure they need to begin the decentering process, and the skills and knowledge to understand and interpret these experiences in order to achieve decentering. The study of language exposes learners to another way of viewing the world as they develop flexibility and independence from a single linguistic and conceptual system through which to view the world (Byram, 1989a; Kramsch, 1993a).

The Intercultural: Understanding Language, Culture, and their Relationship

The interrelationships between language and culture in communication will be discussed on the basis of the diagram presented in Figure 2.2. Language mediates cultures; however, in perceptions of human practice there is a perception that some aspects of practice are more "cultural" and others are more "linguistic." Figure 2.2 presents the language–culture interface as a continuum between aspects in which culture is the most apparent construct through to those in which language is the most apparent construct, but recognizes that regardless of the superficial appearance, both language and culture are integrally involved across the continuum. Figure 2.2 represents a number of ways in which language and culture intersect in communication, from the macrolevel of world knowledge, which provides a context in which communication occurs and is interpreted, to the microlevel of language forms.

At its most global level culture is a frame in which meanings are conveyed and interpreted and at this level apparently is least attached to language (Liddicoat, 2009). Culture as context comprises the knowledge speakers have about how the world works and how this is displayed and understood in acts of communication. This cultural knowledge has probably been the best covered in most approaches to culture in communication (see e.g. Fitzgerald, 2002; Levine and Adelman, 2002; Thomas, 1983, 1984). The linguistic dimension of world knowledge is often ignored, although such knowledge of the world is associated with and invoked by language (and other semiotic systems). This means that the message itself is not simply a sum of the linguistic elements of which it is composed, but it also includes additional elements of meaning that are invoked by, but are not inherent in, the linguistic elements. For example, the English term "sacred site" at the lexical level indicates only a location that has a religious or spiritual association or where a religious activity is carried out. In Australian English, however, it has very specific associations that are not inherent in its lexical meaning. The term sacred site applies only to sites that have associations with traditional indigenous religious beliefs. The determination that a place is a sacred site has legal consequences for a native title claim because it evidences indigenous land ownership. The identification of sites as sacred is located within a framework of contested political, historical, and legal ideologies about the nature of land ownership, the rights of indigenous people, and the legal doctrine of

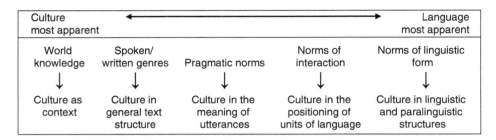

Figure 2.2   Points of articulation between culture and language in communication.
Source: Liddicoat, A. J. (2009) Communication as culturally contexted practice: A view from intercultural communication. *Australian Journal of Linguistics*, 29 (1): 115–133. Adapted from Crozet, C. and Liddicoat, A. J. (1999) The challenge of intercultural language teaching: Engaging with culture in the classroom, in *Striving for the Third Place: Intercultural Competence through Language Education* (eds J. Lo Bianco, A. J. Liddicoat, and C. Crozet), Language Australia, Melbourne.

terra nullius – the belief that Australia had not been subjected to any form of sovereignty before it was claimed by Europeans. For a speaker of Australian English, the use of the term "sacred site" comes packaged with this nonlinguistic information, which affects both its use and interpretation (Liddicoat, 2009).

Cultures also give specific, local meanings to language by adding shared connotations and associations to the standard denotation of terms. In this way, culture can be understood as a form of community of practice (Eckert and McConnell-Ginet, 1992; Holmes and Meyerhoff, 1999) in which certain meanings are privileged above other possible meanings in ways that are relevant to the purposes and histories of the communities of practice. World knowledge is by nature embedded and complex, but its operations can be seen through specific instances of communication in which assumed shared world knowledge is fundamental to the message being communicated. As Bakhtin (1981) argues, discourse always represents a worldview. When language is used in communication, it is used within and for this worldview and the worldview is as much constitutive of the message as the linguistic forms and their "agreed meanings." For example, the French word *didactique* and the English word "didactic" both have denotations related to instruction; however, the French term is a neutral word referring to the processes of teaching and learning, while the English word usually has negative connotations of excessiveness and tedium. The connotations appear to be more or less reversed in the pair "pedagogy" and *pédogogie* in which the English term is neutral but the French term has negative connotations.

The intersection of culture and communication is not simply one of the content or meaning of messages; it also applies to the forms of messages, and the ways in which these forms are evaluated and understood. In a given society the forms used in communication tend to be perceived as belonging together to form a class or genre, with each genre being understood as a type of communicative event (Hymes, 1974). Like other parts of language, texts are cultural activities and the act of communicating through speaking or writing is an act of encoding and interpreting culture (Kramsch, 1993a). Culture interacts with the forms of communication in three broad ways:

- the (oral and written) genres which are recognized and used;
- the properties of the textual features used in communication;
- the purposes for which these textual structures are used (Liddicoat, 2009).

Malinowski (1960) indicates that genres are socially and culturally significant and have an important function in the maintenance and cohesion of the culture. They can be considered to be a mapping of language forms onto recognizable types of communicative activity in which genres are formed by the cultural traditions of the community (Oring, 1986). In viewing genre as culturally contexted, genre ceases to be simply text and becomes activity (Shopen, 1993). The implications of culturally oriented perspectives for genre analysis are that any study of genre must treat genre as culturally situated, culturally defined, and culturally defining. For a particular genre to have importance it must have some sort of prominence within its culture.

Within a culture, members recognize the function and purpose of a text from the textual characteristics that are regularly associated with the text. This means that the forms of a text are cues to how texts are to be understood and responded to, and help to locate individual texts within genre. For example, Kirkpatrick (1991) has shown that letters of request written in English by speakers of Mandarin Chinese usually adopt a different structure than those written by British speakers of English. Request letters contain two main components: the request itself and reasons for the request. Writers of both English and Chinese are able to sequence these in any order: request then reasons or reasons then request; however, each culture appears to have different preferences for how such letters should normally be structured. Chinese favors reasons then request while British English favors request then reasons. The choice of structures is based on perceptions of communicative effectiveness. British English speakers believe that effective communication is achieved if a reader knows the purpose of the communication and can use this knowledge to interpret the text as a whole. Chinese speakers, however, believe that effective communication involves preparing the ground for a request and only producing the request when the need for the request will be understood by the reader.

Moreover, whereas some genres exist in all or most cultures as recognized patterns of purposeful communicative behavior, for example stories and conversations, not all genres are found in all cultures. For example, Shen (1989) describes a genre of scholarly literary criticism that exists in Chinese, *yijing*, but which has no parallel in English academic writing. *Yijing* involves constructing an imagistic response to a text that captures the affective and aesthetic impact of the text on the reader. A translation of a *yijing* text into English can be read and appreciated as a literary work by an English speaker, but would not be recognized as an academic text of literary criticism.

In pragmatic norms and norms of interaction, the effect of culture on communication can be seen more immediately in intercultural communication than in text structures. In considering norms, the effect of culture is on what "equivalent" units mean in contexts of use, and the sorts of interactional trajectories that are established by these contexts of use. Pragmatic norms refer to norms of language use, especially to politeness. They encompass knowledge of the ways in which particular utterances are evaluated by a culture. For example, French *Donne-moi le livre* and English "Give me the book" may mean the same thing, but they cannot be used in the same contexts. The French version would be considered adequately polite in a broader range of contexts than the English version would be (Béal, 1990). Norms of interaction refer to what it is appropriate to say at a particular point in a conversation, and what someone is expected to say at this point. This concerns issues such as the appropriate and expected answer to a question such as "How are you?" and the appropriate thing to say before eating, how acceptable it is to be silent or to be talkative (Béal, 1992; Kerbrat-Orecchioni, 1993). In all of the cases discussed here, the interpersonal and interactional meaning of any particular utterance is not determined solely by its linguistic composition. Instead each element is understood within a cultural framework that guides the process of interpretation. The communicative value of any utterance is then not strictly a property of language, but of language in its cultural context (Liddicoat, 2009).

From an intercultural perspective, linguistic form is not simply a structural feature of language. Instead, "every language embodies in its very structure a certain world view, a certain philosophy" (Wierzbicka, 1979, p. 313). Acts of communication are made up of structural elements: lexicon, morphology, syntax, etc. Each of these forms part of a culturally contexted system of meaningful elements that embed any utterance within a particular cultural frame. The influence of culture on linguistic forms is best recognized in the lexicon, in which words are seen as embodying culturally contexted conceptual systems. Lexical items are used to organize a social and physical universe and to construct patterns of similarity and difference between categories. For example, the Japanese word *aoi* is normally translated as "blue" in English. This translation, however, does not accurately reflect the ways in which *aoi* is mapped onto the color spectrum, as the color category "*aoi*" is not identical with the colour category "blue." *Aoi* is the color term used to describe traffic lights and apples, which in English would be classified as "green" rather than as "blue." In morphology, differences can be seen between Spanish and English in the ways that an event indicated by the verb is conceptualized in the grammar of the languages. The Spanish sentences *"Buscamos una persona que tiene pelo largo"* and *"Buscamos una persona que tenga pelo largo"* would both be translated into English as "We are looking for a person who has long hair." The Spanish versions contain two different conceptualizations of the event. The first, which has the indicative verb *tiene* "has," indicates that the speakers are looking for a definite known person, while the second indicates that the person they are looking for may not exist. The description of the person, which is rendered in the same way in English, encapsulates very different understandings about the nature of the world depicted by the sentence. Linguistic structures therefore can be seen as culturally embedded elements that represent different conceptualizations of the world of experience. This means that the relationships between the forms of two languages are not simply of translation equivalence (Eco, 2003; Venuti, 2006), but involve a remapping of the world of experience onto linguistic form. The result is that any translation does not capture the meaning of the original with fidelity, but necessarily adds or omits information that is salient and fundamental to the understanding of a meaning in the languages involved. This means that even at the most basic level, intercultural communication becomes an engagement with a conceptually different construction of experience.

In language teaching it is possible to identify a distinction between a cultural perspective and an intercultural perspective (Liddicoat, 2005b). A cultural perspective implies the development of knowledge about a culture, which remains external to the learner and is not intended to confront or transform the learner's existing identity, practices, values, attitudes, beliefs, and worldview. An intercultural perspective implies the transformational engagement of the learner in the act of learning. The goal of learning is to decenter learners from their preexisting assumptions and practices and to develop an intercultural identity through engagement with an additional culture. The borders between self and other are explored, problematized, and redrawn. In taking an intercultural perspective in language teaching and learning, the central focus for culture learning involves more than developing knowledge of other people and places (Liddicoat, 2005b). It involves learning that all human beings are shaped by their cultures and that communicating across cultures involves accepting that one's own and one's interlocutors' assumptions and practices are formed within a cultural context and are influenced by the cultures in which they are formed, also acknowledging the diverse ways that assumptions and practices are at play in communication. Learning another language can be like placing a mirror up to one's culture and to one's assumptions about how communication happens, what particular messages mean, and what assumptions one makes in daily life. Effective intercultural learning therefore occurs as the student engages in the relationships between the cultures that are at play in the language classroom. Such learning involves much more than developing knowledge about some other culture and its language. A main difference, then, between a cultural and an intercultural perspective is that a cultural perspective emphasizes the culture of the other and leaves that culture external to the learner, whereas an intercultural perspective emphasizes the learners' own cultures as a fundamental part of engaging with a new culture (Liddicoat, 2005c).

Such a view of the intercultural places learners as language users and social actors at the center of language learning, along with the languages and cultures they bring to that learning (Kern and Liddicoat, 2008). Language learners are positioned between languages and cultures and have communicative needs derived from the positioning. As a result, the communicative capabilities they need to develop may be different from those required of a first language speaker, and the native speaker is an inappropriate target norm in SLA (Byram, 1989a; Crozet and Liddicoat, 1999; Kasper, 1997; Kramsch, 1999; Saville-Troike, 1999). Kramsch (1999) argues that the very concept of native speaker is outdated and inappropriate, given the large-scale variations in linguistic norms and linguistic competence among "native speakers" of the same language (Davies, 1991; Widdowson, 1994). Instead of focusing on the native speaker as the target norm, many researchers now argue that the focus should be placed on the "intercultural speaker" as the target for second language teaching and learning (Byram and Zarate, 1994; Kramsch, 1998; Liddicoat, Crozet, and Lo Bianco, 1999).

Various researchers have argued that there is a need for different models of communicative competence for production and interpretation of a second language (Crozet and Liddicoat, 1999; Kasper, 1997; Saville-Troike, 1999). In terms of interpretation, learners need to know what native speakers are doing in their communication and to have an understanding of the native language norms that allow messages to be interpreted appropriately. For production, however, the situation is more complex. It may be that learners need to know how to produce language that can be interpreted by native speakers, but which at the same time acknowledges their own place as members of another culture along with the identity issues that relate to their first language cultural frame of reference as nonmembers of the target language community. Taking a slightly different approach,

Kramsch (1998) argues that learners need to develop a native-speaker–like competence in understanding the pragmatic force associated with linguistic structures (Thomas' (1983) pragmalinguistic competence), but should have choices about whether or not to adopt native speakers' understandings of the size of imposition, social distance, and relative rights and obligations when involving these linguistic structures (Thomas' (1983) sociopragmatic competence). Pauwels (2000) has argued that there needs to be a greater awareness of the importance of interactions, when using languages such as English as *linguae francae* in which communication may equally be between nonnative speakers from different cultural backgrounds as between native speakers and nonnative speakers. Pauwels criticizes the current approach, which assumes that intercultural communication is necessarily between learners and native speakers, as the communicative and cultural needs of such learners are different from native-speaker targets.

Rather than focusing only on communicative competence, it is also useful to consider the needs of language learners in terms of their development of "symbolic competence" (Kramsch, 2006; Kramsch and Whiteside, 2008). Symbolic competence involves more than the ability to use language to engage in communication with others and recognizes the needs of language users to develop new contexts for participation: "Symbolic competence is the ability not only to approximate or appropriate for oneself someone else's language, but to shape the very context in which the language is learned and used" (Kramsch and Whiteside, 2008, p. 664). This involves recognizing the symbolic value residing in language because of its subjective, historical, and creative associations. This involves recognition of the complexity inherent in language and its variability, which in turn allows for the recognition of alternate modes of thinking about and acting in the world. Kramsch and Whiteside (2008, p. 668) see symbolic competence as a "mindset that can create relationships of possibility" and note that this requires learners to come to see themselves from multiple perspectives. This entails recognizing the ways in which one's embodied history and subjectivity shapes perceptions of self and how the self is perceived through the history and subjectivity of others. It also involves considering the reciprocity of such perceptions – what is true of the self is also true of the other. Symbolic competence is thus an element of a repertoire that enables action within contexts of linguistic and cultural diversity.

These considerations mean that there is a need for language teaching to take into account norms related to bilinguality and interculturality rather than focusing exclusively on the native speaker as the target language norm. This shift of focus means redefining the nature of linguistic competence in SLA in order to add new dimensions to psycholinguistically determined models, with their emphasis on the development of linguistic structures, by emphasizing more socioculturally determined models of language as communication (Firth and Wagner, 1997; Liddicoat, 1997b). Learning about culture in the language classroom needs to involve a considerable element of learning how to learn from one's experiences of and reflections on language and culture in trying to create and interpret meanings. Developing the ability to learn beyond the classroom is probably more important than acquiring particular information about another culture during schooling. Learning how to learn about culture means that as people engage with new aspects of culture's variability, they develop their knowledge and awareness and find ways of acting according to their new learning.

3

Second Language Acquisition, Language Learning, and Language Learning within an Intercultural Orientation

Introduction: Two Families of Theories

In this chapter our attention turns to the process of learning language. Just as it is necessary to consider diverse conceptions of language and culture in relation to an intercultural orientation to language teaching and learning, so too it is necessary to consider diverse conceptions of the process of learning itself. A recent volume has drawn attention to the need in applied linguistics to understand both the different conceptions of learning to which different schools of SLA subscribe and to the way in which discussion of language learning depends on how language itself, as the substance or object of learning in second language learning, is understood (Seedhouse, Walsh, and Jenks, 2010).

Before beginning to discuss understandings of language learning, it is important to recognize a difficulty with the use of the key terms: "acquisition" and "learning." Although we recognize that SLA (with emphasis on acquisition) is the field of applied linguistics that addresses the question of how language is learned, the word "acquisition" may be interpreted in a traditional sense to refer to a view of learning understood only as the gaining of "knowledge" as object, or facts, or subject matter, abstracted from context, as opposed to also involving the learner, processes of learning, and situatedness. Our use of the term "learning" includes both senses. These distinctions become meaningful in the discussion of the two families of theories that we consider below. Understanding learning within an intercultural orientation entails an expanded view of learning that extends beyond traditional views of learning in SLA.

It is also important to consider the distinctiveness of language itself in education and learning, for it is both an area of learning in its own right (i.e. the substance of learning in second language learning), and one of the major mediums through which people learn. Language itself is integral to learning as the means through which people make personal meanings intrapersonally and through which they negotiate social relationships and share

Intercultural Language Teaching and Learning, First Edition. Anthony J. Liddicoat and Angela Scarino.
© 2013 Anthony J. Liddicoat and Angela Scarino. Published 2013 by Blackwell Publishing Ltd.

meanings and values interpersonally with others. Halliday (1993), writing about first language learning (although equally relevant to second language learning), explains that learning a language is not simply learning a particular domain of knowledge like all others. He sees learning a language as learning the "foundation of learning itself" (p. 93) because language is a crucial medium through which people make meaning, and it is this meaning-making that characterizes learning. He states: "Language is not a *domain* of human knowledge (except in the special context of linguistics, where it becomes an object of scientific study); language is the essential condition of knowing, the process by which experience *becomes* knowledge" (p. 94; emphasis in the original).

In this chapter we consider briefly some aspects of the history of SLA, leading to a central debate in the field that emerged through the 1990s and continues to the present time. The debate is about the nature of SLA and second language learning (see Block, 1996; Lantolf, 1996; van Lier, 1994) and is captured in two families of theories: the long established, traditional, cognitively oriented family of theories and the more recent socially and socioculturally oriented families of theories. In naming these "families of theories" we acknowledge the diversity of theories within both. In a seminal paper Firth and Wagner (1997) provided a catalyst for questioning, in a fundamental way, the very nature of SLA and the act of language learning. Describing the current state of play as "a bifurcation between cognitive SLA … and sociocultural/sociointeractional SLA," they called for a reconceptualization of SLA by inviting a consideration of alternate perspectives on learning. The notion of "bifurcation" suggests that the field is at a crossroad where the paths separate. This image raises the important question of what the relationship or balance between these different families of theories might be. Firth and Wagner also introduce the characterization of the alternate family of theories as social, cultural, and interactional, thereby highlighting the social dimension of learning and the central role of interaction.

Prior to the 1990s, SLA was viewed essentially as a matter of individual cognition, as a process that occurs in the mind of the learner, prompted by input that was seen to activate general cognitive processes. From the mid-1990s onwards, within social and sociocultural theoretical orientations, SLA has also come to be seen to involve "doing" or "action," in context, in social interaction with others; it has come to be seen as a process that involves becoming a member and extending participation within communities of language users (Kern and Liddicoat, 2008). The debate pertaining to these two families of theories challenges the traditional distinction in SLA research between language learning and language use (Kramsch and Whiteside, 2007), which, in turn, relates to the competence–performance debate in applied linguistics more generally. This debate will be revisited in Chapter 8 where we consider ways of conceptualizing the construct of interest in assessing language learning within an intercultural orientation. The debate is also reflective of current debates in learning theory in education (see e.g. Bruner, 1996; Hargreaves, 2005; Kalantzis and Cope, 2008; Shepard, 2000).

In this chapter we consider key understandings relevant to the two families of theories and trace briefly the history of the development of these families of theories. We then discuss Sfard's (1998) two metaphors of learning – acquisition and participation – and her argument for complementarity, that is, that both are needed in understanding and developing learning. This complementarity, however, also implies sufficiency. In arguing against the sufficiency of these two metaphors, we discuss the need to further expand views of learning within an intercultural orientation in order to capture the process of learning to communicate in a second language as "moving between" linguistic and cultural systems, and to acknowledge the essential role of interpretation in using and learning to use language for communication across languages. It is these two requirements, we argue, that best characterize language learning within an intercultural orientation.

Key Understandings of SLA and Language Learning within Diverse Families of Theories

In considering the theoretical pluralism that characterizes SLA in contemporary times Ellis (2010) presents a comparison of cognitive and social SLA which provides a useful framework for understanding the two diverse families of theories. He summarizes differences between these families in relation to nine key dimensions: language, mental representation, social context, learner identity, learner's linguistic background, input, interaction, language learning, and research methodology (Table 3.1).

The value of this presentation resides in the way it captures, in summary form, the major differences between the two families of theories as discussed within the field of SLA. Clearly, it is important to recognize that language itself and its representation, as the substance of learning, are integral to an understanding of how it is learned. Notably, however, in Ellis' account there is not an equal recognition of the importance of culture and its relationship to language and its role in understanding second language learning. This absence signals that in both families of theories within the field of SLA, the emphasis with respect to the substance of second language learning remains on learning the system of the language itself. If learning language also involves learning its fundamental meaning-making potential, then culture is integral to its theorization because it is culture that provides a lens through which to interpret and create meaning, both in the act of communication and in the act of learning. Language learning within an intercultural orientation needs to attend not only to the exchange of language but also to the exchange of meanings. Ellis highlights the different understandings of the role of context in both families of theories. In the description provided, however, it is the context of situation that is implied and not equally the context of culture. Ellis describes the difference between cognitive SLA and social SLA with respect to the learner identity category essentially as difference in terms of being singular or multiple, and static or dynamic. Although these are important characteristics that distinguish the families of theories, equally important is the notion of identity positioning, that is, the role of the learner and the way the learner is positioned in the learning process, that is, who it is that the learner is invited to be in both the target language being learned and in his or her own language(s). The learner's linguistic background category distinguishes how the two families of learning theories understand the learner's linguistic background as being monolingual or plurilingual, but it does not render how it is that the linguistic, and indeed cultural, "background" is, in fact, foregrounded or brought into play in the learning process itself. The learner's linguistic and cultural backgrounds can be seen as providing an already-structured position or standpoint or life-world that shapes subsequent learning.

Table 3.1 Comparison of cognitive and social second language acquisition (SLA)

Dimensions	Cognitive SLA	Social SLA
Language	Language viewed as either a set of formalist rules (as in Chomskyan linguistics) or as a network of form–function mapping (as in functional models of grammar of the Hallidayan type)	Language viewed not just as a linguistic system but as "a diverse set of cultural practices, often best understood in the context of wider relations of power" (Norton and Toohey, 2002, p. 115)
Mental representation	Two views: (i) as a set of rules that comprise the learner's linguistic competence; (ii) as an elaborate network of connections between neural nodes	In some social theories representation is not considered at all. Vygotskyan approaches emphasize the semantic ("conceptual") rather than the formal properties of the language that learners internalize
Social context	A broad distinction is made between "second" and "foreign" language contexts. Social context is seen as influencing the rate of acquisition and ultimate level of proficiency achieved but not affecting the internal processes responsible for acquisition	The social context is seen as both determining L2[1] use and developmental outcomes (as in variationist studies) and as something that is jointly constructed by the participants. The social context is where learning takes place
Learner identity	The learner is viewed as a "nonnative speaker". Learner identity is static	The learner is viewed as having multiple identities that afford different opportunities for language learning. Learner identity is dynamic (see Norton, 2000)
Learner's linguistic background	The learner has full linguistic competence in his/her L1[2]	Learners may be multilingual and may display varying degrees of proficiency in their various languages
Input	Input is viewed as linguistic "data" that serves as a trigger for acquisition. Input is viewed as related to but distinguishable from "interaction"	Input is viewed as contextually constructed; it is both linguistic and nonlinguistic
Interaction	Interaction is viewed as a source of input	Interaction is viewed as a socially negotiated event and a means by which learners are socialized into the L2 culture. Input and interaction are viewed as a "sociocognitive whole" (Atkinson, 2002)
Language learning	L2 acquisition occurs inside the mind of the learner as a result of input that activates universal cognitive processes	L2 acquisition is "learning-in-action"; it is not a mental phenomenon but a social and collaborative one. It is an "interactional phenomenon that transcends contexts while being context dependent" (Firth and Wagner, 1997, p. 807)
Research methodology	Typically atomistic, quantitative, and confirmatory – aims to form generalizations about groups of learners	Holistic, qualitative, and interpretative – focuses on individual learner and specific interactional sequences

[1] Second language.
[2] First language.
Source: Ellis, R. (2010) Theoretical pluralism in SLA: Is there a way forward? In P. Seedhouse, S. Walsh, and C. Jenks (eds), *Conceptualising "Learning" in Applied Linguistics*, Basingstoke, Palgrave Macmillan.

The input category captures well the distinction normally made between the two families of theories; between linguistic and nonlinguistic input and between input as separate from or integrated with its construction in interaction; it does not capture, however, how the families of theories understand the ways in which the input is interpreted, processed, and used by the learner, in other words the personal and interpersonal meanings that learners make of the input provided. The interaction category is one of the major characteristics that is used to distinguish the two families of theories. Neither account provided by Ellis, however, recognizes sufficiently the act of learning a second language as an act of mutual interpretation and exchange of meanings in interaction, that is, that students learn what it means to interpret the world and others in the world and to be interpreted by others through the horizon of the linguistic and cultural system that is their own while gradually and increasingly coming to understand the linguist and cultural system that they are learning. The two positions on language learning described by Ellis do not acknowledge that learning also involves learners coming to understand how they themselves interpret knowledge through their positioning in their own language and culture.

In each of these nine categories, Ellis identifies the current state of play with respect to the defining characteristics and distinctions that are made between the families of theories. In relation to each of these categories we argue that when language learning is understood within an intercultural orientation each of these categories needs to be expanded further to recognize learning as interlinguistic and intercultural (Byrnes, Maxim, and Norris, 2010) and as interpretive (Scarino, 2010). Interestingly, in the research methodology category outlined by Ellis, the interpretive characteristic is captured within the social SLA.

Before discussing more fully the nature and value of such an expanded view of learning, we provide a brief history of the development of these families of theories of SLA to better situate our understandings of second language learning.

A Brief History of the Development of Theories of Language Learning

Cognitive theories of language acquisition developed as a reaction to behaviorism. The behaviorist view was challenged by Chomsky (1959), who claimed that children are born with a capacity for language, just as they are born with an ability to learn to walk, and that it is neither taught nor learned but it just grows. This innatist view of language acquisition states that beyond imitation and practice children have a language acquisition device in the brain which allows them to discover the rules of a language system; experience of natural language activates the device, which enables learners to discover the structure of the language to be learned by matching the structures of language in their environment with their innate knowledge of basic grammatical relationships. This capability, related to innate knowledge of principles of Universal Grammar, enables children to develop their language ability beyond the actual input that they have received. This is the creativity of language; children create sentences that they have never learned before. The evidence for this view comes from the fact that all children successfully learn their home language, that they do so under highly diverse conditions, and that they learn to use language beyond the instances of their immediate experience. The evidence that they are applying rules rather than imitating language around them comes from utterances such as "she goed to the shop." While Chomsky essentially worked within first language situations, there has been subsequent consideration about whether his theory also pertains to SLA and, if so, how exactly it is that Universal Grammar works in the learning of subsequent languages (e.g. White, 2003). At this same time there was a shift from structural linguistic, which considered the surface structure of language, to generative linguistic, which considered language as rule-governed and creative.

A more comprehensive innatist theory of SLA is the influential theory proposed by Krashen (1982). It is based on five tenets. The first is a distinction between acquisition (which he describes as the process through which people naturally and subconsciously acquire language to which they are exposed, guided by their innate ability) and learning (which entails a conscious process of learning form, through instruction and correction). In this theory, acquisition is the process that yields natural, spontaneous communication, while learning plays a less important role in that it serves as a "monitor" of speech and writing, understood essentially as grammar, to ensure correctness. Krashen maintains that there is no interface between acquisition and learning; these are seen as separate processes. The second tenet relates to monitoring, which is the process of editing language use. Krashen holds that grammatical rules can be learned but that doing so is only useful as a monitor. The third tenet of Krashen's theory is that acquisition can occur only through receiving abundant *comprehensible input* that is designed to be linguistically just beyond the learner's level of competence ($i+1$). The fourth tenet is that learners acquire language in predictable, developmental sequences in terms of structures and complexity, and this natural order cannot be altered by direct teaching. The final tenet is that learners learn best when the "affective filter" is low, that is, when they are not anxious, stressed, uncomfortable, and therefore unmotivated. While Krashen's claims have not been substantiated through empirical research, his theory remains influential, particularly in language teaching, as a theory that has supported communicative language teaching. This remains the dominant approach to language teaching in many contexts because it foregrounds communication above learning as a process of learning and activating rules. Nevertheless, the relationship between communication and form remains a problem in language learning.

Van Lier (2004) argues that each of these five tenets can be considered more expansively. With regard to the acquisition–learning distinction he observes that when Krashen (1982) talks about learning he is referring to meaningless drill approaches, that is, learning language by learning grammar, and this is the reason for his no-interface position between acquisition and learning. Van Lier suggests that a weak interface position might be more reasonable or indeed an emergentist position in which both incidental learning (or acquisition in Krashen's sense) and focused learning can contribute to the emergence of linguistic abilities. Van Lier expands the monitor hypothesis (tenet 2) beyond a conception of a supervisory center in the brain that inspects or analyzes every utterance to monitoring as a constant and necessary accompaniment of language use. With regard to the natural order hypothesis (tenet 4), van Lier suggests that despite the notions of learnability and processability it is possible that learners store rules learned in a rote manner for retrieval later in language use. With regard to the input hypothesis (tenet 3) he notes the problem of the computational metaphor that suggests learning is the processing and storage of fixed pieces of language as information in the brain, thereby neglecting the socially active learner. With regard to the affective filter (tenet 5), van Lier notes that Krashen's (1982) metaphor encourages a view of it as a single variable that is open or closed by "a passive, asocial learner who just sits around soaking up comprehensible input" (2004, p. 140). This fails to take into account the learner as a social being, participating emotionally and motivationally in interaction in learning where social interaction involves a risk to identity at every point (Ashworth, 2004). Van Lier (2004) expands the notion of affect, recognizing that it is integral to all cognitive and social work, and that a learner must be receptive to learning in order to invest in it. He further problematizes the notion by recognizing that because emotional factors do not have a uniform relationship with learning, emotions cannot be simply categorized as positive or negative in relation to learning. Although Van Lier proposes a more expansive view of language learning, his attention remains focused on language learning essentially as the learning of grammar, which restricts the substance of learning.

More recent cognitive theories have adopted an *information processing* view of human learning. Within this view students begin by attending to particular words or items and gradually build up or construct a system. Some items of knowledge are rapidly brought into use, so that they become automatic, thereby creating mental space for students to attend to other aspects. In this context, in contrast to Krashen (1982), Schmidt (1990) highlights the role of "noticing." He argues that conscious noticing is the first step towards coming to know a language. If learning is to take place, learners need to pay attention to language features and forms. Attention, however, entails attending to language itself and not the various aspects of an expanded view of language.

The theories described so far give salience to the internal processing of information in the mind of the individual learner. Further theoretical work on language learning considers the role of interaction. Building on Krashen's (1982) notion of comprehensible input, Long (1985, 1996) proposes an interactive view of input whereby learners work at understanding each others' meanings in interaction. Essentially, within this view comprehensible input becomes available in situations of social interaction. This is because the context of interaction provides opportunities for the negotiation of meaning. Through the process of negotiation, input becomes comprehensible as native speakers adjust or modify their language until learners show signs of understanding. This is not only a process of simplification, but also a process of clarification, elaboration, emphasis, or providing further contextual clues. The adjustment involves negotiation in order to clarify and confirm meaning in the particular instance in response to difficulties experienced by the learner. Long (1996, pp. 451–452) sees the negotiation for meaning that takes place in interaction as connecting input, internal learner capacities, particularly selective attention, and output in productive ways. The interactivity here remains focused on language understood as grammar, and is aimed at resolving communication problems: improving the comprehensibility of input, attention, and the need to produce output, within a computational metaphor. Interaction is needed to facilitate cognition and learning; it is a means to a learning end but not constitutive of learning itself in the sense of learning how to interpret, create, and exchange personal meanings. Furthermore, the link between increased opportunity for negotiation of meaning and improved learning is yet to be demonstrated empirically (Littlewood, 2004).

Another important development in relation to interaction-based approaches to language learning is the recognition that output plays an important role in acquisition (Swain, 1995). Speaking and writing forces learners to attend to aspects of form that they do not need for comprehension purposes alone, and in the process of speaking and writing learners identify gaps, make hypotheses about how language works, and obtain feedback towards extending their understanding of the language. Within these interaction-based views, interaction plays a mediating role in learning in that it stimulates students to seek scaffolds or supports from peers or the teacher in order to fill gaps or extend their learning (Littlewood, 2004).

In the theories discussed above, the emphasis is on cognitive processes that underlie second language learning. They are psychologically oriented theories that consider learning as developing in the mind of the individual. Interaction becomes the vehicle for stimulating various kinds of mental processes within the individual. It is one of the conditions for learning. Context is considered to be important but it is understood only as the immediate setting in which interaction takes place; it is not seen as shaping the interaction towards the exchange of meaning. Furthermore, language itself remains the substance of learning rather than also including significant "content" that is derived from other domains of knowledge and culture(s) of the target language being learned or the personal knowledge of the students themselves.

Sociocultural theories, as the second family of theories, have developed in reaction to cognitive theories. They consider the relationship between thinking and the wider social, cultural, historical, and institutional context in which it occurs. The context itself is seen to be constitutive of learning. Within these theories social interaction is seen as the major means through which learning occurs. As Lantolf explains, "sociocultural theory holds that specifically human forms of mental activity arise in the interactions we enter into with other members of our culture and with the specific experiences we have with the artifacts produced by our ancestors and by our contemporaries" (2000, p. 79). Within the sociocultural family of theories the mental and the social are not seen as a dichotomy but rather as being in a dialectic relationship where each is shaped by and shapes the other.

Learning within the social and sociocultural family of theories occurs through the learner's interaction with more knowledgeable others. The social process of interaction is understood as a process of co-construction through language as well as other social and cultural systems and tools. It mediates the construction of knowledge and leads to the development of individuals' frameworks of knowledge and reference. It is through these frameworks that learners make sense of experience that is congruent with the cultural system in which they and the learning are situated. It is through social and cultural processes that learners are socialized to act, communicate, and "be" in ways that are culturally appropriate to the groups in which they participate as members, and through which their identities are formed. The goal is to become a knowing member of a particular community.

Sociocultural theories draw upon the work of Vygotsky (1978) who, with a particular concern for development in learning over time (i.e. understanding both the current character and level of learning and the potential for further learning), developed the notion of the *zone of proximal development*. This zone refers to domains of performance that the learner cannot yet achieve independently but can achieve with scaffolding, that is, with assistance that is provided in a variety of ways. Further, as van Lier (2004, p. 156) clarifies, the "co-constructed, dialogical language is no longer limited to approved bits of the standard language as promoted by textbooks and tests, but it includes a variety of ways in which learners find their own voice, their right to speak, including their right to draw on their first language." The prior understanding of learners, already prestructured in and by their experiences of their first language and culture, comes into play as they engage with learning a new language and culture; in so doing they need opportunities to experiment with who they are and can be in the new interlinguistic and intercultural reality. It is in this sense that identity theories come into play; learners are constantly "organizing and reorganizing a sense of who they are and how they relate to the social world" (Norton, 2000, p. 11). The value of the social and sociocultural family of theories resides in their recognition of the significance of the social and cultural context, that is, situatedness, in an understanding of learning that traditionally has been predominantly psychologically driven. A fundamental difference between the two families of theories relates to whether knowledge is seen to reside in the mind or in the social and cultural context and whether learning is an individual or social accomplishment.

Within sociocultural theory interaction involves complex activity on the part of the individual, drawing upon mediational tools (the most important of which is language) and the social context as constitutive of learning. As Swain and Deters state:

> [Sociocultural Theory] views language as a tool of the mind, a tool that contributes to cognitive development and is constitutive of thought. Through *languaging*, defined as the use of speaking and writing to mediate cognitively complex activities, an individual develops cognitively, and … affectively. The act of producing spoken or written language is thinking in progress and is key to learners' understanding of complex concepts. These understandings are reached through interacting with others, ourselves, and social and cultural artifacts. (2007, p. 822)

In this way, complex language learning emerges through the learner's engagement in human interaction in activity with artifacts and tools and in social, cultural, and historical practices. In the interaction, language combines with gesture, images, and objects in context, all of which support language use. Through the zone of proximal development learners participate socially in interaction with more knowledgeable interlocutors, thereby learning firstly on a social, interpersonal plane and then making the learning their own through internalization on an individual, intrapersonal plane (Vygotsky, 1978).

Van Lier discusses interaction in his description of an ecological approach to language learning:

> From an ecological perspective the learner is immersed in an environment full of potential meanings. These meanings become available gradually as the learner acts and interacts within and with this environment. Learning is not a holus-bolus or piecemeal migration of meanings to the inside of the learner's head, but rather the development of increasingly effective ways of dealing with the world and its meanings. Therefore, to look for learning is to look at the active learner in her environment, not at the contents of her brain. (2000, pp. 246–247)

The learner in his or her environment is engaged with understanding all aspects of interpreting and understanding human interaction, and not only language itself. The context is not just a source of input for the receiving learner, but rather, it provides the condition for interaction for active meaning-making together with others who are more or less competent with respect to language. This kind of social interaction in context is best seen as a relational view of learning where participants relate to each other and the tools and resources in context to generate language use and reflection on language use. This knowledge is socially distributed and has a social history. In this way, as Firth and Wagner state, "a reconceptualized SLA will be better able to understand and explicate how language is used *as it is being acquired through interaction* and used resourcefully, contingently and contextually" (1997, pp. 296; emphasis in the original).

Thus the two families of theories differ in their definition of what is being learned, that is, their conceptualizations of language as well as the nature and processes of learning itself. There are also differences in how the *relationship* between the two families of theories and the bridging of the social–cognitive divide might best be understood. This relationship is discussed by Sfard (1998) and in the further consideration that her influential paper has stimulated.

The Acquisition and Participation Metaphors

Sfard's (1998) discussion of learning as two dominant metaphors, *acquisition* and *participation*, has increasingly entered into discussions of second language learning. It is important to note that the understanding of "acquisition" here is different from the particular meaning that Krashen gives to the term. Sfard proposes a relationship of complementarity between the two ways of thinking about learning, which she describes as two metaphors. Within the acquisition metaphor, knowledge is conceptualized as a commodity and learning is seen as the process of receiving, accumulating, or gaining possession of that commodity. Within the participation metaphor, knowledge is conceptualized as an aspect of practice, activity, and discourse. The concept of "knowledge" (a noun) as an entity or state within the acquisition metaphor becomes "knowing" (a verb) within the participation metaphor so as to render the notion of process. Within the participation metaphor, learning involves a process of active construction and becoming a participant in communities of shared practice and shared discourse, through a process of enculturation.

Sfard (1998) clarifies that the distinction between the two metaphors is not, in fact, based on the distinction between individual and social views of learning. Rather, she sees the distinction as a difference in the way knowledge itself is conceptualized in learning. She sees both the traditional view of learning as the reception and transmission of knowledge *and* the sociocultural constructivist view of learning as the internalization of socially and culturally established concepts as belonging to the acquisition metaphor (Sfard, 1998, p. 7), in that they both represent perspectives on how learning occurs. The difference between the two metaphors that she highlights relates to the nature of learning itself rather than the means through which it arises. Within the acquisition metaphor, whether the knowledge is acquired through transmission or construction, individually and/or socially, there is an assumption of the objectification of knowledge, regardless of whether the knowledge is the knowledge of rules of grammar or the internationalization of social concepts. Knowledge within this metaphor is something that can be acquired, owned, transferred, and that can become part of the human make-up. The notion that knowledge is transferred requires a view of knowledge as an entity, as something that *can* be transferred or changed. The participation metaphor, on the other hand, highlights people in action where "being in action means being in constant flux" (Sfard, 1998, p. 8). This metaphor focuses on the activity; success is expressed in relation to the activity rather than the person's store of knowledge or traits. Learning is situated in these activities of participation. By presenting context as central in the sense of being constitutive of learning, and by not objectifying knowledge, the participation metaphor (taken on its own) loses explanatory power in relation to the notion of *transfer* or change. This is because context is infinitely variable and, as such, it is not amenable to generalizability and because there is no entity that can be transferred. Yet, as Sfard observes, despite the context-dependent nature of any activity and the problem of transfer within the participation metaphor, "something does keep repeating itself as we move from situation to situation and from context to context" (Sfard, 1998, p. 9). It is for this reason that she concludes that neither metaphor is sufficient on its own but that both, taken together, can be seen as offering differing and complementary, rather than competing perspectives. Furthermore, she highlights the value of having more than one metaphor as permitting productive argument that leads to a more critical process of theory building with respect to learning.

In line with Sfard's view of the value of argument, debates have emerged relating to the meaning of the metaphors that she has proposed and their relationship for the purposes of accounting for learning. These are discussed below.

Working on developing models of innovative knowledge communities, Paavola, Lipponen, and Hakkarainen (2004) propose that beyond characterizing learning through Sfard's (1998) two metaphors there is need for a third aspect, which they designate as the *knowledge-creation* metaphor. They argue that this metaphor allows for mediated processes of *collective knowledge creation* for developing new and shared knowledge. This metaphor extends learning beyond adding to, or changing, **or** reorganizing ready-made existing knowledge (i.e. acquisition) and the passing on of knowledge and practices to future generations (participation), to advancing *new* knowledge and solving problems in a way that can be achieved only communally, and in a way that extends the overall knowledge and know-how of the community of participants. This creativity may involve drawing upon people's tacit knowledge and transforming it into explicit knowledge, experimenting with new conceptual modeling (with a focus on *re*conceptualizing) and new theory building beyond current levels of understanding. In summary, Paavola, Lipponen, and Hakkarainen state:

> Learning is not conceptualized through processes occurring in individual's minds, or through processes of participation in social practices. Learning is understood as a collaborative effort directed toward developing some mediated artifacts, broadly defined as including knowledge, ideas, practices, and material or conceptual artifacts. The interaction among different forms of knowledge or between knowledge and other activities is emphasized as a requirement for this kind of innovativeness in learning and knowledge creation. (2004, pp. 569–570)

The value of the knowledge-creation metaphor resides in the fact that it goes beyond notions of situated cognition and social practices to emphasize communal, social, mediated activity to create new practices or artifacts. Drawing attention to a third metaphor opens the possibility of generating additional metaphors that capture further aspects of the process or further characteristics of learning. Having added a third metaphor, however, Paavola, Lipponen, and Hakkarainen (2004), like Sfard (1998), assume that the combination of the three metaphors provides a sufficient account of learning. We question this sufficiency in the context of second language learning.

The notion of drawing together strands from diverse families of theories is a pragmatic stance that is taken by several researchers, both in education in general and in languages education. Working in education, Shepard (2000) among others (see also e.g. Gipps, 1999) sees that it is some kind of merged theory that accounts for cognitive development in terms of social experiences that will inform practice in teaching and learning. She states:

> The constructivist paradigm takes its name from the fundamental notion that all human knowledge is constructed. … scientists build their theories and understandings rather than merely discovering laws of nature. Similarly individuals make their own interpretations, ways of organising information and approaches to problems, rather than merely taking in pre-existing knowledge structures. … an important aspect of individual learning is developing experience with and being inducted into the ways of thinking and working in a discipline or community of practice. Both the building of science and individual learning are social processes. Although the individual must do some private work to internalize what is supported and practiced in the social plane, learning cannot be understood apart from its social context and content. (Shephard 2000, p. 18)

Both families of theories see learning as active construction, that is, that learners are engaged in making sense of the learning from their own points of view, integrating it into their own way of understanding in social interaction with others. The characteristic of "prior knowledge" is important in that it recognizes that new learning is built upon prior learning, that is, the ideas and concepts (conceptions *and* misconceptions) as well as prior social and cultural experiences and knowledge that learners bring. These prior understandings and cultural experiences are not simply a part of learners' backgrounds, but rather, they constitute the students' social and cultural life-worlds that they bring to and that shape new learning. The characteristic of metacognition, or awareness about how one learns is integral to learning. Learners come to understand how it is that they learn, and how and why they interpret phenomena as they do and develop self-awareness of themselves as learners.

In applied linguistics several researchers have addressed the question of the relationship between Sfard's (1998) metaphors specifically in relation to language learning. Larsen-Freeman and Cameron (2008) explain that they do not accept the acquisition–participation dichotomy as representing an adequate account of language learning. They apply complexity theory to language learning, recognizing learning as a "complex, dynamic, non-linear, self-organizing, open, emergent, sometimes chaotic and adaptive system" (p. 4). Larsen-Freeman (2010) presents what she describes as a "middle ground" position (p. 52) based on complexity theory. She conceptualizes Sfard's (1998) metaphors as the two ends of a continuum, where at one end there are theories that represent language learning as "having" something while at the other end there are theories that represent language learning as "doing" something. She argues for a doing/having view that sees language as a complex adaptive system in which every use of language changes the language resources of the learner/user and the changed resources are then potentially available for the next speech event. In this way learners constantly adapt their linguistic resources, as a whole, in the service of meaning-making in diverse contexts. She sees complexity theory as a means for reframing our understanding of learning. The emphasis on learners mobilizing their linguistic resources as a whole and learning from the holistic experience of doing so is valuable in understanding learning. In this account, however, it is important to clarify how expansively the linguistic resources are seen to be, and how it is exactly that learners learn how to create new learning.

In describing ecological perspectives in language learning, Kramsch (2002) focuses on language learners as language users whose participation in semiotic (and not just linguistic) interactions in natural environments creates affordances for language acquisition. The learner is not a computer or an apprentice but a *negotiator* of multiple meanings, stances, and identities. She argues that the metaphor of ecology is "a convenient shorthand for the post-structuralist realization that learning is nonlinear, relational, human activity, co-constructed between humans and their environment, contingent upon their position in space and history, and a site of struggle for the control of social power and cultural memory" (Kramsch, 2002, p. 5). Learning involves not only one person interacting with another person, but a whole history of experiences and memories interacting with another history of experiences and memories (Kramsch, 2009). In this conceptualization, language learning is a profoundly human activity focused on meaning.

Expanding Learning: Recognizing the Role of Interpretation in "Moving Between" Linguistic and Cultural Systems

Both complexity theory and ecological theory propose views of language learning as dynamic, complex, and holistic, and irreducible to sets of elements and factors. These theories also suggest that while the two (or more) metaphors are relevant, they may not be sufficient as an account of the complexity of language learning.

The question of sufficiency is also raised by Ortega (2009) who, based on the postcolonial theories of Homi Bhabha, proposes "in-betweenness" as an additional metaphor for second language learning. She sees "in-betweenness" as an exploration of moments or processes that are produced in the articulation of cultural differences. The notion of exploration here includes an examination of the role of power and the possibility of building new identities in new sites of collaboration and contestation. Our notion of "moving between" is closely aligned to Ortega's "in-betweeness." However, while we acknowledge that there are issues of power in education, our notion of "moving between" is intended to highlight the phenomenology of learning to work within at least two linguistic and cultural systems when learning an additional language.

Second language learning within an intercultural orientation, we argue, is best seen as a process that necessarily entails a *movement between languages and cultures* in communicating with others in the target language being learned and in the process of learning itself. Participants in communication bring to it their own linguistic and cultural biographies, their distinctive frames of reference that come from their history of prior experiences, their meanings, and values. In the act of communicating, they engage in mutual interpretation to negotiate their own meanings in relation to those of others. This interaction is focused not only on the description, analysis, and interpretation of phenomena shared when communicating but also on active engagement in interpreting self (*intraculturality*) and others (*interculturality*) in diverse contexts of social and cultural exchange (Papademetre and Scarino, forthcoming). Learners do not just speak or write, but in communication in speaking and in writing they are also interpreting themselves and others in an ongoing way. This movement between languages and cultures also comes into play in *learning to communicate*. Through their learning learners develop an understanding of the interrelationship between language and culture and their role in the interpretation and construction of meaning. Thus, an intercultural orientation to language learning involves communicating and learning to communicate in and through an additional language *and* learning to understand the process of communication itself across languages and cultures, recognizing the linguistic and cultural construction of the interpretation and creation of meaning. It recognizes that learning is always referenced to the languages and cultures of the learners, which are part of their repertoires of communication and cultural experiences. The value of learning within a community is that the experience necessarily foregrounds diversity, the variability of people in terms of what they bring to interactions, and their use of language and interpretations of meaning. The diversity of perspectives generated within the community offers the potential for new learning and, at times, unlearning, questioning, and problematizing one's own understanding, which, in turn, leads to further learning. Learning languages within an intercultural orientation involves referencing language use and learning across diverse languages and cultures, understood as meaning systems.

This understanding of language learning resonates with Kramsch's (2009) view of developing *symbolic competence* as a cluster of abilities that includes awareness of the symbolic value of words, an ability to grasp the larger social and historical significance of events and the cultural memories evoked by symbolic systems, an ability to reframe issues from diverse perspectives, and the ability to find the most appropriate subject position. Intercultural language learning involves learners' experiences of reciprocal interpretation in meaning-making towards understanding one another.

Understood in this way, language learning incorporates hermeneutics as a theoretical resource for an interpretive view of learning. In this view, learning is best understood from the point of view of the learner as a process of interpretation, a hermeneutic process (Ashworth, 2004). The learner is an interpreter working towards achieving understanding. Two hermeneutical principles are central: that all interpretation is governed by tradition (or history) and that all interpretation is linguistic. For Gadamer (2004), interpretation involves a dialogue or conversation between two participants who are trying to come to an understanding about the particular subject matter. He sees learning that grows out of dialogue as a "fusion of horizons" – the horizons reflected in the learner's initial presuppositions and the horizon of the other person or text. Gadamer describes the process of reaching understanding as follows:

> Reaching an understanding ... necessarily means that a common language must first be worked out. This is not an external matter or simply adjusting our tools; nor is it even right to say that the partners adapt themselves to one another but, rather ... to reach an understanding in a dialogue is not merely a matter of putting oneself forward and

successfully asserting one's point of view, but being transformed into a communion in which we do not remain the same. (2004, p. 371)

Gadamer does not view language as a superficial tool for learning or coming to understand, a tool which people share, or as a simple process of adaptation to the dialogue partner. To understand requires a mutual process of making sense of each other's contribution (the subject matter) and at the same time each other (the person). To the process of making sense, learners bring their own histories of experiences, their own languages and cultures and ways of seeing the world. In other words, Gadamer reminds us that learners come with their own fore-understandings. Learners use dialogue (talk, language) to achieve a "fusion of horizons" with the other and each experience of doing so transforms their understanding of the subject matter, themselves, and others. In this sense, learning means not only acquiring new knowledge and participating in communities of users of that knowledge, but also recognizing that learning itself is interpretive and that learners are both interpreters and creators of meaning. In learning a second language, learners are interpreters in multiple senses. They work towards interpreting and creating meaning *in vivo* in interaction in using the language they are learning; at the same time and in so doing they are interpreters of another linguistic and cultural system and learning to be themselves in this system that is not their own; in addition, they are interpreters of the experience of learning itself. In all these interpretive senses, Gadamer highlights that the learner's interpretations arise, indeed, can only arise from the standpoint of the learner. In working across at least two linguistic and cultural worlds, second language learners are constantly moving between the two (or more) worlds. It is this view of learning as interpretive and as requiring the constant movement between languages and cultures in diversity that characterizes learning from an intercultural perspective.

Gallagher (1992), who draws on hermeneutics to develop an educational theory that acknowledges the interpretational nature of the learning experience, makes clear the important relationship between language and learning. He explains that understanding is not an abstract, mental act but a linguistic event because language has a central role to play in understanding the world. He emphasizes that "interpretation is the attempt to get to the meaning of something. In the same sense, learning also involves meaning. Whatever is learned is meaningful. Even if one sets out to memorize nonsense syllables, meaningless series of letters, the learning takes place within some context that bestows meaning on their meaninglessness" (p. 120). Thus, returning to the question of the sufficiency of the metaphors of learning within an intercultural orientation, we highlight the value of an interpretive dimension. Beyond acquisition, language learning involves learning to interpret language and knowledge for oneself. Beyond participation in social practices, language learning involves performing and interpreting oneself and others in social practices. It is the interpretive work itself that generates learning.

Conclusion

In the previous two chapters we have argued for an expanded view of language, culture, and learning that is necessary for teaching language within an intercultural perspective. In relation to all three we argue for the acknowledgment of the interpretive nature of communication (language use in the context of situation and culture) and of learning. Thus, in relation to language, learning language within an intercultural orientation requires an understanding of language as word, as a structural system, and as social practice, highlighting not only the practice itself but also the reciprocal process of interpretation of the language and the person. In relation to culture, it requires an understanding of culture as facts, artifacts, information, and social practices as well as an understanding of culture as the lens through which people mutually interpret and communicate meaning. In relation to learning, it requires the acquisition of new concepts and participation in the use of these concepts as well as an understanding of learning as learners becoming aware of how they themselves interpret their world through their own language and culture.

4

Language Teaching and Learning as an Intercultural Endeavor

Introduction

So far, we have argued for an expanded conceptualization of the core concepts of language education – language, culture, and learning – as a foundation for an intercultural perspective in language teaching and learning. In this chapter we turn to the intercultural nature of language learning as an educational activity. At one level this may seem an unproblematic endeavor; many regard language learning as inherently intercultural, because it involves an additional culture. That is, language learning is seen as isomorphic with interculturality (Liddicoat, 2004a). Such simplistic understandings of the intercultural, however, are indeed problematic when considering how language learning can contribute to the intercultural development of learners. In spite of claims they may have made about their aims and objectives, many approaches to language education have effectively marginalized culture and the intercultural by focusing solely on the linguistic system and the use of materials that are sanitized of cultural complexity. In order to understand language learning as intercultural, we need to problematize the relationship between language, culture, and learning in language education and to develop new ways of understanding the ways in which language education can be a fundamentally intercultural endeavor.

In the previous chapters we have made an argument that highlights interpretation as a fundamental feature of how we understand language, culture, and learning, and it is the integration of this interpretive dimension that is a core feature of our stance. The act of interpretation is a core element of the processes of both communication and learning. Both are language games – the speaking of language is a part of both activities (Wittgenstein, 1953). The language game is a union of language and action: *"Ich werde auch das Ganze: der Sprache und der Tätigkeiten, mit denen sie verwoben ist, das»Sprachspiel«nennen"* [I shall also call the whole, the language and the actions into which it is woven, the "language-game"] (section 7).

Intercultural Language Teaching and Learning, First Edition. Anthony J. Liddicoat and Angela Scarino.
© 2013 Anthony J. Liddicoat and Angela Scarino. Published 2013 by Blackwell Publishing Ltd.

Language games involve equally the supporting language practices that enable learning through language use and the whole of a language in its context of social practice. In communication and in learning, language is integrated with action in order to achieve local aims. The differences lie in the purposes of the interactions, not in the nature of interaction. Wittgenstein, in fact, makes a direct link between language use and the act of learning – learning involves the induction into a language. In this way, communication and learning can be seen as facets of the same process. They also parallel each other in that they involve a process in which each participant has only partial access to the meanings of other participants. That is, in both communication and learning, participants are confronted with ways of interpreting language that are context-specific and which shape meanings within that context. There is a need to access frameworks of meaning and understanding that go beyond the strictly linguistic in order to understand how the language is used and what linguistic actions mean.

In a language game, participants have access to words, actions, and the constitutive rules of the game, but access to and knowledge of these potentially differs between participants, although the difference in access and knowledge is particularly highlighted in the teaching–learning relationship. There is a constant process of returning to the contextualized act of communication in order to confirm meanings, to provide interpretations, and to monitor emerging understanding. This means that the activities required of participants are reciprocal – there is a mutual monitoring and mutual responsibility for monitoring that is required of participants for communication to take place and for communication to be effective. Although such processes are central to teaching and learning, language education has rarely considered the interpretations that learners make of themselves, of others, and of learning as a part of the teaching–learning process. In language education, where language is both the object of learning and the medium through which learning occurs, such interpretations have a particular prominence. In teaching and learning language from an intercultural perspective, these processes of interpretation are in fact the lynchpin that holds the process together. By virtue of their membership of a particular culture or cultures and speaking a particular language or languages, language learners come to the act of learning with established, but often unconscious or unarticulated, interpretations of themselves, of others, of language, of culture, and of learning. They engage with other established, unconscious, or unarticulated interpretations of the same constructs, during the act of language learning. They are at the interstices of interpretations and their learning is an act of reinterpretation and renewed interpretation as they encounter new experiences mediated through new or additional languages and cultures.

The intercultural in language learning

As we argued above, there are two orientations to the teaching of culture found in discussions of language education: a cultural orientation and an intercultural orientation. In a cultural orientation, culture is an object studied as an entity in its own right and the development of knowledge about culture focuses on the accumulation of knowledge about the entity identified as a culture (Liddicoat, 2005b). The culture remains external to the learner and does not confront or transform the learner's existing practices, values, attitudes, beliefs, worldview, and identity. Beacco (2000) finds this to be the dominant approach to culture in much language teaching material and remarks that the body of knowledge taught is often limited, overgeneralized, and subordinated to the teaching of language structures. An intercultural orientation focuses on languages and cultures as sites of interactive engagement in the act of meaning-making and implies a transformational engagement of the learner in the act of learning. Here, learning involves the student in a practice of confronting multiple possible interpretations, which seeks to decenter the learner and to develop a response to meaning as the result of engagement with another culture (Kramsch and Nolden, 1994). Here, the borders between self and other are explored, problematized and redrawn. Although writers often conceive a focus on culture as intercultural, our stance is that developing a static body of knowledge is not equivalent to developing an intercultural capability (cf. Zarate, 1983). Instead, we believe that the learner needs to engage with language and culture as elements of a meaning-making system that are mutually influencing and influenced. This means that language learning becomes a process of exploring the ways language and culture relate to lived realities – the learners' as well as that of the target community.

Bryam and Zarate (1994) have articulated aspects of the interculturality involved in language learning through the notion of *savoirs*. *Savoir* (knowledge) refers to knowledge of self and others, of their products and practices and the general processes of interaction. Individuals bring to interactions a knowledge of their own language(s) and culture(s) and those of their interlocutors, and knowledge of the process of interaction. Individuals are socialized into knowledge of their own language and culture and of the processes of interaction as a result of their interactions within the cultures in which they have grown up and been educated. This knowledge may be held consciously or unconsciously. Knowledge of the other can come from experiences of interlocutors from another culture or from experiences of learning about another language and culture. Byram (1997) notes that such knowledge is relational – it is acquired within the processes of the original language and culture of the learner and often understood in terms of contrast with characteristics of one's own group. *Savoir* constitutes a body of knowledge on which other operations can be performed. These further operations are described by Byram and Zarate (1994) as:

- *savoir être*: an attitudinal disposition towards intercultural engagement manifested in approaching intercultural learning with curiosity, openness, and reflexivity. Byram (1997) notes that this *savoir* particularly deals with attitudes towards those who are perceived to be different from oneself and one's own social group and that may exist as prejudices or stereotypes, but which need to be opened up for exploration. The attitudes which are needed for successful intercultural interaction are curiosity and openness, a willingness to suspend disbelief and judgment about others, and a willingness to suspend belief in one's own meanings in order to be able to view them from the perspective of others.
- *savoir comprendre*: learning how to interpret and explain texts, interactions, and cultural practices and to compare them with aspects of one's own culture. Acts of interpretation involve the use of both conscious and unconscious knowledge and therefore some of the knowledge that is used in interpretation may not be fully realized by the person making the interpretation. Learning how to interpret and explain the texts or practices

of another culture involves learning to understand the knowledge that is drawn upon in the act of interpretation as well as how this knowledge is used.

- *savoir apprendre*: the ability to make discoveries through personal involvement in social interaction or in the use of texts. The ability to make discoveries from the language and actions one encounters is manifested when the individual has only partial existing knowledge to draw on in the processes of communication and interpretation. It engages the language learner in a continuous process of knowledge building through understandings reached during engagement in and with languages and cultures.

Byram (1997) adds a further dimension, *savoir s'engager*, which refers to the ability to make informed critical evaluations of aspects of one's own and other cultures. It is the capacity for critical cultural awareness that includes investigating and understanding one's own ideological perspective in communication and engaging with others on the basis of this perspective. It is also derived from interpreting and understanding the ideological perspectives of others as they are communicated through the language and behavior one experiences.

The model of *savoirs* has been influential, but some limitations have been identified in the way it constructs the intercultural. Sercu (2004) proposes that the model of *savoirs* be extended to include a metacognitive dimension, that is, self-regulating mechanisms that enable students to plan, monitor, and evaluate their own learning processes. This would add a stronger educational dimension to the *savoirs* and integrate reflection on learning into the model in addition to reflection on action. In addition, Liddicoat and Scarino (2010) argue that the model of *savoirs* does not elaborate on the important ways in which language affects culture and culture affects language, and how the learner understands this.

An intercultural ability includes awareness of the interrelationship between language and culture in the communication and interpretation of meanings. Our understanding is always informed by the past and present of a particular language and culture and, in intercultural contacts, it is necessary to recognize the same in others (Liddicoat and Scarino, 2010). This means that intercultural language learning calls for understanding the impact of such situatedness on the process and practices of communication and on social relationships between interlocutors. It includes both knowledge and awareness operating in relationship to each other. The relationship between awareness and knowing is not, however, a unidirectional one in which awareness precedes knowledge, but a multidirectional one in which knowing contributes to expanded awareness and awareness contributes to expanded knowing. Through experiences of and engagement with languages and cultures, the intercultural learner can develop an increasingly complex sense of self as a user of language and as a cultural being, acting on and in the world. Understood in this sense, developing the intercultural includes not only developing awareness but also developing the ability to analyze, explain, and elaborate this awareness; that is, it involves a meta-level of awareness (or meta-awareness). However, interculturality is not simply a manifestation of awareness and knowing, it also necessitates acting. The intercultural is manifested through language in use, through interpreting and expressing meaning across cultural boundaries in dialogue with self and others, drawing on awareness and knowledge gained through previous experience, and recognizing the possibility of multiple interpretations of messages and the culturally embedded nature of meaning (Liddicoat and Scarino, 2010). In this conceptualization of the intercultural, the learner is both participant and analyzer in interaction, both learner and user of language and culture (Kern and Liddicoat, 2008; Liddicoat and Scarino, 2010). The intercultural communicator does not simply communicate in contexts of diversity but also monitors, reflects on, and interprets what is occurring in communication. Although it is not true that the participant and analyzer roles are always present to the same degree in any act of communication, the capacity to draw on, integrate, and move between these interactional identities is a fundamental element of the intercultural.

The Learner as Focus

Language teaching and learning from an intercultural perspective places the learner at the meeting point of languages, cultures, and learning. That is, intercultural understanding is not an abstract, but rather an embodied process. Individual learners, with their own linguistic and cultural positionings and identities, are involved in an encounter with alternate positionings and identities that they need to understand and evaluate. Such a focus on the learner recognizes the multiple roles of the language learner in the act of learning – roles that may not be realized in all learning contexts.

Language learner as learner

Most obviously, the language learner is positioned as a learner. The learner stands in relation to some unknown that must in some way become known, usually through interaction with a more knowledgeable other. As such, the learner is involved in a linguistic and cultural process of mediation of knowledge (Vygotsky, 1978): "Mediation is the process through which humans deploy culturally constructed artifacts, concepts, and activities to regulate (i.e. gain voluntary control over and transform) the material world or their own and each other's social and mental activity" (Lantolf and Thorne, 2006, p. 79). In the act of learning therefore, the teacher and learner use cultural products as tools to assimilate, create, or produce new knowledge and understanding. The most significant of these cultural products is language, whether written or spoken. Learning, then, is an interaction between language and culture for and within each learner. In language learning, however, the positioning of the learner is more complex, as encultured understandings derived from the learner's home culture encounter the encultured understandings of the target-language community. All the languages and cultures the learner encounters play a role in the mediation processes involved in learning, and in this way the learner is positioned in an intercultural space in which multiple languages and cultures are the tools through which learning is achieved. For particular groups of learners, the ways in which these multiple languages and cultures are distributed across the social contexts of learning varies. Within the broad diversity of possibilities, three particular possibilities can illustrate some of these complexities. For some, the language and culture of the home and the school may be congruent and the target language and culture represent the main point at which the intercultural may be encountered in the act of learning. For others, the target language and culture may be congruent with those of the school but different from the language and culture of the learner. In this situation it may be that the learners' use of the main mediational tools of the learning context is the most salient point for intercultural engagement. Similarly, for some learners, the language and culture of home, school, and the learning target may all be different and there are multiple possible alignments and misalignments between the cultural products that mediate learning. This complexity means that the positioning of the learner as a learner is itself complex, with different learners standing in different relationships to the cultural products they encounter through their learning.

A related positioning for the second or foreign language learner is as nonnative speaker of the new language. This positioning as *language* learner effectively locates the learner as being in some ways deficient in relation to his/her polar other – the native speaker (Davies, 1991; House and Kasper, 2000). The native speaker envisaged by much work in language education has been a monolingual, monocultural entity who functions faultlessly both linguistically and culturally in his/her own context. In this case, the learner is positioned in relation to the new culture in problematic ways – the dimension that is most clearly articulated is that of an outsider and as a less competent outsider at that. It is a positioning in terms of what the learner is not. This positioning is known and perceived both within the educational context and without, but the consequences of such positioning are not usually considered in the learning context: "Being a learner, as one role a person can assume, has hitherto been all too frequently over-emphasized such that nonnative speaker use was exclusively viewed with an eye to native speaker norms" (House, 2008, p. 15). This means that an important point of what it means to be a language learner is simultaneously attended to – the learner is often evaluated in terms of his/her performance in relation to a native-speaker model and is judged lacking in terms of this model – and ignored; the consequences of being a nonnative speaker, the power relations implicit in nonnative-speaker status, and the consequences for self-understanding as speaker of a language are rarely considered.

These positionings emphasize one dimension of the language learner and privilege the classroom as the proper locus of identity. Such identities are a real part of the language learners' experience of learning, but they can eclipse other possible identities. Where this happens, the learners become sidelined as the focus of learning and the emphasis is placed on things external to the learner – language, native-speaker status, and so on.

Language learner as language user

An additional way to understand the language learner is as a user of the language being learned (Kern and Liddicoat, 2008). This means understanding the learner as using and being able to use language for personal expression through which the learner has opportunities to develop a personal voice in the target language. This positioning of the learner as language user focuses attention more clearly on the learners themselves and on what each learner brings to the act of learning and what the learner needs to attend to as a user of a new language.

This perspective has not always been fully recognized in language learning contexts (Firth and Wagner, 1997). In the act of speaking in a second language, the learner is required to perform in the language. This is an act of language use, although the use can be constrained by the tasks that the learner is asked to perform. The learner may therefore be positioned as a legitimate language user – as a speaker who produces or receives language in order to create, communicate, and interpret language – or as a pseudo-user – a person who produces or receives languages for purposes other than communication. In reality, in classrooms many learners have to switch between instances of legitimate and pseudo-language use as an element of their learning culture. Moreover, aspects of their possible positioning as a language user may be disallowed in language classrooms; for example, students may not be able to decide what talk to produce or be able to produce talk on topics of his/her choice. In this way, the language learner as language learner has multiple relationships between the languages and cultures available and the possibilities for enacting language use, with some languages having very constrained possibilities for use in the classroom context. Ideally, the positioning of learner as user engages the language learner in acts of communication in which she/he needs to reconcile the linguistic and cultural demands of communication between and across languages and cultures.

Here, the language learner is positioned not simply as a language user but also as an intercultural speaker (Kramsch, 1999). This is a positioning which does not focus on what language learners are not, as "nonnative speaker" does, but focuses on what they are and what they are becoming. The intercultural speaker stands in a complex relationship with languages, cultures, and communities, as insider or outsider and, to varying degrees, recognized as a member of many speech communities. Intercultural speakers live and communicate within complex frameworks of interpretation and use the rules of interpretation available to them in a knowing and reflective way in both the various interactions in which they are engaged and in the various linguistic and cultural contexts in which they occur. Kramsch argues that being a competent language user is characterized by "the adaptability to select those forms of accuracy and those forms of appropriateness that are called for in a given social context of use" (Kramsch, 1999, p. 27). Such an understanding of the intercultural language user recognizes the complexities involved in being a speaker of multiple languages and the potential influence of all available languages and cultures on the act of interpretation, regardless of the actual language being used to communicate. They allow for movement between languages and cultures. These multiple languages and cultures are both a resource and a challenge for communication.

Understanding the language learner/user as intercultural speaker requires moving beyond the lens of the native speaker. The native speaker lens, which constructs learning in terms of the monolingual, monocultural native speaker, does not begin to capture the reality into which a language learner is being introduced. The intercultural speaker needs to be able to engage with, reconcile, and reflect on multiple languages and cultures. This is not required of the monolingual, monocultural native speaker. None of this implies in any way that the intercultural speaker is in some way inferior to the native speaker, but rather that the native speaker is not a legitimate model against which judgments about capability should be made. The intercultural speaker needs capabilities that the native speaker does not, and these capabilities are at the heart of the lived experience of being an intercultural speaker.

Central to the concept of the intercultural speaker is the idea of mediating between cultures (Byram, 2002; Gohard-Radenkovic *et al.*, 2004). That is, the intercultural speaker is involved not only in participating in interactions with members of other cultures, but also in a process of interpretation. This means that the intercultural speaker is required to engage in a different form of meaning-making from that experienced by the monolingual, monocultural native speaker because she/he is involved in making meaning within and across different languages and cultures. It is an active engagement in diversity as a meaning-making activity. This mediation happens in different ways. First, intercultural speakers need to be able to interpret the meaning of diverse others for themselves – they must analyze meanings that are constructed by others within a different cultural framework and respond to the cultures they encounter in interaction. To do this they must adopt an external perspective on themselves as participants in interaction in the process of interaction itself and in an ongoing process of monitoring, analyzing, interpreting, and adapting (cf. Byram, 2002). Second, intercultural speakers are mediators for others – they provide those who do not have the means to understand what occurs in interaction with the means to understand diverse others (Gohard-Radenkovic *et al.*, 2004). This means that intercultural speakers must stand in complex relationships to the languages and cultures they encounter and use. They are simultaneously insiders and outsiders in each culture and language and connect communicators across cultural and linguistic boundaries.

The learner as person

The language learner is also positioned as an individual with a unique personality and identity, who is engaged in the act of learning a language. In the act of language learning, the learner is always more than a generic construct. Rather, each learner brings to learning relationships with languages and cultures and a personal history formed through and in relation to languages and cultures. The individual can be positioned in the act of learning in different ways. When using one's own language within one's own culture, whether as a learner or otherwise, a learner is typically positioned as himself/herself; that is, they have a real identity as a person, which is relevant in the context of learning. In language learning, this real identity may be submerged in a pseudo-identity constructed for the purposes of language learning. The individual identities of language learners have been treated in different ways in teaching and these treatments construct different intercultural possibilities.

The ways in which learners can be positioned by the act of using language in classroom contexts can be seen in examples drawn from language teaching practice. In the first example, students in Australia are interacting in a conversation directed by the teacher. The teacher is providing students with situations in which they communicate as they develop an interaction and students have to determine the Indonesian language they need in each situation.

TEACHER:	OK, so now you go home and tell Mum and Dad, "I've seen an old friend from school."
MARK:	*Bagaimana hari ibu?* [How was your day Mum?]
JAXSON:	*Oh, baik.* [Oh, good.]
TEACHER:	Oh, that's nice, asking about Mum's day. Now Jaxson tell him…
JAXSON:	Wait, wait. That's what I'm about to say. *Saya memasak makan malam.* [I'm cooking dinner.]
TEACHER:	How stereotypical is this! There are Indonesian mothers who…
JAXSON:	I'm in Australia.
TEACHER:	OK, she's Australian now. (Kohler, 2010, p. 179)

In this extract, the teacher formulates the action as involving going home and saying something to one's parents. In this discussion, the student Jaxson is playing the role of a mother and describes his actions as "cooking dinner." The teacher critiques this as a stereotype of Indonesian women – a stereotyping Jaxson rejects because he is enacting his own identity as an Australian. However, Jaxson and his peers are being positioned in particular ways in relation to their use of Indonesian. The message this teacher projects is that participants in an Indonesian language interaction are necessarily construed as Indonesians, and when speaking Indonesian, students' Australian identities are submerged and they take on Indonesian identities. In a sense, this positions Indonesian people as more legitimate speakers of the language than non-Indonesians and privileges Indonesian as a language that expresses Indonesian realities. In this way, classroom interactions in the target language place the language learners as individuals in a subordinate position to the native speaker and devalue their positioning as a speaker of the language. This positioning claims less relevance for the language learners' own cultural identities in the context of learning and constructs the normal intercultural relationship as one of assimilation to not only native-speaker norms, but also to native-speaker identities.

A similar delegitimizing of learners' identities can be seen in the advice given by teachers to students preparing for their English as an Additional Language in Malaysia examination. Scarino and Papademetre (forthcoming) report that for students in Malaysia preparing for an Australian-based English language examination, issues of positioning are complex. One of the teachers surveyed reported advising students to "Make sure you are not Malaysian." That is, students writing in English for an Australian-based examination should not communicate local identities when using the language. This raises important issues for how language learners can understand themselves as users of the language. One of the teachers in the study reported:

> Sometimes I think my students have a problem with the role that they are supposed to take when they are writing the letter. So when they look at the picture they know it is about something that is happening in Australia; and you get the people in the picture, the background of the picture, this and that. So, I guess sometimes, I think myself, if I put myself in my students' shoes, I would be thinking like: Am I supposed to be an Australian? What is the role? Should I reflect that I am part of the Australian community? Because I have to answer the question, and I can't assume that the picture is happening in Malaysia.

The teacher sees in the act of speaking another language a confusion about which identities can legitimately be adopted when using the language and constructs the learners' actual identities as less relevant for their communication than other pseudo-identities that correspond more closely to the identities available to native speakers.

In the examples discussed above the learners' identity as learner has greater weight and greater value than the learners' individual identity. This focus on native-speaker-like identities in language learning positions learners as remote from the language they are speaking and their identities as being outside the bounds of language acquisition. Such positioning allows learners few opportunities to explore the intercultural dimensions inherent in their own use of the language and instead serves to separate what they bring to the act of using a language from the process of communicating in that language. In this case, positioning of the individual subordinates the individual's identity to his/her identity as learner and effaces the learner's own voice from the communication.

In teaching and learning language from an intercultural perspective, the position of the learner as an individual is central to understanding the teaching and learning process. It is by seeing the individual as a person who is endowed with a language (or languages) and a culture (or cultures), who embodies languages and cultures, who is shaped and formed by languages and cultures, and who expresses him/herself through languages and cultures. The languages and cultures a learner brings to the learning of a new language are a repertoire for meaning-making and a repertoire that is being enlarged in and through learning.

As intercultural speakers, language learners' own thoughts and ideas become a central resource for the process of mediation – it is their meanings and their attempts at meaning-making for others that form the basic resource for mediation. Communicating them in the target language is therefore not just an exercise in language use for the purposes of language practice but an articulation of meanings for new audiences. It is in the communication of one's own meanings for one's own purposes that the processes of analysis and interpretation achieve their greatest salience and in which the challenges of communicating in a new language and in another cultural frame are most effectively realized and enacted.

The learner as focus: Concluding comments

The view of the learner which is presented here recognizes that, in the act of learning, the language learner has multiple positions – learner, language user, and individual. This is not an exhaustive list of possible positions; rather, it aims to highlight the main ways the learner can be understood when engaging in intercultural learning. Fundamentally, these positionings all relate to ways in which the learner is engaged in an interpretive process in which communication affords possibilities for engaging with language and culture. For us, the focus of language teaching and learning from an intercultural perspective is on the language learner as an interpreter and maker of meanings. That is, the language learner is always potentially a learner and a user of language. As learner and user, the language learner is engaged as a performer and as an analyzer of communication. Different positionings afford language learners different possibilities for performance and analysis. The extent to which these possibilities are constrained limits the potential for an intercultural perspective in language teaching and learning.

Principles for Teaching and Learning Languages from an Intercultural Perspective

The discussion in this book so far gives rise to a particular set of principles that underlie an intercultural perspective of language teaching and learning. Five core principles can be considered as a base for language learning: active construction, making connections, social interaction, reflection, and responsibility (Liddicoat, 2008; Liddicoat *et al.*, 2003; Papademetre and Scarino, forthcoming). These principles are not themselves fundamentally intercultural, but they can be seen as preconditions for an intercultural perspective.

Active construction refers to a way of understanding how learning happens in language learning. The teacher creates opportunities through which learners come to make sense of their encounters with language and culture and how they relate to each other. Learning then evolves from purposeful, active engagement in interpreting and creating meaning in interaction with others, and continuously reflecting on one's self and others in communication and meaning-making in variable contexts. For students, it is more than a process of absorbing facts; it is continuous development as thinking, feeling, changing intercultural beings. Every language experience afforded to a language learner is considered to be potentially open to interpretation, an artifact of the culture in which it was created and a communication of that culture. Teaching for active construction means providing opportunities for students to recognize the cultural embeddedness of their experiences of language, to develop and explore their own interpretations, and to identify the cultural constructedness of their own responses.

Making connections is a principle that acknowledges that languages and cultures are not acquired or experienced in isolation. In coming to engage with a new language and culture, a learner needs to connect the new to what is already known. This means first articulating his/her own starting position for engaging with the new, including the *intracultural* experiences they bring to the learning, that are already developed within the individual's existing linguistic and cultural frames and multiple memberships in a variety of social domains. This intraculturality represents a first point of connection between the learner and the new experience and provides a first interpretive position in relation to the new. The new itself has an intracultural dimension – each interactant with whom the learner communicates (teacher, text, co-learner, native speaker, etc.) also brings intracultural positions to their communication. Learning involves making sense of these positions and connecting the intraculturality of others to one's own. These connections in language learning are also *intercultural* in that learners are required to engage beyond their own intracultural positions and interpret meanings across linguistic and cultural boundaries. This means making connections with diverse cultures, identifying similarities and differences between the known and the new, and establishing complex interrelationships between the similarities and differences that are perceived.

Social interaction is a principle that recognizes both that learning is a fundamentally interactive act and that interaction with others is the fundamental purpose of language use. Learning and communication are social and interactive; interacting and communicating interculturally means continuously developing one's own understanding of the relationship between one's own framework of language and culture and that of others. In interaction participants engage in a continuous dialogue in negotiating meaning across variable perspectives held by diverse participants, and continuously learn from and build upon the experience. One of the important understandings which underlies an intercultural learning of language is that there is a reciprocal relationship between one's own linguistically and culturally contexted interactional system and other such systems that the learner encounters. Ideally, then, the learner is continuously in dialogue with diverse ways of communicating in each experience of language and is always therefore a language user, regardless of other goals that may attend the act of language use in a pedagogical context.

Social interaction includes processes of negotiating understandings, of accommodating or distancing from understandings presented by others, of agreeing and disagreeing with the understandings of others, and understanding of the nature and causes of such agreements and disagreements. A process of refinement allows for expressing understanding, challenging ideas and renegotiating understanding in response to challenges. Learning emerges from the sorts of purposeful language use that Swain (2006) calls languaging – "the process of making meaning and shaping knowledge and experience through language" (p. 89). Languaging is a process of deep and significant communication; it contrasts with the often trivialized way communication has been treated in some approaches to language education. The language learner is involved in interactions about language, about culture, about learning, and about intercultural mediation as a constituent part of the learning process. There is also a continuing dialogic development of ideas and understanding as each act of languaging itself becomes available for further languaging and thus increasingly complex learning about the substance of the languaging.

Reflection is fundamental to any teaching and learning process that focuses on interpretation. Learning from reflection arises from becoming aware of how we think, know, and learn about language (first and additional), culture, knowing, understanding, and their relationships, as well as concepts such as diversity, identity, experiences, and one's own intercultural thoughts and feelings. The process of reflection in intercultural learning is both affective and cognitive. It is affective in that every encounter with diverse others has the potential for emotional impact, either positive or negative, and this impact needs to be considered and interpreted by the learner. It is not enough to know what one's reaction to something is; one also has to understand why that reaction is the reaction one experiences. Emotional responses may be triggered by very different cultured understandings of the world being brought together in a way that causes dissonance for the individual. Reflection is cognitive when it involves exploring the attitudes and assumptions that one brings to the act of communication and which one encounters in the communication of others. It is a part of the understanding of self and other, which is central to interculturality. Attitudes and assumptions can also cause dissonance for the individual when different ways of understanding the world are brought together. Such dissonances can lead to a closing down of willingness to engage with diverse others and so need to be available for investigation and interpretation. It is, however, not only dissonance which is the starting point for reflection; instances of consonance, although not as obviously experienced as instances of dissonance, can also be investigated as a way of understanding what one perceives to be consonant between languages and cultures and why.

The reflection being considered here involves a large measure of decentering, of stepping outside one's existing, culturally constructed, framework of interpretation and seeing things from a new perspective (Byram, 1989a; Kramsch, 1993a; Liddicoat and Kohler, 2012). Zarate (1993) refers to the process of engagement with another language and culture as a form of rereading of experience, which has the capacity to see new connections and relationships that are both different from and potentially more insightful than those of native speakers. It is the process of reflection that makes such rereadings available both for analysis by the speaker and for communication to others. The interpersonal and interactional nature of the intercultural requires that the language user is able to decenter from his/her own cultural and linguistic framework in order to see the world from alternate perspectives. Byram, Gribkova, and Starkey (2002, p. 19) describe this as the "ability to make the strange familiar and the familiar strange." Such decentering is a capacity to understand multiple perspectives and a willingness to search for and accept multiple possible interpretations. Interpersonally, interculturality is enacted through reciprocity in interaction, recognizing one's own multiple roles and responsibilities and being sensitive to and accommodating those of one's interlocutors. The intercultural mediator adopts a fundamentally reflective attitude to the ways in which linguistic and cultural diversity is played out in interaction.

Responsibility is a principle that recognizes that learning depends on the learner's attitudes, dispositions, and values, developed over time; in communication this is evident in accepting responsibility for one's way of interacting with others within and across languages and for striving continuously to better understand self and others in the ongoing development of intercultural sensitivity. The intercultural speaker has a responsibility to develop intercultural sensitivity and intercultural understanding. This is an ethical position in which an interlocutor assumes the responsibility not only of understanding what another says but also of understanding what she/he means in saying something and in seeking to be understood by others. The intercultural is therefore manifested as and through an ethical commitment to the acceptance and valuing of language and culture within and across languages and cultures. This ethical commitment requires reacting to encounters with diverse others in constructive ways. It is not a passive, observational approach to difference but an active "being in diversity," in which diversity is not an external reality but communities in which one lives and acts (Liddicoat and Scarino, 2010). As a participant in diversity the ethical commitment of the intercultural individual includes accepting the responsibility to act interculturally, that is, in a way that does justice to, is fair to, and is respectful of other participants in diversity.

These five principles amount to a sociocultural and interpretive theory of learning applied to the context of communication in diversity, in which the intercultural is manifested through language. They are therefore starting points for an intercultural pedagogy, not an intercultural pedagogy itself. Each of these principles requires development into practice.

Practices for Intercultural Learning

Practice for intercultural learning can be conceptualized in a number of different ways. Different ways of understanding what it means for language education to be an intercultural endeavor can be seen in considering practice from the perspective of learning and from the perspective of teaching.

Practices in learning

One way to understand the practice of intercultural teaching is as a cycle of interconnected processes in which the learner engages in experiences of languages, cultures, and their relationship (see Figure 4.1). This is a learning-oriented view of the practice of intercultural language teaching and learning.

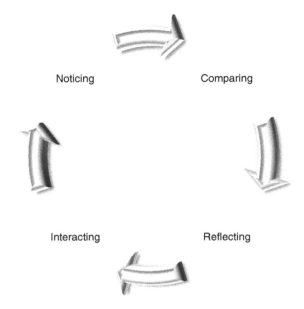

Noticing   Comparing

Interacting   Reflecting

Figure 4.1 Interacting processes of intercultural learning. *Source*: Scarino, A. and Liddicoat, A. J. (2009) *Language Teaching and Learning: A Guide*, Melbourne, Curriculum Corporation.

Figure 4.1 describes the learners' engagement with the intercultural as four processes. These processes do not have a necessary beginning point as each is interrelated with other processes. One possible entry point is through noticing aspects of language and culture as they are presented through the activities in which the learner is engaged. At any point, learners may become aware of things that challenge their current assumptions, spark interest, raise questions, or provide points of connection. The process of noticing is fundamental to learning (Schmidt, 1993). In intercultural language teaching and learning it is important for learners to notice cultural similarities and differences as they are made evident through language, as this is a central element in intercultural language use beyond the classroom. When they are introduced to something new, learners need to examine the new information in their own terms and seek to understand what it is they are experiencing. While noticing is potentially always present for language learners, it is not necessarily a naturally occurring activity in the classroom. Rather, noticing is an activity that occurs in a framework of understandings that regulate what can and should be noticed. Teachers' questions are therefore important in helping students to develop the sophistication of their noticing and to become independent noticers of lived experiences of language and culture.

When students notice something in their experiences of language learning, what they notice becomes available for other processes. At its most basic level, comparison takes the form of identifying similarities and differences. The process of comparison is multilayered: it needs to allow space for comparisons between the learner's background culture and the target culture but also between what the learner already knows about the target language and culture and the new input she/he is noticing. By inviting the identification of similarities and differences, the comparison process can be seen as a way of entering into opportunities for developing greater complexity of thinking. However, it is important to note that the act of comparison itself is not the endpoint of intercultural learning – intercultural understanding cannot simply be identified with a set of identified similarities and differences between languages and cultures. Like noticing, comparison provides opportunities for further development.

Comparisons provide a resource for reflection. As a classroom process, reflection is a core element in developing interculturality (Kohonen, 2000), requiring several considerations. It is a process of interpreting experience: this does not mean, however, that the learner is being required to draw "the right conclusion" or simply to explore his/her feelings about what has been discovered, but that the learner makes personal sense of experiences and constructs an evolving understanding of them. It is therefore a way of making sense of experience and understanding the experience from multiple possible perspectives. In the act of reflection, the language learner thinks about the significance of what has been observed, of his/her reactions to this, of the dimensions of comparison that are being brought to bear on understanding, of ways of enlarging the field of inquiry, of relationships between new knowledge and existing knowledge, and planning ways to test ideas and understandings. The learner reflects on what one's experience of linguistic and cultural diversity means for oneself: how one reacts to diversity, how one thinks about diversity, how one feels about diversity, and how one will find ways of engaging constructively with diversity. The results of reflection then need to become action.

Reflection takes its ultimate shape in the context of interaction. Interculturality is not a passive knowing of aspects of diversity but an active engagement with diversity. This means that the intercultural learner needs to be engaged in interacting on the basis of his/her learning and experiences of diversity in order to create personal meanings about his/her experiences, to communicate those meanings, to explore those meanings, and to reshape them in response to others. There are multiple dimensions to interaction, using the understandings developed through reflection in designing performance in a language, articulating those reflections for others, and negotiating meanings and understandings of phenomena from multiple perspectives. In this way, interaction can be understood as a process of languaging about one's personal accounts and experiences of language and culture and about the current state of one's learning. Interactions in turn are experiences of language and culture that provide renewed opportunities for noticing, comparing, and so on, and form part of an ongoing cycle of developing increasingly complex understandings.

These activities themselves are important to learning how to learn about language and culture. The processes are not linear in relationship; all processes may be co-present in any instance of teaching and learning. Moreover, they do not represent a linear process of learning by which one passes through each "stage" to reach a final outcome. They are a set of processes through which intercultural learners pass many times as they develop greater complexity of understanding.

Conclusion

In this chapter we have argued that the expanded view of language and culture presented in Chapter 2 and the expanded view of learning presented in Chapter 3 have implications for how language learning can be understood as an intercultural endeavor. It is a view of language learning that focuses on the acts of meaning-making and interpretation as the central concern for language education. The identities of the learner and the learner's subjective engagement in meaning-making and interpretation have a fundamental place in the way that both language learning and intercultural understanding are understood. In the remaining chapters of this book, we will work through some of the implications of these ideas for practice in language teaching, learning, and assessment.

5

Designing Classroom Interactions and Experiences

In this chapter, we consider the implications of the expanded view of language, culture, and learning discussed so far, for designing classroom interactions and experiences for language teaching and learning. In traditional Communicative Language Teaching and its further development as Task-Based Language Teaching this is understood as "tasks" for teaching and learning, where tasks are intended to capture a shift from a focus on the language itself to a focus on language use and meaning. We argue that teaching and learning language within an intercultural perspective requires an expansion of the notion of "tasks":

1 to highlight the nature of interaction as the reciprocal interpretation and creation of meaning;
2 to acknowledge that for learners these interactions constitute *experiences* along a trajectory that contribute to the development of communication as well as to the development of an evolving understanding of what it is that communication entails, and ultimately, the learners' development of self-awareness as communicators.

In this context, we discuss extending the concept of "tasks" to focus on interactions and experiences. We see the nature of interaction in teaching and learning languages from an intercultural perspective as more than a means through which learners acquire linguistic form; we see it as social, as personal, as the capability of "moving between" languages and cultures, and as interpretive at every turn. The focus on experiences, in the sense of both lived, real-life experience, and experiential learning complements, extends and reframes communication and learning to communicate. We also discuss some examples that illustrate features of students' actions/interactions, interpretations, choices, judgments, and understandings. Finally, we consider the implications for teachers and learners of the expanded conception of interacting and experiencing language learning.

The goal in language learning within an intercultural perspective is for learners to participate in communication to exchange meanings and to discover, in and through experiences

Intercultural Language Teaching and Learning, First Edition. Anthony J. Liddicoat and Angela Scarino.
© 2013 Anthony J. Liddicoat and Angela Scarino. Published 2013 by Blackwell Publishing Ltd.

of interacting in communication with others, the variability in meaning-making, the linguistic and cultural assumptions made in constructing knowledge and, ultimately, to develop self-awareness of their own interpretive system, as they make meaning of the world around them and share it with others, within and across languages and cultures.

Expanding "Tasks" to Focus on Interaction and Experiences

In the history of language teaching, Communicative Language Teaching and its subsequent development as Task-Based Language Teaching represented a shift from a structural view of language teaching and learning to language teaching and learning that focused on meaning more than on form (Bygate, Skehan, and Swain, 2001; Ellis, 2003; Nunan, 2004; Prabhu, 1987; Skehan, 1998; Willis, 1996), and on "real language use." The concept of "task" has become and remains a central construct in second language teaching and second language syllabus or course design. Although there are differences among, for example, communicative language teaching (Brumfit, 1984; Littlewood, 1981), procedural syllabuses (Prabhu, 1984), and process syllabuses (Breen, 1987; Candlin, 1987), all give salience to active, integrative use of the target language, in other words, learners learn to communicate by communicating through tasks, with tasks representing a microcosm or instance of active language use. Despite the focus on language use, all the formulations of Task-Based Language Teaching accord no more than a limited place to culture. We retain "task" as a construct because it provides an integrative unit of analysis that brings together participants, purposes, contexts, and interaction in communication to achieve particular goals. However, this integrative unit needs to include additional characteristics when learning is understood within an intercultural perspective.

In all of these related developments there has been much definitional work that seeks to describe the nature of tasks. This is especially so in the context of classroom language learning, where there has been much discussion about the extent to which this environment is or can be a site for real-world communication. Nunan (2004) has developed a framework for Task-Based Language Teaching in which he describes tasks along a continuum of degrees of affinity with the real world (see Figure 5.1). He describes the "real-world or target tasks" as "the hundred and one things we do with language in everyday life" (Nunan, 2004, p. 19). He then proposes that in order to create opportunities for learning in the classroom, these "real world tasks" need to be transformed into "pedagogical tasks," which he places on a continuum "from rehearsal to activation tasks" (Nunan, 2004, p. 19). The "rehearsal tasks" emulate in the classroom a task that is likely to be carried out also outside the classroom. Interestingly, describing these as "rehearsal" suggests that the classroom setting itself is not seen as "real." The "activation tasks" are tasks that require students to engage actively in using language of their choice (i.e. not being constrained to use particular lexical or grammatical resources), but they are created specifically for the classroom, rather than emulating a task to be performed beyond the classroom. This distinction is based on choice or connection with specific lexical and grammatical items. Nunan's framework also includes form-focused work, presented as

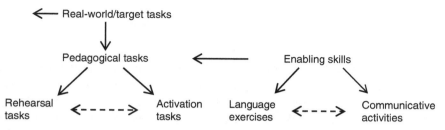

Figure 5.1   A framework for Task-Based Language Teaching. *Source*: Nunan, 2004 *Task-Based Language Teaching*, Cambridge, Cambridge University Press, p. 25.

enabling skills that are designed to develop the knowledge and skills that subsequently will be drawn upon in authentic communication (Nunan, 2004, p. 22). Within this category he also distinguishes between language exercises and communicative activities. He describes the former as focused on practicing and developing the lexical, phonological, and grammatical systems of the target language; he describes the latter as a: "half-way house between language exercises and pedagogical tasks. They are similar to language tasks in that they provide manipulative practice of a restricted set of language items. They resemble pedagogical tasks in that they have an element of meaningful communication" (p. 24).

Nunan's framework seeks to capture the various distinctions made in efforts to define tasks. Ellis (2003) describes the debate surrounding the nature of tasks for language teaching and learning as follows: "'Tasks' are activities that call for primarily meaning-focused language use. In contrast 'exercises' are activities that call for primarily form-focused language use. However, we need to recognize that the overall purpose of tasks is the same as exercises – learning a language – the differences lying in the means by which the purpose is achieved" (p. 3). What is needed for learners is not only the development of integrative language use through tasks and understandings of language form, but also for teachers to develop in learners an understanding of the systematic *relationships* between form, meaning, and use (Larsen-Freeman, 2001). This entails incorporating a reflective and interpretive dimension that allows students to consider the phenomenon of the reciprocal interpretation and creation of meaning in interaction both within and across languages and cultures. Furthermore, notwithstanding Nunan's (2004) effort to distinguish between "tasks" in the real world and in the classroom, we maintain that the classroom is a site where real communication takes place between the teacher and the learners and among learners as peers, and that participation in this setting is an integral part of learners' enculturation into the linguistic and cultural system being learned, through comparison with their own system. Teacher and students are co-performers as they shape the reality of classroom experience through interaction. This interaction in communication and in learning in the language classroom (as indeed it is beyond the classroom) is an interchange of words and meanings as well as an interchange of interpretation (Gallagher, 1992). As such, both communication and learning to communicate both within and across languages and cultures are inter-interpretive. We now turn to a discussion of this interpretive dimension in interaction and in its relationship to experience.

The Nature of Interaction

In Chapter 3 we discussed the different theoretical understandings of the nature of interaction, depending on the family of learning theories. Within a cognitive perspective on interaction and "task" (e.g. Skehan, 1998, 2003), interactions are a source of input oriented towards promoting attention and cognition. Within a sociocultural perspective, interaction and "task" are oriented towards promoting the co-construction of meaning and performing in socioculturally appropriate ways. These accounts of interaction and "task" do not address an interpretive, reflective, dimension that teaching and learning within an intercultural perspective highlights. The nature of interaction in language teaching within an intercultural perspective involves learners in mediating across languages and cultures, in the reciprocal negotiation and interpretation of meanings through the use of language in diverse contexts. It is simultaneously:

- social, that is, *interpersonal* – communication among people who are reciprocally performers and audience, i.e. interpreters of meaning;
- personal, that is, *intrapersonal* – communication or inner dialogue with self;
- *interlinguistic* and *intercultural* – movement between two or more linguistic and cultural systems, i.e. inter-interpretive.

Through participation in interaction learners come to understand that the interaction itself is shaped by all participants present. Because participants are both performers and audiences in relation to each other, the interactive talk can change how they see themselves and others. They come to understand that interactions can be variably interpreted. Each participant will have his or her own individual experience of the interaction. In any interaction in the classroom or beyond, for example, all participants are able to observe each other and manage their contribution for the benefit of others, making changes according to how they wish to be seen. In communicating interculturally, learners come to understand the reciprocal relationship between their own social, linguistic, and cultural systems and those of others. This is a particular kind of negotiation of meaning that includes, but also goes well beyond, the transactional sense of "getting things done" in language or exchanging information. It extends to developing an understanding of the self and the other in communication, in response to variable perspectives. These variable perspectives are available, *inter alia*, to be accepted, rejected, modified, compared, and synthesized. Interaction in this sense includes ongoing reflection on the variable ways in which people interact and communicate and the knowledge/understanding and identity they bring to and develop through communication.

The Experiential Dimension

Learning a language within an intercultural perspective includes an experiential dimension. Kohonen (1992, p. 36) describes the value of experiential learning as providing "the basic philosophical view of learning as part of personal growth." Experiential learning expands the notion of "task" by focusing on personal growth. This means understanding experience as meaningful to the learner and his or her development. As discussed in Chapters 2–4, we see language learning as a process of interpretation, that is, as a hermeneutic process. Language use in both communication and learning to communicate entails interaction and reflection on the reciprocal interpretation and creation of meaning. The learner as communicator/interpreter lives the *experience of communicating* using the target language being learned. The learner as learner/interpreter also lives the *experience of reflecting* on the process and thereby developing an increasingly deep and elaborated capability to understand communication. Developing this capability and understanding is not just a cognitive process, but it is a part of experiencing and interpreting the world of the classroom and beyond. We highlighted in Chapter 3 that two principles are important within this interpretive view of communication and of learning. First, all interpretation is governed by history, meaning the history of a person's experiences. In other words, present communication and learning are always referenced to prior experience. Second, all interpretation is linguistic and cultural. Interpretation involves a dialogue between participants who together come to understanding through a fusion of horizons (Gadamer, 2004). This fusion requires the interaction of fore-understandings, which we describe as the framework of interpretive resources that people bring to interaction in seeking to understand. It is these fore-understandings that both enable and limit understanding. In other words, the learners' historicity and situatedness in experience, mediated through their language and culture, inform their interpretations in coming to understand both in the process of communication and in the process of learning. Each experience of this "fusion" that learners have transforms their understanding of the subject matter, of language and culture themselves, and of others. In learning additional languages, therefore, learners continually:

- interpret and create meaning *in vivo* in interaction with others;
- interpret another linguistic and cultural system that is not their own, while referencing it to their own;
- interpret the experience of communication and learning, through processes of reflection.

It is in this sense that we prioritize the notion of experience. A crucial connection between language, knowing, and experience is also made by Halliday (1993, p. 94), who states that "language is the essential condition of knowing, the process by which experience becomes knowledge." Human experience is the basis for learning, understood as coming to know, and this learning and knowing is construed in language.

The process of learning a language within an intercultural perspective is an iterative one of interpretation and reinterpretation. As such it is also an intertextual dialogue with self and others, in which meanings are reframed, recontextualized in an ongoing way. Lave and Wenger (1991) describe the continuous process of experiencing and reflecting upon and learning from experience: "Activities, tasks, functions, and understanding do not exist in isolation; they are part of the broader systems of relations in which they have meaning. ... Learning then implies becoming a different person with respect to the possibilities enabled by these systems of relations" (p. 53). Language, always open to interpretation, gives expression and meaning to interactions with others and reflection on the experience of communicating in the world. Equally, languaging (Swain, 2006) gives expression and meaning to experiences of learning.

Considerations in Developing Interactions and Experiences

Tasks, understood as interactions and experiences as described above, are purposeful and contextualized instances of using language for communication, that is, the reciprocal interpretation and creation of meaning, as well as for reflection on the meanings and the processes involved in both communication and learning. In developing tasks for language teaching and learning within an intercultural orientation, it is necessary to consider the principles described in Chapter 4 in relation to the following set of dimensions.

Purpose   What is the purpose of the task? How will the purpose be understood by diverse participants? Why are learners being asked to do this task? What ideas and concepts are involved in this task? (*making connections*)

Context   Who are the participants and what is the role of each and their relationship to each other? How are the participants positioned in the particular context? What are the circumstances of the task: the setting, the social, psychological and affective circumstances, the realm of relevant ideas, concepts, knowledge. (*active construction, making connections*)

Process of interaction and interpretation   What is it that participants are to think about and do in interaction with people, texts, and other forms of representation, and mediating technologies to accomplish the task? What are they invited to notice, compare, question? How are they invited to explore their own ideas, experiences, and practices relative to those of others? How are they encouraged to act upon the contribution of others? (*making connections, social interaction, reflection*)

Product   What products or actions will result from the interaction? (*active construction, social interaction*)

Reflection   What are learners invited to reflect upon? How are they asked to decenter? What connections are they invited to explore? How do they reflect upon their own linguistic and cultural situatedness and that of others, their own positioning and that of others, their ideas and those of others, their values and ethical dispositions and those of others, their ways of learning and those of others? (*reflection, responsibility*)

Through the process of reflection learners consider and come to understand the social, linguistic and cultural construction of knowledge, multiple ways of knowing, and the power of language and knowing. They also reflect upon and become aware of themselves as communicators (Clark, Scarino, and Brownell, 1994; Papademetre and Scarino, forthcoming).

Tasks as opportunities for interaction and reflection are valuable as episodes in their own right as well as in their connection and relationship backwards and forwards in experience. Figure 5.2 depicts the process of carrying a task understood as interacting and reflecting on the experience. It depicts an episode of communication (and, equally, learning to communicate) as an act of interpretation of purpose and context, including processes of interaction and interpretation, that result in actions or productions. Reflection on the process of communicating and learning to communicate leads to awareness of both the use and learning of language within an intercultural perspective.

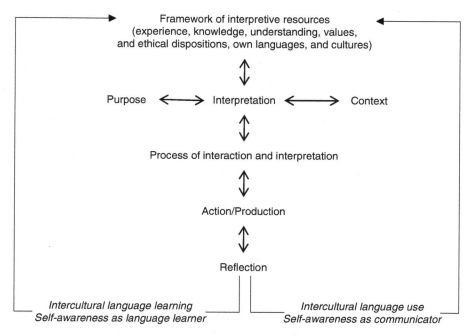

Figure 5.2 Process of carrying out a task: interacting and reflecting on the experience.
Adapted from Clark, J. L., Scarino, A., and Brownell, J. A. (1994) Improving the Quality of Learning.
A Framework for Target-Oriented Curriculum Renewal in Hong Kong, Hong Kong,
Hong Kong Institute of Language in Education.

It also develops the learners' self-awareness as communicators and language learners. Each episode is in itself a valuable instance of learning to engage with the variability of language use and learning in context. Because the processes of communication and of learning are iterative and cumulative, each episode is also valuable in relating backwards and forwards in learners' experience of communication and learning to communicate. In learning language, learners are constantly moving between instance and systems and it is this dialectic that constitutes learning.

In the expanded sense of interaction and experience discussed above, a task encompasses:

- observation, description, analysis, and interpretation of phenomena shared when interacting and communicating;
- consideration of ways in which language and culture come into play in:
  (a) interpreting, creating, and exchanging meaning
  (b) recognizing and integrating into communication an understanding of self and others as already situated in their own language and culture when communicating with others;
- active engagement with the interpretation of self and others in diverse contexts;
- understanding that interpretation can occur only through the evolving frame of reference developed by each individual, as experience is cumulatively reconsidered and rearticulated.

Examples

The examples provided below in two languages (Chinese, Indonesian) illustrate aspects of interaction and experience. They come from teachers' experimentation with language teaching and learning within an intercultural perspective. Each example provides a different instantiation of learning language that is appropriate to the particular learners involved, and to the subject matter and related language being learned. We describe the context and purpose of each example and we use the five principles for teaching and learning languages from an intercultural perspective (active construction, making connections, social interaction, reflection, and responsibility) as a framework for discussing features of each example.

We consider, in particular, the nature of the interaction and experiential work: the nature of comparing, moving between and analyzing the process of moving between systems of meaning-making, and the nature of reflection.

Example 1: Year 10 Chinese – examining translation

This example is a unit of work designed for Year 10 students of Chinese in an all-girls school. The class comprised eleven students, seven of whom had recently traveled to China (Foster, 2007). Within the group, four students were also studying French and one was studying Italian. It was the profile of the students themselves that was the starting point for the teachers' work in developing this unit. The teacher is a highly experienced Australian teacher of Chinese. The purpose of the unit, as described by the teacher, was to invite students to "decenter, that is, to see languages and cultures from inside and outside, to show understanding of others' linguistic/cultural perspectives and to see the new from the inside and the familiar from the outside." The specific questions that the teacher posed her students were:

- What are the skills needed for translation?
- How accurate is online translation?
- How translatable are languages? What is lost in translation?
- What does it mean to "translate interculturally?"
- How important is this?

These kinds of questions are in line with the recent revival of translation described by Cook (2010). Translation can be seen as a natural context for "moving between" systems of meaning-making. The series of tasks and the teacher's rationale for each follow:

Box 5.1   Tasks and rationale

1   Look at the China hotel English site http://www.chinahotelsreservation.com/ Shanghai/Shanghai_Huang_Jindao_hotel.html
    Students read the hotel description. Respond in writing to the question: Would you choose to stay in this hotel? Why? Why not? Follow with discussion on aspects of the description: what do you know about the hotel from this site?

2 Look at examples of Chinglish in signs found in China. Respond in writing to the question: Are these good translations? Why?
Rationale. This is to help students work towards their own understanding that mistranslation can have a big impact on peoples' understandings, responses to texts, and also their impressions of other cultures.

3 Give a list of sentences in English with at least one word students do not know – students look up in the dictionary, give the translation in Chinese. Followed by discussion on the appropriateness of their word choice. Students then reflect on issues of translation they experienced. Written response to the questions: Does translation simply require a knowledge of the two languages? What else is needed to be an effective translator?
Rationale. This is to help students come to the realization that context and cultural values are also important considerations when translating.

4 Present two translations of one Chinese text. Students comment on what is lacking, and what is added in each text. What do you make of the different translations? http://zhidao.baidu.com/question/57422440.html

5 View article on http://olympics.blogs.nytimes.com/2008/08/13/lost-in-translation-a-chinese-cheer/ and its translations. Discuss the implications of the different translations and what do we need to consider when translating?
Rationale. To help students see that there is more than one possible way of translating (even of simple phrases) and to identify what makes some translations better than others, reinforcing the importance of context and cultural values.

6 Using online translators to translate sentences given in previous lesson. Class discussion on following question: What are the advantages of an online translator? What are the limitations of an online translator? How then should we use online translators?
Rationale. To help students to see the limits and dangers (the things that online translators cannot do that a person can when translating) of relying heavily on online translators and to better understand how to use them effectively.

7 Students find examples (either from internet, books, their own sentences, etc.) of one example of a poor translation, one example of a good translation. They reflect why they chose these examples, what is it about each one that makes them a good example?
Rationale. For students to identify and be able to articulate what makes a good or poor translation and to begin thinking of how they might apply this to their own translations.

8 Class discussion following individual reflections – What makes a good translation and a poor translation? What are the implications of a poor translation? To what extent is culture an important part of translation?

9   Write a guide for themselves on what is needed to be an effective translator. What do they need to be aware of? How will they use the tools available? What steps will they follow?
     Rationale.   For students to develop their own ideas on how they can translate more effectively.

10   Students are given a Chinese paragraph to translate into English and an English paragraph to translate into Chinese. Students are invited to reflect on the process.
     Rationale.   For students to show how they understand the importance of intercultural understanding in translation.

11   Final reflection on their own learning.

Source: Cook, G. (2010)

In each task in the series, learners are invited to interact with texts and with the teacher and each other in discussion. The focus on translation affords an opportunity for "moving between" and comparing languages. The reflections on consequences (Tasks 1 and 8), issues in translation (Task 3), comparisons (Task 4), implications and considerations (Task 5), advantages and limitations (Task 6), choices (Task 7), and processes (Task 10) provide an opportunity for reflective analysis, that is, for students to consider translation through the lens of their own personal experience – past and present.

Throughout the process of working on this unit, the students and their teacher engaged in continuous cycles of experiences of interaction and reflective analysis: group consideration and pooling of ideas, noticing, questioning, and comparing. In order to give a sense of continuity to the work, the teacher provided a "guided reflection journal" in which students recorded their own work on researching, investigating, and practicing translation (active construction) and their reflection on the process (reflection). This journal provided a mechanism for recording ongoing participation and cumulative, reflective commentaries and, importantly, making connections, thereby building coherence and depth in learning (making connections). The teacher provided a final reflection: "Looking back over all of our activities, discussions and also your previous reflections, comment on how your own understanding of translation has changed. What do you now feel makes a 'good translation'?" This reflection provided an opportunity for students to draw connections cumulatively across all the interactions and consider their own experience of translating and learning.

Figure 5.3 shows a response from one of the students to the reflection for the third task: "Does translation simply require a knowledge of the two languages? What else is needed to be an effective translator?" As can be seen, the student articulates her initial thoughts (see 1); the teacher interacts individually with the student seeking expansion or elaboration (see 2) and the student extends her response, as prompted by the teacher (see 3).

The teacher interacts individually with her students through their journal writing, inviting them to expand or elaborate on their initial formulations, or to summarize or synthesize

(1)

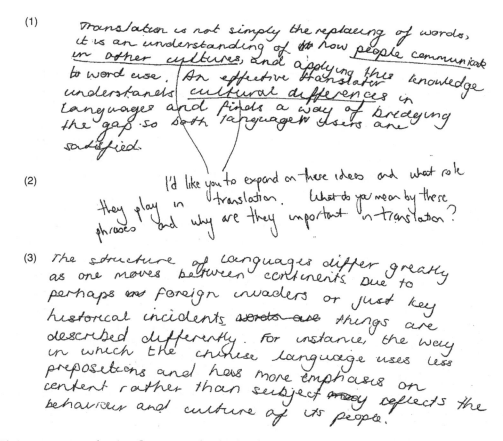

Translation is not simply the replacing of words, it is an understanding of how people communicate in other cultures, and applying this knowledge to word use. An effective translator understands *cultural differences* in languages and finds a way of bridging the gap so both language users are satisfied.

(2)

I'd like you to expand on these ideas and what role they play in translation. What do you mean by these phrases and why are they important in translation?

(3)

The structure of languages differ greatly as one moves between continents. Due to perhaps foreign invaders or just key historical incidents things are described differently. For instance, the way in which the chinese language uses less prepositions and has more emphasis on content rather than subject may reflects the behaviour and culture of its people.

Figure 5.3 A student's reflection on the third task. *Source*: Foster, M. (2007) Assessing the Intercultural in Language Learning. Unpublished Project Report. Research Centre for Languages and Cultures, University of South Australia. Adelaide, SA.

their cumulative experience and learning (active construction, making connection, reflection). The experiential dimension in the interactions and reflections that the teacher provides can be seen in the way the teacher invites the students to experience the use of online translations (Task 6) and select their own examples of good and bad translations (Task 7). All the reflections invite personalization (active construction) and connection (making connections) to their own experiences of being in China (as a recollection of their experience of being *in situ*) or researching the virtual world of China. The interactions and reflections invite students to participate in reading, interpreting, and creating translations and, at the same time, focus on interrogating the entailments, processes, outcomes of translation, and its consequences or significance (active construction; social interaction). The students continually compare and move between texts. The texts and tasks themselves are real-world, contemporary documents and practices. The ongoing classroom interaction and discussion affords further possibilities in terms of comparing diverse perspectives and experiences (social interaction; reflection; responsibility).

The extract below provides the teacher's own commentary on her students' learning.

Box 5.2   Teacher's commentary

In terms of decentering, while students wrote mostly as observers of translation and of culture, their own experiences in the translation activities led them to a greater appreciation of what they, themselves, must consider when translating and also the limits of their own cultural understanding when working between Chinese and English. This, I think, is an example of them looking back inwards with new perspective and being more aware of how others may perceive them through their translations. The consideration students took when making language choices in the translation exercise is also evidence of this. Students really deliberated over these choices and tried to seek advice from me on the best choice and were not always comfortable when I did not offer advice and instead asked them to use their own knowledge and experience of Chinese culture and language to make their choices. Some evidence is in Emma's reflections, she particularly struggled with this and commented that she "wasn't sure how to translate … and have it still make sense." However, she showed excellent development in this when she took the phrase "by the way" and "changed it to 'before I forget'" to try to keep the original meaning. This was a big step for Emma and showed that she was prioritizing meaning-making in her translation rather than just focusing on the word and phrase level.

The discussion revealed to the students and myself how much we might judge people and/or places by the level of language fluency. In the hotel website, students were mostly in agreement that because the use of English was inaccurate, this reflected on the quality of the hotel facilities and its receptiveness to English speakers. They were quite negative about this hotel's level of service and yet, when I took some of the girls to China last year, we stayed in hotels of the same star and of similar facilities and they were more than happy with this. For one student, this translation unit led her to be "less critical of people who make bad mistakes when translating," to be less judgmental. I think this is a big step in her intercultural journey. This was a big step from her earlier comment that "because of poor translation, a country or culture could get a bad reputation." To me, this shows that she now realizes that there is more than one person responsible for negotiating meaning in interactions. Not only does the translator have a responsibility to consider the culture of the language being translated into, but also the reader also needs to consider the culture of the original language when reading the translation.

The teacher highlights her students' understanding of the role of language and culture. She comments on the process of decentering as a fundamental part of the interactive and reflective work of teaching and learning within an intercultural perspective. She comments on her students' own direct experience of translating, highlighting the importance of concurrently participating in language practices and reflecting on the experience, recognizing their personal limits, as learners, moving between Chinese and English. The reflections thus entail simultaneous reflection on self as a language user and as language learner, highlighting the importance of the intracultural dimensions in intercultural interaction.

In the set of tasks that form this unit of work, the teacher provides opportunities for a range of related interactions, experiences, and reflections that draw upon and extend the students' experiences, both past and present. All the interactions and experiences require moving between and reflecting upon Chinese and Australian English linguistic and cultural systems captured in a journal recording, experiences of translation, and cumulative commentaries and reflections on these experiences.

Example 2: Year 11 and 12 Indonesian: Developing intra- and intercultural understanding

This example is drawn from a whole program of work designed for Year 11 and 12 students of Indonesian, in which the teacher was experimenting with developing students' *intra-* and *inter*cultural understanding (Gould-Drakeley, 2005). In Table 5.1 she maps what she calls "key intra- and intercultural concepts," which provide a conceptual overlay to language development in her program as a whole. Framing this dimension of the program through questions directed to the students (see examples in italics) provides an indication of the interactions that she plans to use in drawing upon and building students' experience.

The teacher's mapping of themes, questions, and topics shows a range of cultural practices that are always treated within a comparative linguistic and cultural perspective. Although this is a planning document and therefore a somewhat abstracted representation of classroom teaching and learning, the framing in terms of direct questions to students invites narrative accounts of their own personal histories of experiences and reflections. Narrative is important as an expressive embodiment of experience and as a form for understanding the world. The intracultural dimension highlights the importance of moving from comparisons across Indonesian and Australian English language and culture to the meaning and significance that this holds for the individual.

The teacher has developed a conception of "the intercultural person," which she shared with her students, as a culminating goal that connects all interactions and experiences that she develops with her students.

The intercultural person

The intercultural person actively uses and analyzes language and culture as they are used in communication. S/he knows how to read meanings in texts and is aware that any incidence of speech or writing carries with it embedded assumptions and implications which contribute to the actual meaning of language in use. S/he also acknowledges that meanings are problematic, that any use of language may be interpreted in multiple ways, and that linguistic and cultural background are important things that shape how messages are produced and understood.

An intercultural person is one who is able to see things from more than one perspective. S/he is able to see that his/her own assumptions are not universal and that similar messages or behaviours may mean different things to other people. S/he is able not only to see others from his/her own perspective, but is able to reflect on his/her own culture from the perspective of others, seeing that the familiar may be strange. S/he is mindful, in the sense of bearing in mind the influences that come to bear in interaction to communicate and negotiate meanings and actively brings this awareness into play in dealing with others.

Her goal is to connect with the students' trajectory of prior experiences in life and in language learning. For all participants (her students and herself) language learning is

Table 5.1 Year 11 and 12 Indonesian: Intra- and intercultural concepts

	Year 11 Module 1	Year 11 Module 2	Year 11 Module 3	Year 12 Module 1	Year 12 Module 2	Year 12 Module 3	Year 12 Module 4
Identity	Who are you? How do you represent yourself to others? What is important to you? What are your values? What do you notice is important to different Indonesians?	Identity – How does your job reflect who you are and what status you have? What do different Australians and Indonesians value about work? What are your aspirations? Compare this to aspirations of Indonesian youth	Identity – multiple identities. Examination of ethnicity, nationality. How do different Indonesians represent themselves? Symbolism of art and craft Change – traditional vs contemporary practices	Religious identity and values, self, and communities in Australia, Indonesia and other countries as relevant	Making choices and reflecting on their implied values. How issues affect self/identity. Being a global citizen	Identity of youth and how young people are portrayed by Indonesian and Australian communities	How has your understanding of your identity developed/changed over the past 2 years? How has your new knowledge influenced who you are? Is your identity influenced by your knowledge and understanding of Indonesian life? Have your values changed? How do you measure success?
Social organization	Individual and family life Variability of family structure and composition in Australian and Indonesian contexts	How is education valued? Examine opportunities. What qualities are considered important for an employer/employee in Australia/Indonesia. Examination of jobs in both countries	Motto: Unity in diversity Examination of ethnic variability in Indonesia. Explore similarities and differences between rural and urban life in Indonesia and Australia and other countries	Church, mosque, temple and other places of spiritual significance. Special occasions	Government and nongovernment organizations, environmental clubs	Rites of passage. School, family, marriage, issues – smoking, alcohol, drugs	Birthday parties, ceremonies, graduation

Interpersonal relationships	*What do you need to know to engage with and understand others? What do you value in a friend? How do you like to spend your leisure time? How similar/different is this for an Indonesian teenager? How will the register of the language you use vary according to whom you interact with?*	*How do you interact with peers and teachers at school? What would you need to consider if you were to go on a student exchange to Indonesia? What would an Indonesian student need to know about school life in Australia? Examine similarities and differences between Indonesia and Australia (and other countries)*	*How would you interact in a social situation in Indonesia? Consider setting – e.g. in a home, at an event, etc, as well as other factors including a person's ethnicity, religion, age, gender, status, etc. How would interacting with a Javanese be similar to or different from a Balinese? Why is this the case? Examination of etiquette and ritual*	Interacting with people of different religions in everyday setting, special occasions, etc. Interfaith relationships	Discussing issues with different people; friends, family, teachers, Indonesian people of different ages and background. Impact of issues and how they affect lifestyle	Friendships. Relationships with parents, teachers, others. Making arrangements. Invitations	Understanding how to relate to a wide variety of Indonesians. Understanding of interrelationship between language and culture. Able to define "third place"
Change	*What type of global citizen do you want to be?*	*Changing nature of work and values of work. Discussion of gender, status, technology in relation to change. Examination of work/study options of the future*	*Change in contemporary society – changes, language, etiquette, values, housing, architecture, arts and craft, cuisine, etc.*	Changes in choice of religion, marriage, influence of different religions, politics, etc.	Globalization, rural–urban shift in Indonesia. "Sea/tree change" phenomenon in Australia, climate change	Change – shifts in perception of youth Demographic changes, technology.	Future aspirations, transition from school to work/university. Change in intra- and intercultural understanding

Source: Gould-Drakeley, M. (2005) Intercultural Language Teaching and Learning in Practice Project. Unpublished Report, Research Centre for Languages and Cultures, Adelaide, SA.

interpersonal, intrapersonal, experiential, and reflective in relation to each instance and cumulatively. In line with this stance, she draws connections continuously across the interactions and reflections that form her program. From the abstracted program described above, the teacher develops sets of interactions. Here we include those that she envisages for listening and responding and reading and writing in the interpersonal relationships module.

Box 5.3   Interactions for "listening and responding" and "reading and writing"

Listening and responding

1   Listen and respond to Indonesian texts from *Jak, Suara Siswa, Bersamasama 2* (Ch 8). Discuss the purpose, audience, and context of these texts. In pairs students discuss, register language used, and whether language is informative, persuasive, etc. Link this to text-type. From the texts, students consider how being polite in Indonesian is not necessarily the same in English.

2   Listen to and view Indonesians being interviewed by (name of school) students. Discuss concepts presented in the DVD. Students notice the type of language used by different interlocutors when referring to parents. Why does this difference exist? (Is it related to age, gender, ethnicity, personal choice or other factors?)

3   Complete a cloze activity for the song about love *Cinta Kilat*. Discuss, in Indonesian, the concept of relationships as presented in the song. Is this similar to the type(s) of relationships teenage Indonesians may experience?

4   Listen and respond to the song about unemployment *Sarjana Muda* (Iwan Fals). With other students, discuss main issue raised in the song.

5   Listen and summarize the song about sibling relationships *Sebelum kau bosan*. What does this say about sibling relationships in this situation? Is this similar to your own experience?

6   View, listen to, and extract information from videos in which a range of Indonesians discuss friendship. In Indonesian, students discuss and explain the important qualities of friendship to them as individuals.

Reading and responding

7   Read various texts which contain how to accept/decline invitations. Students are asked to notice the language used and discuss cultural implications. Compare this to how they accept/decline invitations in their own languages.

8   Read *Kawan karibku* from *Suara Siswa*. In groups, discuss what values arise from these texts about friendship. What qualities are considered to be important? Summarize this in Indonesian.

9   Read Indonesian advertisement for ideal partner. Students consider their own personal values and consider what factors influence their values. Students write their own advertisement for an ideal partner.

Source: Gould-Drakeley (2005)

The set of tasks asks students to interact with a range of texts, peers, and the teacher in different ways (social interaction). The discussion dimension of the tasks invites students to compare ideas, language, and cultural practices across languages and cultures, and to draw connections with their own experiences and perceptions and judgments of experiences (making connections, reflection). An ongoing task accompanies the tasks included in the teacher's program. This is a year-long reflective journal in which students are encouraged to reflect on their experiences of the interactions (making connections, reflection). The teacher interacts with students individually so as to encourage deeper reflection (active construction) and connections with previous experiences and reflections (making connections).

The extract in Box 5.4 is from one of her students' journal reflections. The student moves from description to comparison to questioning herself to the recognition of variability and to deeper questioning (active construction, making connections). She concludes with an insightful recognition of her own limits in seeing (reflection). This is an example of the way the students accomplish the kind of understanding that emerges from "moving between" diverse linguistic and cultural systems and learning to reflect on self and others – characteristics of language learning within an intercultural orientation (reflection, responsibility).

Box 5.4   Student journal: the Fulla doll

In the half yearly examination section 2 reading and responding we were given a text, an article, on "barbie disaingi boneka berjilbab!" I found this to be so interesting as it clearly demonstrates and reflects the cultural opinion of the Islamic Indonesians. I find particularly interesting the differences outline between Barbie and the "Fulla" doll. They are as follows:

Barbie: wears mini skirt, revealing clothing, has a boyfriend, made by a western country
Fulla: wears loose clothing, pray rug, jilbab, doesn't have a boyfriend, made by an Indonesian company.

It is remarkable to note that from these descriptions the "Fulla" doll has been made based on the Islamic guidelines.

I am unsure whether the "Fulla" doll would be popular to children within Indonesia as our modern generation of children have been largely influenced by western cultures eg: from Australia. However I believe that the "Fulla" doll will be popular for Muslim parents in particular as, in my opinion it portrays the "perfect" Muslim character being "nice, honest and respectful".

I wonder, has this doll been made with the concern that the Islamic culture is being pushed aside due to the western influence??

I was shocked when reading about the 'wanita karir' as her main career choices were a doctor and a teacher. I did not know that in the Islamic culture that these jobs were considered important role model jobs for children. In fact I did not think that particular work was important in the Islamic religion. I pose the question is the 'wanita karir' doll in fact driven by western influence, my culture?? Or is it simply that status within Indonesia is important in the Islamic culture??

As Barbie is so popular in Australia, apart from having equivalent dolls such as Bratz dolls, I find it interesting that we do not have a doll for our main religions such as Christianity. What would be the response if the "Fulla" doll was sold in Australia, how would other religions react?? Is it simply that Islam is the main religion that controversy hasn't occurred in Indonesia?? Or has it?? Is it in fact my own culture that has driven the creation of a Islamic doll? Have I been involved in such strong westernization in Indonesia, creating Barbie etc?? Is the way in which the company portrays the "Fulla" doll our perception of Islamic people??

Source: Gould-Drakeley (2005)

An example of a student e-mail response follows:

Box 5.5　An example of a student's response

"sebelum aku datang ke sini aku kira bahwa agama Islam nggak menerima agama lain." (Before I came here I thought that Islam didn't accept other religions). … *Di Australia aku berprasangka tentang semua aspek agama Islam. Aku berpendapat bahwa mereka nggak membolehkan aku ikut perayaan mereka. Akhirnya, Ucy berkata: 'tergantung dari kamu."*

[In Australia I was prejudiced about all aspects of Islam. I thought that they wouldn't allow me to take part in their celebrations. Finally Ucy said: "It's up to you."] (Alana had asked Ucy in her interview if, as a Christian, she would be able to participate in the fasting month of Ramadan.)

Ucapan yang selalu aku dengar adalah "Selamat Hari Raya. Maaf lahir batin." Ucapan ini menarik; penting bahwa yang muda mengunjungi yang tua untuk sungkem kepada mereka dan minta maaf. Aku ngaak sungkem, sedangkan Ucy dan kakaknya sungkem kepada ortu-nya. Bisa kamu membayangkannya?

[The expression that I always heard was "Happy Hari Raya. Please forgive me in body and soul." This expression is interesting; it's important for young people to kneel before their parents and request forgiveness. I didn't kneel whereas Ucy and his older brother knelt before their parents. Can you believe it?]

Embedded in this e-mail text are a student's (imagined) personal experience of participating in the practices of Islam and reflection on the experience. Her observation "Can you believe it?" indicates simultaneously her own observation and her assumption that her fellow interactant will hold the same view.

The layers of the program demonstrate the continuous cycle of interactions, experiences, connections (active construction, making connections), questioning, and reflection that create the culture of experiential, personalized learning for this teacher and her students (reflection, responsibility).

The examples provide evidence of the incorporation of the five principles of language learning within an intercultural perspective that we proposed in Chapter 4. Within an intercultural perspective, it is necessary to consider the nature of the interactions and experiences that involve different ways of "moving between" languages and cultures, diverse ideas, practices, and perspectives that students consider relative to their own, and the nature of reflection. These examples also show the need to build connections within and across interactions and experiences: between students, between prior and new experiences, between the languages and cultures available in the learners' repertoires, between texts, between interactions and reflections, and more.

This expanded concept of task for language learning within an intercultural orientation affords opportunities for communicating to exchange interpretations and meanings. In addition, it provides opportunities for understanding the variability of:

- contexts of situation and culture;
- ideas, opinions, perspectives, practices, and plans;
- ways of perceiving experience within and across languages and cultures;
- ways of acting upon the variability in communication.

From participating in these tasks, students learn about the consequences of choices in communication and adjust their choices of what they say and how, in order to respect the "other" when communicating across cultures. They develop a sensitivity to the diversity of the rich, dynamic world around them and their ethical responsibilities as communicators, within and across languages and cultures.

Implications for Teachers and Students as Participants in Language Learning

The expanded conception of task discussed in this chapter has implications for teacher and student roles in the interactions and experiences of communication that are made available for language learning. Both students and teachers bring their own interpretive resources, and their own stance to language learning – how they see the subject, the language, and culture being learned, the process of learning and themselves and their roles as interactants. They undertake their personal experience of language learning together. As expert, the teacher has a distinctive role in facilitating connections, that is, in building the fabric of the target language and culture and the lived culture of learning that is being created continually with students within and beyond the classroom. It is the teacher who also invites the noticing, comparing, the making of intertextual and interexperiential connections, and prompts reflection on the nature of language, culture, communication, and learning in diversity. Interactive questioning is a powerful means for building these connections and inviting questioning, problematizing, and inquiry. The teachers in the examples discussed above (see e.g. the teacher commentary in Example 1 and the teacher's account of "the intercultural person" in Example 2) interrelated each student's variable intraculturality, bringing each to recognize through interaction and reflection that his or her way of experiencing, seeing, interpreting, and understanding is always understood interactively, with reference to others. Teachers draw upon learners' emotions, not just their cognition (Kramsch, 2009). They listen actively to learners and ask them to attend to the interpretations and meanings of other contributors. Together, teachers and students draw connections over time, across contexts, texts, experiences, and all aspects of language using and language learning, in increasing complexity and sophistication. They consider each others' interpretations and meanings as part of the continuing dialogue of communicating and learning to communicate in the target language. Teachers and learners need to resource themselves with a wide range of experiences and sources that permit the creative, comparative, connection, and reflection that teaching and learning languages within an intercultural perspective require.

6

Resources for Intercultural Language Learning

Resources, in whatever form they take, provide language learners with experiences of language and culture that then become available for learning. Traditionally the main resource for input has been the textbook, and this may be supplemented by authentic texts from a range of sources: written texts, video or audio texts, music, multimedia and so on.

Traditional models of second language teaching and learning have treated resources as instances of language that present the learner with material to develop learning. They are a way of exposing learners to different modalities of language use (spoken, written, technologically mediated) and to different registers, and of broadening the input beyond the teacher. Resources may also be used as ways of promoting output, either verbal or written. Such resources form a starting point for language use and may be linguistic (e.g. oral or written texts and websites) or nonlinguistic (e.g. artifacts, games, and images), and are used to prompt discussion and description. More recently, there have been a number of new technological resources that provide opportunities for both input and output by permitting interaction: e-mail, chat, and text messaging. Such resources allow for the possibility of receiving input from another participant and require output from the learner. These will be considered in the next chapter. Resources that provide scaffolding for learning may provide models to guide learners' language use. These may be exemplars of a particular spoken or written text type, or frameworks for developing a text, which provide partial structures to speaking or writing. Resources used as input can also be used for scaffolding either through modification or through different ways of using the text to focus beyond surface elements of grammar and vocabulary.

It is important, however, to think about resources as doing more than providing linguistic input and output. Resources also represent engagements with culture through language. Resources are not just language samples – they are also cultural products. They are produced within a cultural context for consumption by others and are imbued with the cultural positionings, identities, assumptions, and worldviews of their creators and their intended audiences. As cultural products, they open new ways of engagement that use the

Intercultural Language Teaching and Learning, First Edition. Anthony J. Liddicoat and Angela Scarino.

language of the text as an entry point to new cultural realities. This means it is important to consider not just what a resource provides linguistically, but also what the language of the resource affords for deeper learning. Consideration of what lies within the language of a resource builds the possibility that resources can be used to stimulate reflection. This is different from using a text simply to generate language use that may be descriptive or narrative, because reflective work is deeper and introspective. Such resources do not need to be different from the resources used for input. It is rather a case of using resources differently by developing questions and activities around the resource to stimulate deeper thought, affective response, and analysis of feelings, conclusions, and interpretations.

There is no neat mapping between purposes and resources. Rather, resources can be used in multiple ways. The key is to have resources that open up multiple possible uses rather than resources that are limited or constrained and which narrow the possible teaching and learning opportunities available. Each resource should be used as effectively as possible and each resource should allow for flexibility and creativity in teaching and learning.

Textbooks as Resources for Intercultural Learning

Traditionally the starting point for resourcing language learning has been the selection of a textbook and for many teachers this is still their main resourcing task. By their nature, textbooks pose some problems for resourcing language learning as they are not adapted to the particular context and the needs, desires, and expectations of particular learners and so are not able to respond to local needs or provide locally relevant content.

Kramsch (1988), discussing textbooks, argues that there is a fundamental complexity in the use of any resource for teaching a new language and culture to a group of learners within an educational context. Any such resource is expected to serve a fundamentally intercultural educational goal but is located within an essentially monocultural educational frame. This complexity reveals itself in a number of ways that have implications for how resources are chosen and used.

A resource for intercultural learning needs to enable access to and insights about the language and culture that is being learned. This means not only providing access to the forms of the language but also to the logic of the performance of the language used by native speakers. That is, resources need to provide opportunities for learners to make target-language-relevant inferences about elements of language used in the resource and build target-language-relevant connections between them. Kramsch (1988) argues that it is difficult for a resource to achieve such target-language relevance if it is embedded only within the learners' educational culture. Such learning requires that target-culture perspectives and discourses also become available to the learner as part of engaging with the resource. That is, any resource needs to be addressed in multiple ways, not only developing further the cultural discourses that already exist for the learner but also providing opportunities for engagement with new discourses.

Kramsch (1988) also argues that there is complexity in what should be included within the focus of the resources that are provided to learners. This complexity emerges when there are disjunctions between the focuses of similar groups in different societies. For example, the events, issues, and ideas that are of central concern to an analogous group in the target language community may be different from and unrelated to those that are a concern of the learners. Should the resource give learners insight into the issues that affect people like them in the target language or should it deal with issues with which learners themselves connect? For whichever focus a resource is chosen, it is important that it also capture the integration of language, culture, and learning in the target language, as this is what enables the learner to go beyond static appraisals of content and opens the resource to deeper interpretation and more complex possibilities for intercultural learning.

A third issue that Kramsch (1988) identifies is the nature of the culture to be taught through the selection of resources provided. Even the most complete resource is necessarily a selection and the process of selection limits the diversity and variability that can be found. This raises the issue of whose culture is represented in texts and how this constrains ways of engaging with the culture. The representations of the target culture tend to be highly selective. For example, Elissondo (2001) demonstrates that representations of Latino cultures depict middle-class, light-skinned Europeans and that where indigenous or black groups are included, they are included as exotic "color" or have assimilated to the otherwise homogeneous cultural image. She also demonstrates that the activities with which the dominating middle class group engage are those of globalized world culture or stereotypical activities associated with particular societies, with little representation of the complexities of people's lives in Latino societies. These people engage in social relationships that are "smooth, neutral, friendly and peaceful" (Elissondo, 2001, p. 80). These representations have consequences for how learners are positioned in engaging with a new culture. Abdullah and Chandran (2009) have reported in Malaysia that the middle class focus found in Malaysian English textbooks meant that students in middle-class schools engaged with the text while those in lower class schools did not, as the text offered no point of connections for them.

Many of the representations of the target culture in textbooks are those of a touristic encounter with the county or countries concerned, often depicting well-known geographic and historical material. In so doing, the texts position language learners as "superficial tourists who travel from one country to another without any serious engagement with those cultures" (Elissondo, 2001, p. 74).

One common feature of textbooks is that they are often developed with reference to the culture of the learner rather than to that of the target community (Kramsch, 1987a). One reason for this seems to be to protect the learner from the perceived discomfort of encountering different ways of living in and viewing the world. That is, textbooks are designed to provide a comfortable encounter with a language rather than a nuanced encounter with a culture. This means that the intercultural objectives of language teaching and learning become minimized in resources that are designed to promote such learning. For example, Kramsch (1987b, 1988) noted that in German language textbooks used in the United States the German and American cultures are presented as being only slightly different and the differences between the two are obscured. In some cases, local culture may dominate the language textbook, excluding the culture related to the language being learned. In these cases, the textbook is designed to promote a form of learning that is distinctly not intercultural, but which serves a local ideological purpose. Lui (2005) notes that English language textbooks in China are designed to project particular images of Chinese culture rather than engaging with the cultures of the English-speaking world. The textbooks impart a dominant ideology that embodies the interests of the government and the cultural elite and reify official interpretations of Chinese society. Similarly, in Japanese English language textbooks, McKay (2004) notes that Japanese cultural norms predominate and Westerners (typically Americans) and their perspectives are typically introduced in contexts where the Westerner is being introduced to some aspect of Japanese culture. That is, English is to be used to interpret Japanese culture to non-Japanese, not for engagement with other cultures (cf. Liddicoat, 2007). Adaskou, Britten, and Fahsi (1990) note that in Morocco, the inclusion of Western cultural content in language textbooks is considered problematic, as the resulting comparisons between cultures may lead to disaffection and because some Western practices are unacceptable within the local context. In this way, language is taught in a way that isolates the learner from the target culture. In Saudi Arabian textbooks, the desire to protect locals from Western culture is seen in the deliberate removal of all cultural information inconsistent with local practice (Al-Asmari, 2008).

Where textbooks do present the culture of the target language community, they do it in a way that reduces the culture to information about aspects of context. That is, they present a static view of the culture in a body of factual knowledge about a country, and this is done uncritically and with limited engagement between the learner and the culture being presented for learning. As Elissondo (2001, p. 92) argues, "students passively consume factual information about natural wonders, prominent architecture, regional food and dances." Such presentations of culture can be seen in Figures 6.1 and 6.2.

Figure 6.1 is taken from the cultural awareness sections of a textbook designed for early secondary level learners of Italian in Australia. It presents cultural information in English, with the occasional use of Italian words, such as *il Circo Massimo, il Colosseo, il Patalino,* and *igladiatori.* The image presented is both historical and touristic, The presentation of ancient Roman culture is linked superficially to the modern word in the final sentence of each section – the Circus Maximus is used to celebrate the Italian World Cup victory, Romulus and Remus are represented in statues and on postcards, and the Colosseum is a home to feral cats. This is cultural information and does not provide opportunities for interpretation and deeper learning – these images of Italy provide no connection point between cultures except to reinforce students' awareness of Italy as the site of ancient Rome. An attempt to move from the cultural to the intercultural is found in the section "Moving between cultures" at the bottom right of the page. In the three questions contained here, it is not clear what the nature of this movement is, or which cultures the movement is between. That is, in this material, interculturality as the movement between cultures is claimed but not realized.

Figure 6.2 is from a German textbook for early secondary level learners in Australia. It is presented in the form of an e-mail explaining aspects of German life. Like the Italian example in Figure 6.1, the base language of this information is English, with German used for a few lexical items and some phatic language closing the text and is also found in the written text in one of the images of the e-mail. According to the contents for the chapter, the chapter's cultural focus is "school in Germany, *Schulelotsen, Schuletüten,* environmental awareness" (Rogan and Hoffman, 2003, p. vi), and the specific focus is on the last two elements of the list. This information is also presented as factual information about practices in Germany and embodies a static representation of the culture. Unlike the Italian textbook, there is no explicit attempt to include an intercultural as opposed to a purely cultural focus in this material. However, some implicit cultural comparisons could be made between

A glimpse of Ancient Rome

The city of Rome is over 2500 years old. In the years between 98 CE and 275 CE, it was the centre of government of the vast Roman Empire and was home to at least a million people. Animals were important in Roman society: the wolf was worshipped; bird flight patterns were used to tell the future; and many other animals were used in sporting activities and for entertainment.

Il Circo Massimo

Built in the sixth century BCE, **il Circo Massimo** was mainly used for chariot racing, the most popular sport in ancient Rome. Chariots were pulled at great speed by two or four specially trained horses. High speeds meant regular accidents and charioteers were often trampled to death. **Il Circo Massimo** held up to 300 000 people – that's almost a quarter of Rome's population at the time, crowded into the stands and on the hills. Much like today's soccer fans, supporters wore their team colours, although there were only four teams to choose from – the Whites, the Reds, the Greens and the Blues. Today, the tradition of celebrating sporting champions at **il Circo Massimo** is still strong – after Italy's success in the 2006 World Cup, **gli Azzurri** made their first public appearance there before a huge, ecstatic crowd.

Il Palatino

Dating back to 753 BCE, **il Palatino** is one of the seven Roman hills and is said to be the founding place of Rome. Rome itself is named after **Romolo**, its first king. According to the story **Romolo** and his twin brother, **Remo**, were abandoned as babies and found by a she-wolf, who fed them. A shepherd then raised the twins until they could look after themselves. As young men, they set out to found a kingdom by the banks of the river **il Tevere**, where their lives had begun. But **Romolo** and **Remo** could not agree on the exact site. In an angry battle on **il Palatino**, **Romolo** killed **Remo** and became the undisputed leader of what was to become the city of Rome. Today you'll find statues and postcards of the she-wolf and twins everywhere in Rome.

Il Colosseo

Il Colosseo was built in 80 CE. Here **i gladiatori** fought gruesome battles with wild beasts and even each other, watched by the emperor and 50 000 loud spectators who decided whether the loser should live or die by signalling thumbs up or down! All sorts of animals were used for these battles, including bulls, bears, lions, rhinoceroses, tigers and elephants. (Today's spectator sport of bull fighting, still popular in Spain and southern France, originates from the battles that took place in **il Colosseo**. You can still find intact remains of amphitheatres modelled on **il Colosseo** in both countries.) These days **il Colosseo** is home to some less ferocious animals – about 200 feral cats.

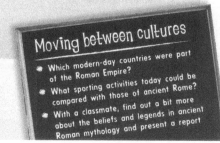

Moving between cultures

- Which modern-day countries were part of the Roman Empire?
- What sporting activities today could be compared with those of ancient Rome?
- With a classmate, find out a bit more about the beliefs and legends in ancient Roman mythology and present a report

Figure 6.1 Cultural awareness material from *Ecco! Uno*. *Source*: Sedunary, M., Posterino, N., Kearns, S., and Tarascio-Spiller, M. (2007) *Ecco! Uno*, Heinemann, Melbourne. Reproduced with permission from Pearson Australia.

Germany and the learners' culture through the description of the environmental practices, which implies that the German practices are newsworthy and therefore not typical of the culture of the reader.

Both of these examples present a superficial, simplified, and essentialized image of the culture of the target-language society. The culture is represented by interesting trivia about

Figure 6.2 Cultural awareness material from *Katzensprung 1*. *Source*: Rogan, P., and Hoffman, F. (2003) Katzensprung 1, Melbourne, Heinemann. Reproduced with permission from Pearson Australia.

a society. These school-level texts therefore reflect Elissondo's (2001) observation that the content of Spanish language texts at college level confirms the ideas about the Hispanic world that students bring to their learning and offers simplistic visuals and narratives that do not encourage participation in or critical thinking about the cultures of the language they are studying. The role of the cultural elements in these books seems to be "entertain or stimulate interest" rather than engage the learner with the culture intellectually. As Elissando observes, "instead of an intellectually provocative experience in the classroom, students often receive an education based on ready-mades devoid of real connection with specific geographies and historical processes" (2001, p. 97). Such texts do not invite comparison and afford few opportunities for real communication with peers about understandings and interpretations of the information presented.

Where textbooks do engage with the dynamism of societies and cultures, they typically essentialize the culture and ignore the ways in which changes are perceived and adopted differently among different groups and by different individuals in a society. This can be seen in the treatment of French culture in Figure 6.3.

Figure 6.3 is taken from a textbook for intermediate learners of French in Australian high schools. It is written in French, reflecting the greater proficiency levels of the target audience than the texts in Figures 6.1 and 6.2. It presents French culture as changing and multifaceted but presents this multifacetedness as a series of simple contrasts: what people do now as opposed to what they used to do, what happens in towns and in villages. However, each of these groups is presented as monolithic and the cultural variability is limited to the variations of groups. Young people do the same things, but these things are different from those that young people used to do. Cities are modern and globalized, but villages are traditional. This means that the image of cultural variability that is made available to students remains one in which variability is reduced and becomes a series of stereotypicalized differences between groups rather than a reflection of the inherent variability within groups. As with the other examples discussed here, the culture treated is as factual information and in all cases the learner is positioned as an external observer of cultural facts rather than as someone who is invited to interpret cultural practices as relevant to his/her communicative repertoire as a language user.

All of these examples also present the target language culture in isolation and without explicit connection to the culture of the learner. This is even the case in Figure 6.1, where the authors include a reference to moving between cultures. The new culture is therefore presented as having little necessary relationship with the learners' own cultures and cultural information is acquired by accumulating facts about the other. Kramsch (1987a) has also argued that textbooks usually have constructed the target-language culture with reference to the culture of the learner either in terms of explicit low-level concepts or in implicit higher level analogies. Textbooks tend to lack connections between factual statements about the target culture and the learners' own cultures and lack explicit higher level interpretations of what is presented about the target culture. This makes it difficult, according to Kramsch, for learners to engage critically with their own culture or to assess the validity of the target language concepts presented in the textbook. Although the texts discussed here do not deal with the culture of the learner explicitly, in some cases that culture is actually implicitly present in a way that is not acknowledged in the texts or necessarily available to learners for critical reflection. In Figure 6.3, the presentation of the globalized French youth culture provides an implicit narrative of cultural similarity between the target culture and the culture of the learner. French practices are presented as being largely similar to the experiences of learners and differences are presented as belonging to an older, rural France. These differences are presented therefore as being not

lecture

La Culture Carrefour

C'est samedi après-midi. Que faire ? Une promenade à vélo ? Non, pas question : il fait un temps de chien. Rien à la télé. Papa travaille sur l'ordinateur. Un coup de fil aux copains. Alors, qu'est-ce qu'on fait ? Bien, on va au centre commercial, à Carrefour. Que faire là-bas ? On cause, on regarde passer les gens, on compare les vêtements, les accessoires et les coiffures, on fait du lèche-vitrine. C'est un spectacle permanent et vous, vous en faites partie. On regarde et on se fait regarder...

Le café du coin, ce n'est plus le lieu de rencontre préféré des jeunes. Finis les diabolo-menthe, finis les jeux de baby-foot, de flipper. De plus en plus, les jeunes Français se réunissent dans les grands centres commerciaux, surtout dans la banlieue parisienne et dans les villes de province.

Qu'est-ce qu'il y a qui les attire chez Carrefour, chez Mammouth, chez Leclerc ? D'abord, il fait toujours bon dans un grand centre commercial. C'est chauffé en hiver et climatisé en été. C'est ouvert sept jours sur sept, du matin au soir. Et il n'y a pas seulement des magasins et des boutiques. Il y a aussi des restaurants et des cafés – ou plutôt des fast-food, le style de nourriture préféré des jeunes. C'est là où on se retrouve avec les copains pendant le week-end.

Les propriétaires de ces grands centres, que pensent-ils de ces bandes de jeunes qui s'y rassemblent ? Eh bien, ils trouvent ça formidable, parce que ces jeunes, ils achètent... Séduits par les étalages, la musique, l'ambiance luxueuse, ils achètent de tout – des vêtements, des accessoires, des CD, des jeux... et à manger bien sûr. Le shopping, c'est un passe-temps.

Cependant, cette 'culture Carrefour' inquiète beaucoup de Français. Il faut dire que dans un grand centre commercial on se demande si on est en France ou aux États-Unis. Avec la globalisation, les pays se ressemblent de plus en plus. La vieille France a-t-elle disparu ? La France des boulangeries, des boucheries, des épiceries, des 'BOF' (beurre-œufs-fromages) et des marchés de rue ?

Eh bien, non. Allez dans n'importe quelle petite ville ou village le jour de marché. On y trouve la même ambiance qu'il y a cent ans et dans la plupart des cas les mêmes produits : les fromages, les vins, les saucissons, les jambons, les légumes et les fruits de saison. Dans les grandes villes, les petites rues de marché sont toujours là et pleines de monde.

Oui, la culture Carrefour existe, mais en parallèle de la France traditionnelle. Le Coca-Cola et le hamburger vivent ensemble avec le croissant et le café-crème. Après tout, la France est un pays tolérant !

78   soixante-dix-huit

Figure 6.3   Cultural awareness material from *Tapis Volant 2*. *Source*: Zemiro, J. and Chamberlain, A. (2004) *Tapis volant 2* (2nd ed.), South Melbourne, Thomson Nelson.

only remote to the learner but also to the experience of those French people who are similar in age to the learner. In Figure 6.2, the focus on specific events in the German school context implicitly indexes the dissimilarities between Australian and German cultures in terms of the early start to the school day (a negative aspect of Germany – "the early starts are killing me"), the *Schultüte* (a positive aspect of Germany – "a really cool custom"), and the environmental practices of German schools (presented as a difference with explicit evaluation). These differences reflect Kramsch's (1987a) observation that there are three main ways of representing the relationship between the cultures involved in language textbooks: emphasizing the similarity of the two cultures, emphasizing the differences between the two cultures, and representing one culture as lacking something which is present in the other. Each of these invites an implicit and unrecognized comparison between cultural practices, which invokes a particular value system through the associations made and these comparisons are reproduced chapter by chapter through the text. Moreover, the account of differences between Australia and Germany in Figure 6.2 represents the differences as something that is lacking in one culture (in this case the learner's own culture) but present in the other: the "really cool custom" of *Schultüten* or the environmental focus of schools. In these cases, as in the negative evaluation of the early start of the school day, differences are presented as value laden. That is, cultural variability is constructed in terms of one culture being in some sense better than another. This means that cultural diversity is not presented as a normal element of human reality with its own internal validity and value, but as something that is to be evaluated from one's own cultural perspective.

As resources for intercultural language learning, textbooks provide material that is often of limited use in developing the sorts of intercultural understanding that an interculturally oriented stance in language teaching aims for. This means that intercultural teaching needs to engage with the issues of resourcing learning in more creative ways and that a textbook alone is unlikely to provide the sorts of language learning experiences that students need to become interculturally aware users of language.

Moving Beyond Textbooks

For most teachers, resourcing learning from an intercultural perspective on language learning requires more than a textbook and it is common for teachers to supplement, or even replace, textbooks with other materials more relevant to their own learners and their teaching goals. Textbooks typically present a single focus on the material that they present, or if they present multiple perspectives on an issue, tend to do so as distinct and contrasting perspectives. In order to develop a more sophisticated engagement with the diversity of values, beliefs, practices, and contexts that exist in any cultural context, it is necessary to provide material that will supplement the perspectives provided in textbook resources. Any resource is likely to present only a single perspective on the language and culture it embodies. Such single perspectives may be construed as the only relevant perspective on what is being presented. That is, what is being presented in the resource is perceived as the "truth" about a language, culture, or people. This is especially the case when information is presented as factual knowledge in authoritative texts, and for many learners all materials provided by teachers can take on such authority. In providing only single or limited perspectives through their selection of resources, language teachers may play a significant role in creating

Figure 6.4   "He! Toi! L'Arabe! Tes papiers!"

stereotypicalized understandings. When teaching from an intercultural perspective there is therefore a need to use language-learning materials to emphasize the variability of cultures and the place of context in understanding the meaning of linguistic and cultural behaviors. Recognizing the variability of culture goes beyond depictions of multicultural diversity or the pluricentric nature of languages, as these are often little more than contextual backdrops against which language learning tasks are presented (Pulverness, 2003).

Resources need to be selected in a principled way to ensure that learners are exposed to a broad range of themes on the culture they are studying. This may include gender, social class, ethnicity, region, religion, political affiliation, and so on, in order to reflect the inherent variability of cultures in any context. However, these themes do not fully represent the diversity found in any culture, as they represent group, rather than individual, perspectives. Such groups are not homogeneous and it is important that a selection of resources for language learning does not present diversity only in terms of groups but also allows insights into the ways individuals participate differently in their groups and have different perspectives on their cultures and societies.

The kinds of distinctions discussed above form part of the context for understanding language as a cultured act of meaning-making (Figure 6.4). That is, participants' identities are a dimension of their meaning-making and need to be considered and understood as part of the communication. In Figure 6.4 it is the context represented by the various identities involved that creates the meaning-making potential of the language itself. The relationship between the police officer and the young man is part of the intended meaning, as is the minority status of an Arab in this context. There are significant issues of power in this relationship – the institutional power of the police in relation to the individual, the ethnic power of the dominant white mainstream and the marginalized minority. This relationship is encoded in particular ways through the language – the invocation of institutional power through *"tes papiers,"* the abruptness of the command given only as a noun, the designation of the individual by his ethnic membership, and the use of *"tu."*

Figure 6.4 can be brought into relationship with standard textbook versions of the use of *tu* such as that shown in Magnan *et al.* (2002, p. 18):

Forms of Address

Use Tu

- With family and friends
- Among peers. Particularly among young people, students, colleagues, and co-workers the tendency is to use **tu** and first names from the start.
- With children even if you have not met them before.
- With pets.

Use Vous

- With all adults you meet for the first time and all adults you address as **monsieur/ madame/mademoiselle**. You can also use **vous** with adults you know, even if you are on a first-name basis, but you will often be invited to use tu.

The list of uses of *tu* given here does not sit well with the interaction in the cartoon and so the textbook itself becomes a site for contention as the rules for use conflict with the situation in which the form is being used. Nonetheless, learners can use the list as a resource to interpret what the use of *tu* means in this context. That is, resources can be related to each other to better understand each resource involved. The interpretation here raises issues of reciprocity in the use of French pronouns that are not covered by the textbook list, which seems to presuppose reciprocal use of *tu* and *vous*. The cartoon therefore can be interrogated according to the possibilities of the policeman's use of *tu* being reciprocated. The use of language in the cartoon is an entry point into understanding what the language means in its context. *Tu* is not fixed in its meaning, but interacts with its context to communicate particular meanings and associations that can be read from context.

The process of resourcing language learning involves much more than selecting the resource. Effective teaching involves being a critical user of all resources and using resources flexibly to enhance learning opportunities. Moreover, it is important to consider how the resource positions the learner in relation to what is being learned. A resource may position the learner as an insider or as an outsider in relation to its content, and can constrain the possible roles that the learner may adopt in relation to the content. Critical evaluation of a resource also needs to consider the conceptual load that the resource imposes on the learner, to match the demands of the resource to the capabilities of the learners in order to allow learners to work with a level of sophistication in interpreting it. Resources are fundamentally learning opportunities and so teachers will also need to consider how a resource scaffolds learning for the student or how to provide scaffolding to allow the resource to become available for learners to use in developing greater complexity in thinking about issues of language, culture, and their relationship. Any resource is only an instance of possible representations of language, culture, and learning and there will always be other possibilities.

The Authenticity of the Resource

One concern for language teachers teaching from an intercultural perspective is the authenticity of resources for language learning. Authenticity is particularly important when language is viewed as an instantiation of culture and the process of learning as the negotiation of this relationship. Many resources developed especially for language learning have tended to edit out or modify aspects of context that are important to understanding the relationship between language and culture and have privileged language as the structural system over the development of culturally contexted meaning. Material developed by speakers of a language for communication with other speakers is heavily contexted and privileges processes of meaning-making over language use for its own sake. Such materials then provide opportunities for investigating language as culturally contexted meaning-making, however, they are not designed for learners of the language but for those who already know it and the cultural messages it conveys in context. This poses a problem for the use of such materials as language learning materials, especially at lower levels of learning, and raises the issue of what constitutes authentic material for intercultural language learning.

Authenticity has been interpreted in a range of ways. Material may be considered authentic because it is designed by native speakers for native speakers – that is, it represents authentic communication between native speakers (Alptekin, 2002). The argument given above, that such language is contexted in the target culture, seems to imply, at least in part, that such authenticity is important in intercultural learning. However, such a view is limited if it is considered the only criterion for authenticity of resources. It is limited because it assumes that the situation of native speakers communicating with other native speakers is the "real" context of language use. This denies the possibility of the nonnative speaker, the language learner, ever being an authentic communicator in the language. There is therefore a need to recognize the intercultural nature of the communication in which language learners engage as constituting part of the authenticity of their communicative needs. Authenticity therefore needs also to be seen in the ways in which cultural realities can be communicated between languages. As Widdowson (1998) observed, language that is authentic for native speakers may not be authentic for nonnative speakers and there need to be points of connection with the lives of the learners themselves and the language resources with which they engage. Alptekin (2002) further argues that the monolingualism inherent in the native-speaker view of authenticity may even inhibit opportunities for intercultural learning. This means resources that demonstrate the engagement of those outside a culture with that culture have an important role as resources for language learning. For example, Pulverness (2003) argues that literature written by immigrants and other outsiders provides a particularly effective way to see what is taken for granted by cultural insiders.

Alternately, authenticity has been considered in terms of what is done with the resource rather than in terms of the resource itself, which may be purpose-made for the task. Widdowson's (1983) understanding of authenticity includes "the communicative activity of the language use … the engagement of interpretative procedures for making sense, even if these procedures are operating on and with textual data which are not authentic in the first sense" (p. 30). From an intercultural perspective, the procedures with which a learner engages are the procedures of negotiating meaning across languages and cultures and we argue that it is in this sense that authenticity needs to be considered. That is, authenticity exists when learners use resources authentically as intercultural speakers engaging in making and interpreting meaning at the intersections of languages and cultures. In such a view, the authenticity of the resource itself is a separate, but not trivial, consideration.

In reality, both forms of authenticity are important in the selection, adaptation, and use of resources. Authentic materials, in the sense of materials designed by speakers of a language for other speakers of the same language, expose learners to actual contemporary ways of language use rather than to idealized or old-fashioned structures. They bring learners into closer contact with the real world of the target language and enlarge their understanding of what language is. Most importantly, they are produced within the cultural context of native speakers and are imbued with the assumptions, values, and ways of communicating of that culture. However, authentic resources do not of themselves guarantee relevant and authentic learning, and resources do not exist independently of the teaching and learning context in which they are used. Arnold argues that the tension between the teaching–learning situation and the original communicative purpose of the resources being used is resolved if several types of authenticity come together: "Authentic materials and learner's purposes, authentic materials and authentic interactions, authentic responses, authentic participants, authentic status, settings and equipment and authentic inputs and outputs" (1991, p. 237). Authenticity as a goal in selecting and using resources for language learning is not a question of the nature of the resource itself but needs to be considered as a dynamic interaction between the resources, their use, and the learning that they are designed to produce:

- Authenticity of purpose: the resource needs to be of intrinsic interest or there needs to be an extrinsic purpose (as in the case of maps, menus, etc.) if it is to engage learners. These purposes can be either a "real world" purpose external to the classroom or an intellectual engagement with the resources to promote new insights and knowledge.
- Authenticity of response or task: learners need to respond to the resource in an authentic way, thus what students are asked to do with a resource is at least as important as its origin. In this response, it is important to consider how the learner is positioned in responding to the class. Is this persona congruent with or in conflict with the learners' identities as learners and users of the language?
- Authenticity of conditions: the conditions for language use need to be reflective of the conditions for use of the resource in the "real world." This real world needs to be understood as the world of the intercultural language user, who mediates between languages and cultures as an inherent part of communication. (Liddicoat *et al.*, 2003, p. 68)

Literature as an Authentic Resource

If an authentic resource is understood as one that has been produced by a speaker of a language for other speakers of the same language, literature can be seen as a highly developed version of an authentic resource for intercultural learning.

There have been a number of studies of the use of literature as a source of cultural learning and the emphasis on literature is unsurprising given the strong association between literature and culture in traditional approaches to language teaching and learning. Such approaches have tended to focus on the study of a text as a work of literature and have implicitly assumed that appreciation of the work as literature was equivalent to engaging with the culture of the text. More recent work on the use of literature has argued that the study of literature needs to move beyond literary criticism and textual study to begin to engage with context (e.g. Byram, 1988, 1989a; Kramsch, 1993a). In intercultural approaches to the use of literature, it is important that the literary text does not remain the object of study in itself, but also becomes the vehicle for deeper reflection and for understanding of self and others. Pulverness (2003) argues that the key use of literature for resourcing intercultural learning is to provide a stimulus for enabling learners to decenter from their own perspectives in reading the text and to come to see their own constructions of reality as strange. He suggests that literary genres, such as science fiction or stories of immigrants' experiences, which seek to make the familiar strange to their readers, provide a useful departure point for reflecting on ways of understanding difference.

Kramsch and Nolden (1994) do not limit the usefulness of literary texts to particular genres but see the possibilities for intercultural engagement with literature as lying in the meeting of cultures inherent in reading a "foreign text." They argue that it is in the process of negotiating meaning in the act of reading that the language learner constructs and explores intercultural meanings. Following Certeau, they see reading the literary text as a form of oppositional practice or "transforming imposed structures, languages, codes, rules, etc. in ways that serve individual or group purposes other than those 'intended'" (p. 29). Kramsch and Nolden identify instances in which students' response to texts indicates that students are relocating meaning from the cultural context of the text into their own cultural context and in so doing are transforming the text as a cultural object. The learners themselves may not be conscious of the cultural transformation involved. Second language readers therefore enter into a dialogic relationship with the text in which they recognize the gaps and dissonances as they read.

Kramsch (1993a) approaches intercultural learning from the perspective of the interrelationships between texts people generate and contexts shaping them or shaped by them. In this work, Kramsch shows the power of textual analysis as a stimulus for intercultural learning by going beyond the text as artifact to explore possible meanings in the text. She identifies five significant elements of context – linguistic, situational, interactional, cultural, and intertextual – and argues that language learning needs to provide opportunities to discover potential meanings through explorations of the context of the discourse under study. Meanings in a text produced in another culture need to be made visible (Kramsch, 1995b) and learners need to explore the cues that signal meanings in the text. Through the investigation of culturally contexted meaning, the language learner comes to see language as culturally shaped and as culturally shaping rather than as an unproblematized process of communication. In this way, texts open possibilities of new and hitherto undiscovered meanings that become possible for investigation (Kramsch, 2003).

In most work on the use of literature for culture learning, the emphasis has been on a two-way comparison between the culture of the learner and the target culture. Carroli, Maurer, and Hillman (Carroli, Hillman, and Maurer, 1999; Maurer, Carroli, and Hillman, 2000) have used a comparative literature perspective in which the same theme is examined through writings in different languages and written in different cultural contexts, thereby producing a richer, multilateral perspective on the theme. They argue that in the confrontation between literature about the Second World War from four languages (Italian, French, German, and English), students learn that the English language perspective with which they are familiar is only one perspective among many. The differences between texts can be located in a historical context that influences how texts and ideas are produced and received. Literary texts therefore become positioned cultural objects and the events they describe can be seen as created and communicated from and within different cultural understandings rather than as objective happenings.

In each of these approaches to literature, the intercultural emerges not from the text as an authentic language resource but through the engagement between the cultural worlds of the text and the language learner. It is in the process of interpretation, of seeing the cultural in the text, that literature becomes a resource for intercultural language learning.

Communities as Resources

Communities of target-language speakers have often been considered to be potential resources for intercultural learning and there has been much attention given in the literature of intercultural learning to the place of ethnography (e.g. Byram, 1989b; Carel, 2001; Corbett, 2003; Jurasek, 1995; Roberts *et al.*, 2001; Robinson-Stuart and Nocon, 1996). Ethnographic approaches to intercultural learning move away from the idea of a learning resource as an artifact that brings language into the learning experience to one in which intercultural interactions themselves become the resource for learning. They involve a shift away from the interpretation of written and audiovisual texts to a way of seeing direct experience of lived reality as a text for interpretation.

The fundamental resource for the ethnographic approach to intercultural language teaching is an experience, typically an out-of-class experience, of another culture, and ethnographic language learning has focused on experiences gained through study-abroad programs – a language learning context that is external to the delivery of language courses in educational institutions. Such experiences engage students in a direct experience of the everyday life of those whose language they are learning with an interpretive reflective component in which students situate their lived experience of the other within a broader sociopolitical context (Roberts *et al.*, 2001). The study-abroad experience is a direct experience of using an additional language in its own cultural context and as such is a process of communicative engagement with another community and its language and culture. Study-abroad programs within an intercultural orientation to language learning offer the opportunity to both improve use of the target language and develop students' intercultural capabilities (Byram, 1989b; Byram and Feng, 2005; Coleman, 1997, 1998; Murphy-Lejeune, 2003; Roberts *et al.*, 2001). Ethnography adds to a focus on communication in language learning and the use of communicative capabilities in real life, the development of conceptual understandings of the cultural processes involved in such communication. The aim of such ethnographies is to encourage "a repositioning of the self both intellectually and at the level of 'felt' reality, the apprehension of relationships and material realities and their impact on us as thinking, feeling beings" (Roberts *et al.*, 2001, p. 6).

Study abroad is not in itself a form of intercultural learning, rather it provides the potential for such learning to occur. That is, not every instance of study abroad results in intercultural learning, or at least, not in positive experiences of intercultural learning (Byram, 1989b). For study abroad to function as a resource for intercultural learning it needs to be supported within an educational learning program (Coleman, 1997; Schmidt and Jansen, 2004). That is, it is not the resource but the way the resource is used that makes the resource effective. Study abroad has the potential to become intercultural when integrated into a process of teaching and learning that gives scope for sustained reflection on the experience. Roberts *et al.* (2001) propose a model for the integration of study abroad into a program of intercultural learning through the Ealing ethnography program. This program combines preparatory classes in which students learn the principles of ethnography before the study-abroad experience and the development of an ethnographic account of the study-abroad experience upon their return. This model therefore allows students to develop the necessary capacity to be participant observers during their time in another culture and requires them to reflect on that experience in a sustained way after the experience. The program described here is in agreement therefore with Corbett's (2003) argument that observing, interviewing, analyzing, and reporting are fundamental to encounters with other cultures and argues that language learners need to learn these as an element of language curricula. This means that language learning resources not only need to provide access to language and culture, but also to the processes required to understand and interpret them.

Ethnographic projects in study-abroad settings have been a particular feature of intercultural programs in Europe, where the proximity of neighboring countries and strong programs of educational exchange have aided student mobility (Byram and Snow, 1997). As student mobility increases, such projects become more feasible in other regions, but for many language learners it is not a readily available source of experience of the culture of another community. However, ethnography as a resource for language learning has not been associated only with study-abroad programs, but it has also been adapted to other learning contexts in which some experience of another culture is possible. This typically takes the form of a small-scale ethnography embedded within a larger language-learning program. One way of including ethnography within language programs has been through the use of ethnographic interviews. The depth to which this may go may be limited compared to the larger scale immersion of study abroad, but the essential aims remain similar to those of larger projects. Such interviews with members of the target-language community are seen as a way of developing contact between the language learner and users of the language in a way that develops similar capabilities for reflection on language, culture, and their relationship. As a language- and culture-learning resource, ethnographic interviews make available to language learners a view of a culture from inside, that is, a description of a culture in its own terms (Damen, 1987), and allow for the discovery of similarities and shared values as well as differences between cultures. In particular, the ethnographic interview is seen as a way of both coming to understand another culture's perspective and becoming aware of one's own cultural positioning (Bateman, 2002).

The ethnographic interview is used in a range of ways in language programs. In some programs, the pedagogical focus is placed on developing ethnographic techniques. Such programs are in line with Pulverness' (2003) argument that resources need to provide opportunities for the development of ethnographic research approaches that would allow students opportunities to investigate and analyze cultures as they participate in them. Robinson-Stuart and Nocon (1996) used ethnographic interviews as a culture-learning tool with Spanish language learners. In this study, interviewing a speaker of the target language was integrated as an element of a regular language program and students prepared a report based on the interview. The authors identify a number of changes in learners' attitudes towards target-language groups resulting from the process of interviewing, but the project they report seems to treat this as an outcome of the project rather than as the focus of the project itself. That is, the intercultural investigation was secondary to the ethnography. Similarly, Bateman's (2002) use of ethnographic interviews sees the development of the ability to conduct and report an ethnographic interview as the main gain from the process of interviewing and the effects on attitudes as resulting from having done the project rather than being the focus of the project. Such ethnographic approaches seem therefore to have emphasized the development of ethnographic research techniques but have focused less on the ethnography as a resource for learning in its own right, with much of the learning reported being incidental to or outside the pedagogical program itself.

Other language teachers have used ethnographic interviews specifically as a form of intercultural investigation. Sobolewski (2009) describes a language-learning task in which investigation of some aspect of culture becomes the focus of the ethnographic interview. That is, the interviewees are positioned explicitly as a resource for promoting the students' own learning and ethnography as a mechanism for exploring an area of cultural interest. In this project, the interview is only a part of an overall research project in which culture is investigated through a range of complementary information sources to develop an enriched understanding of culture. In reporting on the project students were asked specifically to discuss their reactions to their learning, how the experience affected their views of both the target culture and their own. Sobolewski's work reveals an important dimension of the ethnographic interview for intercultural learning – that to be intercultural it needs to focus on the self as well as the other. An interview that gains insight into another culture without offering insight into one's own has not achieved the intercultural project, although it may have had such an outcome as a by-product of engagement with another culture. Knutson (2006) proposes that ethnographic projects for intercultural learning should combine "home ethnographies" as well as ethnographies of the other and should be open to investigating outsiders' perceptions of one's own culture as well as one's own perceptions of the other.

Conceptualizing communities of speakers as a resource opens the scope of intercultural language learning to move beyond texts and audiovisual materials into more interactive engagements with language and culture. By making people a resource for learning, ethnography as a form of language learning begins to develop capabilities that lend themselves to continued learning beyond the confines of the language classroom. However, as the discussion above has argued, the community is a resource for learning and ethnographic methods are simply tools for engaging with the resource. They are not a pedagogy in and of themselves but need to be integrated into processes of reflection and interpretation in order to become effective resources for intercultural learning.

The Classroom as a Resource

One key resource that is available for language learning is rarely adopted by language teachers. This is the languaging produced by learners themselves. This languaging, especially when it involves interpretation and the expression of reflections on the target language and culture, can be a powerful way of generating further thinking and discussion. Languaging about language and culture provides opportunities to explore the life worlds that learners bring to their engagement with a new language and culture, and allows learners to explore the encultured starting points to the process of interpretation. Where learning activities promote open-ended possibilities, different interpretations or responses may be juxtaposed as a way of seeing multiple perspectives of the same issues and of generating commentary and further thinking. This would mean that rather than student's written or oral responses being evaluated and then let go, responses would become the stimulus for further work. Such an approach increases the scope of resources for learning, validates diversity of interpretation, and provides challenges for further learning and reanalysis. The classroom environment is multivoiced in the Bakhtinian sense of a dialogic juxtaposition and interanimation of multiple perspectives and understandings (Bakhtin, 1981, 1984). Individual teachers and learners bring different knowledge, experiences, histories, languages, and cultures to the classroom, and interact through them using the learning opportunities afforded to them. The multivoiced classroom realities can be used as a way of developing learning and interpretation through social interactions in which different conceptualizations are brought into relationship to create new understandings. As Bakhtin argues:

> An active understanding, one that assimilates the word under consideration into a new conceptual system, that of the one striving to understand, establishes a series of complex interrelationships, consonances and dissonances with the word and enriches it with new elements. ... The speaker strives to get a reading of his own word, and on his own conceptual system that determines the word, within the alien conceptual system of the understanding receiver. (1981, p. 282)

Thus the process of interaction is one of interpretation and articulation of ideas within a multivoiced frame of reference in which different understandings are not only present, but are the central concern of communication.

The classroom is available as a resource because it is itself a real instantiation of languages and cultures in which different perspectives are brought into relationship. The value of the classroom community as a learning resource is that experiences of interpretation necessarily foreground diversity in the resources and experiences learners bring to the process of interpretation, and these resources and experiences have different consequences for how the material they are learning is perceived and understood. This means that each classroom is a site for diverse interpretations of the same experience. Coming to understand how this diversity is created and communicated opens new perspectives on diversity as a cultural phenomenon. This means that teachers and learners can use the interpretations of others as a resource for further reflection: investigating why interpretations are made, comparing interpretations and associating them with individual perspectives and experiences, and languaging about the process of interpretation. Through the processes of interaction about interpretation, interpretations can be reformulated, rearticulated, and re-formed in the light of developing understandings of alternates, forming the basis for reinterpretation through deeper understanding of the encultured nature of the starting point for interpretation.

Selecting and Evaluating Resources

The process of selecting any resource is one of evaluation and evaluations need be made in a principled way. Such evaluations go beyond questions such as "Is the resource suitable for the level of the learner?" or "Will students like the resource?" or "Can I use the resource in my teaching context?" although such questions have their place. In considering how resources are to be selected, the principles outlined in Chapter 4 provide a useful set of criteria for evaluation.

- *Active construction* implies that the resource allows students to notice aspects on language and culture and to begin to develop their own understandings through the text. This means that a resource is less a communication about a culture than an opportunity to experience a culture through language in a way that allows the learner to discover personal meanings and ways of interpreting through engagement with the text.
- *Making connections* requires the resource to have within it points of connection to learners' experiences – of their own languages and cultures, of what they have already learned about the new language and culture, or both. This means that resources need to allow for the possibilities of personalization. The aim is not to constrain the connections that learners will make but to open up new possibilities for connection with the resources and across and between learners using the resource.
- *Social interaction* is associated with the opportunities the resource affords for learners to engage with others about it and to express and understand different ways of interpreting it and the dispositions that underlie such interpretations. This requires that a resource provides a basis for interaction. A resource may also afford opportunities to explore interactions in different ways by focusing on the interaction itself and diverse ways of interacting across languages and cultures.
- *Reflection* implies that the resource engage learners in an interpretive process through which they develop and articulate new understandings of language, culture, and their relationship. Reflection is associated with possibilities of recognizing the cultural perspectives with which the resource is imbued and using this in a process of interpretation which engages both the learners' intracultural perspectives and possibilities for diverse perspectives of others.
- *Responsibility* requires a resource to afford opportunities for understanding one's personal responsibility for ensuring communication with diverse others.

It is unlikely that any resource will address all of the principles. Rather, they represent a way of evaluating resources both individually and collectively to ensure that the resources provided for learners provide opportunities to develop each of the principles.

These principles raise a number of further questions to be considered in selecting, adapting, and evaluating resources.

1   What opportunities does the resource provide for exploring language and culture?
2   What opportunities does the resource provide for engaging with language, culture, and their relationship in developing learning?
3   What does the resource contribute to developing meaning-making and interpretation?

4 How does the resource support a developing understanding of the nature of interpretation and the role of language and culture in interpretation and meaning-making?

5 How does the resource allow learners to make connections between their own lives and experiences and the target language and its speakers?

6 What opportunities for exploration does the resource afford students?

7 How does the resource connect to other resources, or how do the components of a resource connect with each other?

8 What sort of learning will the resource enable? What will it build on and what could be done next?

9 What more will be needed to use the resource to its fullest effect?

Adapting Resources

Teachers approach their resources in different ways. For some the resource, especially a textbook, may be considered to be fixed and unchangeable, a resource to be followed faithfully and systematically. For others, resources are starting points for teaching and learning and can be supplemented, adapted, or changed to suit their goals and students' interests (Littlejohn, 1998). In reality, no resource can completely meet the needs of individual teachers and their learners and any resource will require adaptation for use with particular groups of students. Adapting materials allows teachers to achieve greater compatibility and a better fit between the resource and their teaching context, to maximize the value of the resource for their particular learners. Adapting materials applies equally to authentic materials and to materials produced especially for language learning. Authentic resources are not designed for language learning, but are invaluable for promoting learning. Such materials may need to be adapted for use in the classroom, such as by providing:

• additional language support (glossing, explanation of terms, etc.);
• additional information relevant to understanding the resource (e.g. additional resources showing different aspects of the same basic issue);
• scaffolding to assist in using the resource.

Materials developed specifically for learning also need to be adapted. Such materials present a generalized frame for learning, but this learning needs to be placed into a context considering, among other things, the teaching, the interests, needs, experiences, expectations, motivations, and knowledge of the students, the age of the students, their language-learning history, and so on. Textbooks present generalized, fictional material designed to be used by any teacher with any learner anywhere. This means that there may be little that connects directly to individual students' lives and there may be little with which learners can engage. All resources inevitably are directed at a generic student and the key challenge facing teachers is to personalize the resource for their students. This means adapting or supplementing resources to provide links to the learner's life and experiences and permit multiple paths to engagement with the resource. In many cases, personalizing a resource may not be a matter of personalizing the stimulus material but rather the ways in which the learner works with the material, allowing space for interpretation and individual connections as well as connections made collectively as part of the interactive process of learning.

The selection and adaptation of the resource are important, but the most important element of resourcing is planning ways to use the resource. In particular, it is important to consider what learners will actually do with the resource. Each task developed around a resource, or set of resources, constructs a way of engaging with language and culture as presented in the resource. Tasks can limit opportunities for student engagement. For example, a text-reading task may ask students to engage only with superficial issues of locating information in the text; however, the same text could be used for developing interpretation, analysis, and reflection, personal engagement with themes and issues, comparison and connection with other texts, or questioning aspects of the text's message.

Using Resources Critically

Any resource, whether it is a textbook, a published teaching resource, or a resource created by a teacher, needs to be used critically. All resources are developed within a theoretical framework involving the understandings of language, culture, and learning that the resource developer brings to the task. This means that every resource is both subjective and constrained. It is subjective because it represents one individual's (or in some cases a small group's) views and objectives and it is constrained because any resource can present only a limited insight into a language and its attendant cultures.

The subjectivity of resource development is an issue with which every teacher needs to engage. To say that something is subjective is not a criticism; it is a normal part of human functioning connected to the underlying values and theories that a person brings to any situation. When a teacher uses materials developed by someone else, these underlying values and theories may or may not be in accord with those of the teacher using the material. If there is a conflict, the use of the materials may be problematic and they may not achieve the learning the teacher had chosen the resource to develop. Similarly, if we design resources without awareness of the values and theories that we ourselves bring to the design, then we may discover that the material we develop does not work adequately to achieve our purposes. It is missing aspects we value or does not gel with the way we understand the language and cultures we are teaching.

The constrained nature of resources is an inevitable result of the processes of selection, design, and ordering involved in producing a manageable resource. The more a resource is targeted at a generic population, the more constrained it is likely to be, as the designers can assume little shared knowledge with the end-users. As Yoshino (1992) claims, in spite of the best intentions of writers and editors, learning materials, and especially the cultural information in learning materials, are frequently characterized by cultural reductionism and cultural relativism. By cultural reductionism, she means that information is usually presented in a way which strips away the complexity, variability, and subtleness of culture and represents speakers of the target language as homogeneous and stereotypical. Cultural relativism involves the drawing of distinct differences between two cultures, which establishes an "us–them" relationship between the learner and the target language and cultures. This oversimplifies and overemphasizes the differences and makes it more difficult for learners to draw connections between themselves and others and to develop intercultural ways of seeing the world.

Given these considerations, for any resource that is selected, or adapted, or created, it will be necessary to examine it critically in relation to questions such as the following.

- How is sociocultural and linguistic learning included? Is there any bias?
- How is the cultural information linked to the target language?
- How is the cultural information linked to communication?
- Does the resource reflect contemporary or traditional culture?
- Does the resource present a cultural aspect from the locus of the target culture, from another culture's perspective, or from the perspective of the culture's own diaspora?
- Are you in a position to judge? Why? Why not?

Being a critical user does not have to mean that the teacher has to abandon using a textbook or materials developed by others. It does mean thinking carefully about what the resources present to the students using them. It involves seeing the orientation, perspective, limitations, and omissions in the resource and deciding how to deal with these: by supplementing them with other perspectives, by replacing some parts of the resource with new material, by working with students to see the limitations and omissions, and so on.

Relating Resources to Each Other

The relationship between resources is also an important dimension for resourcing language learning. The resources used with a class are often the only experience of the language and culture available to most students. From these resources and the interactions around them, students have to assemble an image of the language and the cultures they are studying. If the resources are coherent and there are relations built between resources and time, then the possibility that students' might develop a coherent image is increased. If the resources are disparate and unconnected, focusing on the momentary learning episode only, then it may be impossible for students to develop any coherent sense of the language and cultures and to see only randomness and fragmentation.

Each resource is a single instance of language, and culture and learning occurs as students draw connections between these instances to establish deeper understandings. For this to happen, the resources for learning need to have connections to provide a rich experience of language and culture. Connections between resources can be of several different types, including resources that:

- add new content;
- develop general knowledge by linking language and content;
- add new perspectives on existing content;
- add new information about aspects of existing content;

- add complexity to interpretations;
- introduce challenges to current understanding;
- introduce personal perspectives;
- respond to learners' questions or interests about content;
- provide opportunities for reflection and identity building.

This means that resourcing needs to be seen as a cumulative presentation of opportunities for learning. In providing resources, teachers need to reflect on what the current resource provides for learning and how resources complement other resources to build learning through a series of experiences of language. Each group of learners may need a different range of resources in order to engage with the culture they are learning, as each group brings different experiences and possible points of connection and engagement to their language learning.

Concluding Comments

Resources are central to any form of teaching and learning and need to have the capacity to constrain or expand opportunities for learning. In selecting, adapting, and using resources, the most important consideration is what learning the resource affords the learner. To be successful, resources need to connect directly to individual students' lives and provide something with which they can engage. This means that a resource needs to be personalized for the particular learners who will use it, which in turn means adapting or supplementing resources so that there are links to the life and experiences of the learners and multiple paths to engagement. The ideal is that learners become resourceful for themselves. They identify and search for material that will help them to expand their understanding in an ongoing way. Language learners as language users need to be engaged in an ongoing process of learning beyond the focus of the classroom and so they need to learn how to resource themselves for further learning. In part, this means coming to see texts, interactions, and other engagements with language as being potentially resourceful for the individual learner through the ways in which they are used. The growth of communication and information technologies provides a powerful means of accessing material that can be resourceful for learning, and we turn to this in the next chapter.

7

Technologies in Intercultural Language Teaching and Learning

Introduction

New technologies have significantly contributed to the ways in which language can be taught as culturally contexted practice. In facilitating communication between distant parts of the world, they have made other languages and cultures more immediately present to language teachers and learners than they have ever been before. Although not usually designed for the purpose of language learning, they provide a useful point of contact between the language learner and the world of target-language speakers. This chapter will examine the roles and uses of technologies in intercultural language teaching and learning.

Windschitl (1998) has stated that access to information and connectedness are the defining traits of the Internet. Consideration of these two dimensions of information technologies is therefore important for considering how they can contribute to intercultural language teaching and learning. Using Windschitl's two traits as a starting point, it is possible to develop a heuristic classification of technologies based on the purpose of the technology.

1   *Information technologies* – technologies that are designed to provide access to information, such as websites (Windschitl's trait of access to information).
2   *Social technologies* – technologies that are designed to enable sociality through interaction, such as e-mail or chat, which afford opportunities to participate in virtual worlds (Windschitl's trait of connectedness).

In reality, the distinction is not clearly defined. As all information exists to be communicated, it is necessarily social. Moreover, some technologies blur the distinction between information and sociality. By giving opportunities for varying the roles of sender and receiver in

Intercultural Language Teaching and Learning, First Edition. Anthony J. Liddicoat and Angela Scarino.
© 2013 Anthony J. Liddicoat and Angela Scarino. Published 2013 by Blackwell Publishing Ltd.

constructing information (e.g. wikis, blogs), they break down the directionality of information provision, hence the purpose is both information and sociality. This blurring of the boundaries between information technologies and social technologies arises in part from the evolution of the web as a source of information or a way of presenting content in the first generation of web technologies, to the more collaborative, participatory technologies of Web 2.0 (Greenhow, Robelia, and Hughes, 2009). Despite the blurring of boundaries, the distinction of purpose between information and sociality is useful for considering how technologies can be used in intercultural language teaching and learning, because it allows different possible functions, uses, and educative focuses to be highlighted. It also allows for consideration of whether an instructional design responds to the technologies' purposes or uses the technology for other purposes. For example, Internet chat may enable social interaction across cultures and languages, but the transcripts of a chat session may be used as a source of information for analysis. That is, the information/social distinction is not simply a feature of technologies themselves, but also characterizes patterns of use of technologies within learning contexts.

Information Technologies and Intercultural Learning

Information technologies provide students with access to a vast information repository that can promote experiences of inquiry for students. This is probably the most obvious way in which technologies can be used for intercultural learning – to make cultural information available to language learners. The particular advantage of technology as an information repository is its potential to provide absolutely contemporary information from anywhere in the world. How contemporary this information is depends on the nature of the technology involved. It may range from websites that are infrequently updated and therefore possibly out of date, to blogs, which may be updated daily, to Twitter, which may be updated every few seconds. This absolute contemporaneity means that technologically mediated information does not exist simply as static information, but has the potential to be a constantly evolving discourse of events and ideas. These rapidly evolving discourses include both information and misinformation, and the publicly accessible nature of information on the web means that information is also subject to bias, stereotyping, and a host of other problems (Sercu, 2008). Such problems are inherently undermining if the purpose of using the information is to gain factual data about a country, culture, or people; however, they are nonetheless real-world instantiations of attitudes, values, and under-standings with which anyone using the Internet needs to engage, and they afford opportu-nities for analysis and reflection. This means that the student engaging with internet-resourced information needs to do so from a critical, analytic perspective. That is, the important focus is not on the information but on how students engage with the information (e.g. checking, validating, contrasting, and critiquing information and information sources). In the focus on process, the issue of reliability of information becomes less crucial. All information is seen as a culturally possible formulation, but only one of many possible formulations, and needs to be understood as part of a world of discourse, not as a pronouncement of fact. The issue here is less whether or not the source is reliable, but rather what the source affords as a learning experience.

Sercu (2008) notes that not all information available on the net yields the same learning experiences for the language learner. In comparing two sites dealing with aspects of France, she identifies different ways in which cultural information is presented and the different possibilities each affords for intercultural learning. The first site – fr.wikipedia.org/wiki/France#.c3.89conomie – presents information about France that is fixed and factual, and constructs a static view of the country. The second – fr.wikipedia.org/wiki/Tour-Eiffel – includes representations of the tower in ways that explore the tower as a symbolically constructed cultural object. The first site presents cultural information as fixed and authoritative; the second presents similar information as constructed and contested. In this discussion, Sercu demonstrates that different websites provide for different experiences of culture and that teachers need to be critical in the materials they select for their students.

An important part of this learning is to consider all Internet-resourced information as culturally positioned and to see the information available as representing discursive constructions of the world through cultural lenses. These lenses are of course not unitary within any given culture and so the student using the information needs to engage with it as contexted within potentially diverse, variable, and contested discourses. It is at the level of culturally contexted discourse that information begins to provide opportunities for intercultural learning.

One way to engage with information as culturally contexted discourse is to examine collections of information taken from websites. For example, the collection of texts in Box 7.1

Box 7.1   Selected texts from *La Libération*

Le débat sur le voile intégral continue

La secrétaire d'Etat aux droits de l'Homme Rama Yade et le président d'honneur du PRG Roger-Gérard Schwartzenberg se sont dits favorables à une loi. Ils affirment vouloir défendre la laïcité et les droits de la femme.

Alors que le gouvernement dit réfléchir à la possibilité de légiférer sur le port du voile intégral, la secrétaire d'Etat aux droits de l'Homme Rama Yade s'est déclarée ce samedi sur Europe 1 «*pas opposée*» à une loi. «*Il faut à titre préventif, à titre de défense de la laïcité, de défense de la dignité de la femme, agir. Quelle que soit la méthode, loi, règlement, décret, peu importe*», a-t-elle estimé.

Roger-Gérard Schwartzenberg, président d'honneur du PRG, a de son côté estimé dans un communiqué qu'il «*serait très utile de légiférer pour interdire le port de la burqa, qui est contraire à nos principes constitutionnels fondamentaux et aux valeurs de la République*». Il souligne que le préambule de la Constitution de 1946 repris dans la Constitution de 1958 «garantit à la femme, dans tous les domaines des droits égaux à ceux de l'homme». Pour lui, ce préambule justifierait donc de légiférer sur le port du voile intégral (burqa et niqab). A l'appui de sa position, il rappelle en outre des propos du recteur Dalil Boubaker, selon lesquels «*le port de la burqa n'est pas une prescription coranique, mais une coutume imposée arbitrairement par une tendance islamiste extrême*».

Le président de la République Nicolas Sarkozy a prévu de s'exprimer lundi sur l'opportunité d'une loi interdisant le port du voile intégral en France à l'occasion de son discours devant le Parlement réuni en Congrès à Versailles.

Responses

A propos

Il faudrait quand même qu'elles finissent par adopter les moeurs françaises. Pas de burka, pas de voile un foulard c'est suffisant dans la rue seulement.

On n'est pas au pays des barbus.

C'est un début d'application de la charia.

Dieu a créer la femme et l'homme et il faut bien qu'ils se voit pour créer un couple.

Je propose que le voile et le reste soit transparent comme pour le mariage de jane Birkin avec serge Gainsbourg.

Et dans l'autre sens?

Donc si on vous suit il faut prendre intégralement les moeurs du pays dans lequel on vit. ... Et donc porter la burqa ou le voile dans les pays musulmans même si ce n'est pas notre croyance ?

Il faut arrêter avec les clichés moyenâgeux les femmes qui portent la burqa en France (et il y en a très peu) le font librement. C'est un choix de leur part et je ne vois pas en quoi c'est dérangeant. Les goûts et les couleurs ne se discutent pas ... Personnellement je vois dans la rue tous les jours des tenues qui me choquent bien plus que la burqa et ce n'est pas pour autant que je vais me permettre de dire aux gens qui les portent d'aller s'habiller autrement. "Liberté", Egalité, Fraternité ...

Quel retour en arrière que d'interdire certaines tenues. On oublie qu'il y a quelques années on se battait pour ne plus porter d'uniforme à l'école ou pour que les femmes puissent elles aussi porter des pantalons!

eh bien je réponds

que dans un pays comme la France, une femme voilée, en burka de surcroît, c'est totalement déplacé.

Une grande gifle dans la gueule de celles et ceux qui ont combattu pour nos droits.

La laicite n'a pas de fanatique ...

C'est un pretexte fallacieux que de vouloir legiferer sur le port du voile au nom de la laicite et de la protection des femmes.

Quand on est laique, on respecte tout le monde et toutes les formes de pensees, etc. ... on ne legifere pas pour interdire. On tolere.

De quel droit a-t-on pour se prononcer que les femmes qui portent le voile le sont contre leur gre?

Source: Retrieved December 18, 2009 from http://www.liberation.fr/ societe/0101575248-le-debat-sur-le-voile-integral (accessed November 1, 2012)

provides a small sample of ideas, values, and issues relating to the debate over the banning of the full veil in France, taken from the website of left-wing newspaper *La Libération*. This set of texts can be considered as a representation of a range of diverse views on a contentious issue of symbolic importance. The texts can be interrogated in a range of ways by examining the rationales represented, the values that underlie them, and the significance of their inclusion on the *Libération* website. From the collection, it is possible to begin to enter into the ways in which not only the main issue, but also a number of key French values, are understood and can be read as a cultural construction of the debate. These texts raise issues such as human rights and secularism, which are invoked to both reject and support wearing the veil and are a way of engaging with the contested nature of values and beliefs:

> *Ils affirment vouloir défendre la laïcité et les droits de la femme.*
> *…« garantit à la femme, dans tous les domaines des droits égaux à ceux de l'homme ».*
> *C'est un choix de leur part et je ne vois pas en quoi c'est dérangeant … Liberté, Egalité, Fraternité …*
> *C'est un pretexte fallacieux que de vouloir legiferer sur le port du voile au nom de la laicite et de la protection des femmes.*

These texts are not in themselves intercultural learning. Rather, they provide a starting point for beginning a process of noticing, comparing, reflecting, and interacting, in which students notice the value systems being presented and the ways in which they are used to both support and oppose a position, to connect the views expressed to their own and those of others in their culture, to explore how their own cultural assumptions influence how they respond to both the issue and the individual texts, and to use the understandings they have gained to communicate with others about the issues raised.

Social Technologies and Intercultural Learning

From the perspective of intercultural language teaching and learning, social technologies have the potential to bring language learners into direct contact with people whose language they are learning. In language education, technologically mediated intercultural communication projects have been established for language learners in order to increase cultural sensitivity and awareness. The technologies permit interaction with others and this interaction can be seen as having the potential to influence values, attitudes, and beliefs. For this reason, it can be expected that "internet-based activities in which students ultimately develop relationships with students in other cultures should have some influence on the learners' sense of the world" (Windschitl, 1998, p. 31). Projects using social technologies have been linked to positive outcomes for perspective taking, critical thinking, sensitivity to cultural diversity, and social cognition (Bonk, Appelman, and Hay, 1996; Bonk and King, 1998; Daniels, Berglund, and Petre, 1999; Vatrapu, 2008). However, they have not been universally successful (Fabos and Young, 1999; Reeves, 2003; Warschauer, 1998). Fabos and Young (1999), for example, found that the results of technologically mediated communication across cultures were "inconclusive, overly optimistic and even contradictory" (p. 249). This disparity of results points to a key problem in the pedagogical use of social technologies for language teaching and learning. The problem is that exposure to interaction of itself does not necessarily equate with intercultural learning. This problem has been identified also for face-to-face contact with other cultures during study abroad. To be able to contribute to learning, the interaction must first become available in some way for students to reflect on and interpret. It is therefore necessary to consider not only what these technologies permit students to do, but also to consider how their experiences may contribute to learning.

One approach to using social technologies for intercultural learning has been to use technology such as e-mail or chat to establish exchanges between people from different cultural groups. There are many studies of these sorts of programs in the literature, which can begin to provide a way of understanding how social technologies can be integrated into an interculturally focused language-learning program. In a pedagogical context, these projects usually use the technology to establish interactions between people from different cultures about cultural topics, using the first language of one group, which is the second language of the other. A small number of examples gives an overview of the sorts of activities that have been done.

In projects using e-mail, students are involved in a synchronous exchange of information that can be staged in particular ways and which allows for the possibility of some classroom interaction around the tasks involved between e-mail contacts. Liaw (2006) used an online discussion forum to facilitate a discussion between Taiwanese students of English and students in the United States. In her project, she asked students to interpret their own culture for members of the culture they were studying. That is, students were involved in an interpretive act that required them to reconceptualize their own culture in order to mediate it to members of another. She observed that these students needed to engage with different perspectives on both their own and on the other culture when formulating ways of communicating their own culture and its assumptions for others. Levy (2007) describes a project in which an e-mail interaction was established between a group of Brazilian second-language speakers of English and a group of Australian English speakers. The exchange began with the Brazilian participants first discussing their own culture and the ways they believed their culture was perceived overseas. This activity involved the participants in reflection about the variability of their own culture and the different perceptions of individuals about their common culture. Levy argues that it also began a process of distancing the participants from their own culture and in this way the task can be seen as the beginning of a process of decentering from their own cultural assumptions and beginning to think about their culture from other perspectives. As the task was a preparation activity, this meant that the process of decentering was begun before the participants had to represent their culture to others through the e-mail exchange. The Brazilian and Australian participants then began to work through a series of tasks that raised issues of cultural understanding as the participants communicated. In this way, the study reported was highly structured and was designed to use the exchange to promote particular types of learning.

O'Dowd (2003) reports on the use of an unstructured e-mail exchange for intercultural learning in which the exchanges sometimes failed when issues of cultural identity came to the fore. O'Dowd's study followed five pairs of Spanish and British students interacting through e-mail over a year. The exchanges were not set up primarily as intercultural learning but rather as a communicative exchange built around a series of language-focused tasks (see Table 7.1). Some of the tasks involved discussion of representations of cultures – Tasks 1, 4, 5, 7, and 9 – while others had an implicit cultural focus – Tasks 3, 6, and 10. In each case the focus is on a generalized version of the representation of the culture.

O'Dowd found that students were actively involved in contesting or defending representations of their own culture and that the discussion of culture had the potential

Table 7.1 Overview of tasks

Task	Title	Description	Aim
1	In-class e-mailing list	Students discuss the image of Spain abroad (Spanish group only)	Accustom students to using e-mail in their learning
2	Introductory letter	Students introduce themselves and tell partner what may be different if they visited the other's home town	Students get to know their partners and reflect on cultural differences
3	Word association	Students write the associations that they have of key words such as "good food," and "bull-fighting." They then compare their reactions with their partners'	Students become more aware of the link between language and culture
4	In-class e-mailing list	Students discuss the image of Britain in Spain and recount their experiences with members of that culture (Spanish group only)	Brainstorming and discussion for future exchange with partners
5	Tourist shop	Students visit a local tourist shop and report back to their partner, telling them what they saw and how accurately this image represents their home culture	Students reflect on how the two cultures are represented to foreigners and how accurate these representations are
6	Comparative expressions	Students complete a list of comparative phrases (e.g. "as good as … as black as…") in their native language. They then explain the possible origins and cultural significance of these phrases	Students examine differing connotations in the two cultures by comparing what nouns are used in comparative phrases
7	Text extracts (1)	Students read text extracts taken from various foreign writers about Spain and the Spanish. The Spanish group reflect on how accurate they feel the texts to be. The British group pose questions about the texts	Using the texts as a springboard, both groups explain to their partners how they view the Spanish culture and people
8	Explaining idioms	Students explain in the target language the meanings of various idioms from their own language. They also look at the idioms' origins and significance	Students look at the link between idioms and cultural values in both cultures
9	Text extracts (2)	Students read and discuss various short extracts about England and the English	Using the texts as a springboard, both groups explain to their partners how they view English culture and its people
10	"The Unfaithful Woman" (source: e-mail mailing list)	Students compare reactions to a fictitious story which brings up issues of morality and sexuality	Discussion of the story leads to comparison of moral values and sexuality in both countries

Source: O'Dowd, R. (2003) Understanding the "other side": Intercultural learning in a Spanish–English e-mail exchange. *Language Learning and Technology*, 7 (2): 123.

to create conflict between the interactants. In fact, the tasks involved do not really generate intercultural learning but tend to focus attention on the formulation and communication of stereotypicalized views of the cultures involved, although with some possibility of questioning these in Tasks 5 and 7. The potential problems for these tasks became apparent early in the interaction, with students reporting annoyance and frustration with others' perceptions of their own culture and saw a role for themselves in fighting against stereotypes and correcting others' views of their own culture. That is, the tasks tended to commit people to defending particular, personally held, views of their own culture rather than encourage them to engage in intercultural learning. O'Dowd's work presents an example of a series of activities that were intended to lead to some form of intercultural learning, but which were not, in fact, structured to support such learning. Rather than fostering the ideas of decentering from one's own cultural perspective and becoming a mediator of language and cultures, the tasks tended to position the students as defenders of their own cultures and identities against the stereotypicalized views of others or as communicators of stereotypicalized views to those others. O'Dowd notes that exchanges that enabled learners to develop intercultural learning were characterized by:

> opportunities to express their feelings and views about their own culture to a receptive audience
> encouragement to reflect critically on their own culture through questions posed by their partners
> engagement in dialogic interaction with their partners about the home and target cultures and leading to a growing awareness of differing perspectives on the two cultures' products and practices. (2003, p. 137)

However, the extent to which students had the opportunities to do these things was dependent on their own and their interlocutors' dispositions and was not a feature of the tasks themselves.

Chat interactions involve students in real-time interactions with members of another cultural group in which issues need to be negotiated and resolved during the interaction itself. Tudini (2007) demonstrates that, while language learning is not the focus of online chat, interactions between native speakers and students, in this case of Italian, provide opportunities for developing intercultural understanding. In Tudini's data, much of what is negotiated is factual information, which causes a problem for the student in understanding a native speaker's contribution to the chat, as in the example below:

NS: *poi abbiamo il ferragosto.* [Then we have the ferragosto.]
L: *che è il ferragosto?* [What is the ferragosto?]
NS: *il 15 agosto considerato il giorno più caldo dell'anno.* [August 15 considered the hottest day of the year.]
NS: *è una festa nazionale.* [It's a national holiday.] (p. 592)

In this exchange, the problem is a culturally contexted lexical item that leads the learner to request an explication, which is then given by a native speaker.

Toyoda and Harrison (2002) show that cultural differences can also promote similar negotiations of understanding:

NNS: *Eeto, nihon-jin tte jiko shuchoo busoku da to omoimasu ka?* [Well, do you think Japanese people lack self assertion?]

NS: *Aite no iken o kiite kara kangae yoo to suru tokoro wa arimasu yo ne?* [We do tend to try and think after listening to the opinion of the other, don't we?]

NS: *Aite no iken to jibun no iken o tatakawase yoo to suru no dewa naku, onaji bubun o mitsukete ukeirete ikoo to suru no dewa nai desu ka?* [Perhaps it is that, rather than trying to argue against the other's opinion with our own, we try to find common grounds and accept the other's views?]

NNS: *To iu ka, boku no iken dewa nihon-jin wa narubeku meewaku o kakenai yoo ni soo suru shuukan ga aru to wakatte imasu ga.* [Or, in my opinion, I already understand that the Japanese customarily do that so they don't cause trouble or inconvenience to others.]

NS: *Aite no iken mo mitomete, jibun no iken mo wakatte morau doryoku o suru.* [Accepting the other's opinion and also making an effort to make the other understand our opinions.]

NNS: *Desu kara, sore wa gyougi ni chikai desu ne.* [So, that is more like a manner/behavior, isn't it?]

NS: *Kyougi, desu ne.* [You mean conferring, don't you?] (p. 95)

Here, the student and the native speaker engage in interaction about a perception that the student has of the Japanese. In this case, the discussion is about something that the student already knows about the culture and involves interacting with a member of the culture to seek an insider's perspective. In both of these, the negotiation between the student and the native speaker first requires one of the participants to detect or introduce an issue. That is, opportunities to explore cultural issues are highly dependent on the unfolding interaction. Moreover, as these exchanges occur in real time, the participants' focus is on the interaction itself, not on aspects of intercultural learning and behavior. This means that opportunities to decenter from one's own cultural perspective or to mediate between cultures arise only when an issue becomes relevant to the interaction itself. Real-time interactions do not give participants time to reflect on the interaction or on how language and culture are relevant to the interaction. Any reflection on these issues that is relevant to the interaction itself may be dealt with quickly in order to progress the interaction.

Furstenberg and her colleagues (Bauer *et al.*, 2006; Furstenberg, 2003; Furstenberg *et al.*, 2001) have worked substantially with a web-based project called Cultura for collaborative intercultural exploration. The focus of Cultura is comparative and involves a closed group made up of two whole classes of language learners in two different countries (e.g. learners of French in the United States and learners of English in France) examining and comparing visual and textual materials originating from both cultures. They view the materials on a shared website and communicate in asynchronous web-based forums in which they analyze and discuss their shared materials. To begin their involvement, students anonymously answer three questionnaires: a word association that probes apparently universal notions such as freedom, work, family, school, individualism, money; a sentence-completion activity that explores relationships and roles; and a set of situations to which students must respond, designed to explore different attitudes and interactions with a variety of people in different contexts. The answers are then collected and posted on the website and become the first set of materials for analysis. That is, the learners themselves become the first resource for learning. The corpus of information made available to the students is then expanded to include materials such as national opinion polls on similar topics, films and their remakes, images, print media, and a variety of parallel texts. New materials confirm, question, or contradict learners' understandings, and so the process is one of challenging understandings of culture and preventing understandings, from becoming prematurely closed. The electronic forum allows students to exchange and develop their respective viewpoints on the material being discussed, to ask for help from speakers of the language they are learning, and to negotiate meanings and interpretations. The aim is to facilitate the active construction of each other's cultures through the process of communication. The technology facilitates this by allowing different materials to be available simultaneously on the same screen. The cultural content is not presented as a fixed body of cultural information but as dynamic, created, and emerging through interaction. Through these exchanges, the students are able to see that insiders' views are not homogeneous, and responses are individual rather than being culturally typical, and that cultural stances can be problematized. At the same time, students can be brought to see coherent patterns in interaction, patterns that allow them to explore diverse concepts, values, and discourses as they become available in the interactions.

Discussion lists enable learners to engage in authentic communication with proficient speakers of a language on specified topics. Hanna and de Nooy (2003) report a study of learners' engagement in an online discussion forum run by *Le Monde*. Forum discussions are very easy to enter and provide ways in which learners can become participants in the discourse world of native speakers. However, Hanna and de Nooy found that the ease of entry can be deceptive, as ease of entry does not guarantee ease of participation. They found that regular participants in the discussion were not sympathetic to language learners and did not always view them as legitimate participants in the discussion. Until student participants could become socialized into the discourse rules operating in the discussions, they were able to make little progress as participants.

O'Brien and Alfano (2009) used videoconferencing to involve students from several countries in intercultural interactions. In this project, students explained culturally located texts or artifacts from their own culture to members of other cultures. The students were then required to produce a collaborative blog discussing aspects of the negotiation. These interactions effectively focus on the intercultural at two levels. The first is the explicit level of interpreting the culturally embedded nature of a text for an audience that does not share that culture. This task requires a measure of decentering learners from their existing cultural perspectives in order to see the unfamiliarity of the cultural representations encoded in the text. The second level is implicit in the process of interaction between the participants themselves as they communicate across cultural and linguistic boundaries. The explicit level is pedagogically constructed and supported by the design of the task, whereas the implicit level is experienced by the learner with less overt pedagogical support. The technology serves as a channel for allowing both the explanation of a highly contexted activity in which meanings are negotiated with a real, culturally diverse audience and through authentic interactions outside one's own cultural context.

Blogs permit the presentation of views and interpretations, often in much detail, with the possibility of receiving comments from readers that confirm or challenge the author's ideas. Elola and Oskoz (2008) used blogs to connect study-abroad students with their counterparts at home to provide connections for the at-home learners with the sorts of experiences afforded by study abroad. In this project, the bloggers were paired members of the same cohort – learners of Spanish in the United States – and the interactions that occurred were thus between members of the same culture. In this study, the blog became a tool for the at-home learners to ask questions of the study-abroad students about topics that were being worked on in class, while the study-abroad students were able to share experiences and new perspectives. They found that there was development of the intercultural abilities of both sets of learners as a result of the blogs, but that the impact on each group was different. Moreover, some of the evidence of learning collected through questionnaires was not always apparent in the blogs themselves. For the at-home students the blog's main value seems to have been in developing a focused connection with the target culture, which was integrated into reflection on cultural differences, whereas it gave the study-abroad students the opportunity to interpret their experiences in-country for their colleagues at home. Carney (2007) investigated intercultural learning in blog projects involving Japan and the United States. He argues that the posts made to blogs do not necessarily show that intercultural learning is happening or that the material posted on blogs will necessarily generate feedback that can be useful to promote further learning. He also found that blogs, because of their post-comment structure, did not facilitate ongoing discussion and that they produced very short exchanges, with a new topic and new exchange occurring every week.

In each instance discussed above, interaction using a social technology has not necessarily resulted in intercultural learning as understood in this book. The technologically focused tasks failed as intercultural learning because the intercultural itself was not a feature of how the tasks were planned and designed. The tasks involved students in exchanges across cultures and placed culture at the heart of these exchanges, but the intercultural learning was supposed to happen as an automatic result of communication or engagement with others. In other words, the tasks were set up as cultural tasks – that is, tasks that focused on factual information, in this case in the form of representations of cultures – rather than as intercultural tasks that involved learners in moving between cultures and reflecting on their own cultural positioning and the roles of language and culture within it. The tasks involved exchange, but reflection on what happened in the exchange was not the learners' central focus during the communication. O'Dowd's (2003) tasks (see Table 7.1) clearly illustrate the risks involved in using social technologies for intercultural learning. Belz (2005, p. 27) describes the risk for learners in such interactions as "retreating into self, reinforcing stereotypes and myths and even creating new, more negative stereotypes when confronted by the unknown."

O'Dowd's (2003) observations demonstrate a very important consideration for using technology to provide direct engagement between cultures, that is, providing opportunities to interact with others is not the same as not as providing a learning experience (Windschitl, 1998). Belz (2002) has also noted that making connections with other learners does not always translate into intercultural learning. She argues that cultural communication differences between participants in a mediated interaction may impede intercultural learning unless students become aware of the existence of the differences and their effect on interactions. Thus, using technology to connect people across languages and cultures is not in itself a form of intercultural learning, although the potential is there. In the case of authentic forms of technological communication, the purposes of engagement in some activities (e.g. chat or discussion forums) may not be pedagogical. When the technologically mediated practices are not themselves pedagogical in nature, the problems for intercultural learning become potentially greater. This is well illustrated in Hanna and de Nooy's (2003) study of online engagement in the *Le Monde* discussion forum. Although the students in this study were highly supported through classroom activities to participate in the forum, they experienced difficulties in participating. As Hanna and de Nooy note, the function of the forum is to provide a venue for debate and discussion, not to teach French. This means that to be accepted as a participant, they have to have the capacity to engage in the cultural practice required for participation. In such contexts, learning how to participate is not the expected intercultural learning. However, Hanna and de Nooy note that in sites such as *Le Monde*, moderators' feedback, both official and unofficial, can function as a form of initiation or of informal teaching about the expectations of the group. They can become sites for intercultural learning outside the act of participation itself when the learner becomes involved in analyzing and reflecting on the ways of participation, the culturally embedded nature of the particular practices involved, and the ways in which these practices differ in different linguistic and cultural contexts.

Kramsch and Thorne (2002) cast doubt on whether the types of communication in which people typically engage in using technologically mediated networks may naturally support intercultural understanding. They argue that the forms of communication found in chat, forums, and so on favor phatic contact and the positive presentation of the self rather than significant engagement with issues and ideas, or with the working through of issues arising in communication. This would suggest that ensuring connectivity between people from different cultures alone cannot be considered an adequate use of technology for intercultural learning. Rather, the technologies make available possibilities that need to be developed as experiences of learning in parallel with the interactions that technology facilitates. As Windschitl notes, "if our goal is to maximize the possibilities for student learning with technology, this will require a critical examination of the intersection of the affordances of information technology, pedagogy, and learning." (1998, p. 28).

If technologically mediated interactions are to become experiences that provide opportunities for learning, the interaction needs to be converted into learning through reflection. That is, learners need to become aware of what it is that they are experiencing and how they understand that experience, and also to be able to decenter from that experience to explore different possible understandings. As part of such a process, learners need to be able to frame and explore accounts of what is happening and to communicate, contest, and respond to these accounts.

Developing the Potential of Technologies for Intercultural Learning

In this chapter, we have argued that technologies have an important role to play in facilitating intercultural language learning but have also argued that technologies alone will not achieve such learning. As a final comment on using technology, it is important to consider different ways in which technologies can be integrated into language learning and what affordances each possibility provides for the language learner. Barab, Hay, and Duffy (1998) have identified five ways of using technology to promote learning:

- information resource
- content contextualization
- communication tool
- construction kit
- visualization and manipulation.

Each of these approaches presents a different perspective of the place and role of technologies in developing intercultural learning.

Technology as information resource

In providing information to support learner inquiry, technology provides access to the language and the culture for learning. Learning is not in itself a direct consequence of access, but technology provides a resource that can be used to promote learning by converting access to information into an experience of engagement with language and culture. Barab, Hay and Duffy (1998) note that the creation of resources is not enough and that in order to be maximally effective, the resources should not be treated as isolated tools introduced in a vacuum but as multimedia environments to be explored in a context of authentic inquiry. Windschitl (1998) has also argued that there is a difference between accessing information and having a learning experience.

Technology as content contextualization

Engaging with language in context is vitally important for intercultural learning, and technologies assist in providing a rich and varied context for understanding culturally embedded meanings. This means that language can be explored through a richer possible range of contexts than is possible with paper-based technologies and also that students themselves can play a role in identifying and analyzing contexts. Technology can provide a real world anchor for what is being learned or investigated and enable information from multiple sources to be integrated to promote the interpretation of meaning.

Technology as communication tool

When used as a communication tool, technology is able to facilitate collaborative and distributed learning. Technologies have the potential to place learners in situations of inter-cultural communication where they can explore the language and culture they are learning in real world interactions. This means that through mechanisms such as e-mail, chat, blogs or computer-mediated audio or video communication, learners are able to engage in authentic instances in which they create and communicate meanings across cultural and linguistic boundaries. In addition, they can use the same technologies, in addition to wikis, to communicate their own understandings of the experience of engagement with another culture and respond to the communications of others.

Technology as a construction kit

By providing mediating devices for building phenomena or understandings, computer technology can be seen as a construction kit. Computer technology can been used as a way of bringing language learners and members of the target language communication into contact for the purpose of language and intercultural learning. However, these interactions can be developed further through manipulation of the observations to create interpretations and expressions of learning resulting from that contact. Furstenberg *et al.* (2001) and Belz (2003), and Belz and Kinginger (2002) report projects in which computer-mediated interactions became input for reflection on language and culture. The technology becomes a resource for collecting data about the target-language community and their communicative practices, which then becomes available for comparison. Carel (2001) describes how she used an interactive computer courseware package to enable students to use ethnographic skills to observe and analyze cultural phenomena and to do virtual fieldwork. In this way, she used technology to overcome the separation of learner and target-language community and sought to replicate the learning possibilities of in-country experience in a classroom context. The computer courseware made it possible for students not only to observe difference but also to reflect on their own culture and their previous views of the target culture as a part of their virtual experience of the target culture and their reflection about language and culture and the relationship between the two.

Technology as visualization and manipulation

Technologies can provide mechanisms through which learners can explore their developing awareness in reflective ways. That is, they can provide ways of making representations of knowledge and interpretation available as resources to be developed, explored, and refined in interaction with others. For example, blogs have the potential to enable ongoing reflection about learning from experiences of language and culture, with the possibility of soliciting and responding to feedback as a component of that learning. Similarly, wikis and discussion groups provide opportunities for the collaborative development of interpretation and the negotiation of understanding of experiences. In this way, technologies provide a way of presenting phenomena for scrutiny and manipulation.

Summary

In reviewing this list it can be seen that technologies, whether used for information or social purposes, have the capacity to contribute to intercultural learning for language students. To maximize the affordances that technology provides for learning, it is important to design learning experiences so as to provide opportunities to use different technologies and to use them in different ways. In particular, technologies provide access to a wider world of experience of language and intensify opportunities for exposure to a greater diversity of contexts. This gives languages and cultures a greater immediacy in learners' lives in ways that are rich with new opportunities for engagement and learning. Because they are not designed as learning experiences but as instantiations of cultures articulated through language for their own members, these experiences are not sanitized for learners and technologies contain the possibility of both positive and negative experiences of the other. Such variable experiences are themselves indicative of the diversities to which learners are exposed and this engagement with the positive and negative through sustained reflection on experiences of language and culture affords enhanced and personalized possibilities for learning.

8

Assessing Intercultural Language Learning

The expanded understanding of language, culture, and learning discussed in Chapters 2 and 3 and their interrelationship discussed in Chapter 4 call for a reconceptualization of the assessment process and the interpretive resources needed to judge learner performance and learner understanding. In working with teachers in exploring the possibilities of teaching and learning languages within an intercultural perspective, the question of how to assess such learning is raised constantly. The question arises for a number of interrelated reasons. The first relates to uncertainty about the construct, emerging in questions such as:

- What exactly is this intercultural capability/understanding, and how can its theorization be operationalized for the purposes of assessment?
- How does the assessment of language relate to the assessment of culture, and conversely?
- What exactly is the language–culture–intercultural capability connection?
- How does knowledge of language and culture relate to intercultural capability/ understanding?

The second reason assessment is queried relates to uncertainty about the nature of the assessment process itself, articulated in questions such as:

- How do we elicit intercultural capability/understanding in language learning?
- Is it integrated with or separate from assessing the language itself?
- What procedures are best suited to the assessment of this capability?
- How do we judge the learning of intercultural capability/understanding?
- What additional interpretive resources are necessary?
- How can the assessment be objective when it involves values?
- Should we be assessing values anyway?

Intercultural Language Teaching and Learning, First Edition. Anthony J. Liddicoat and Angela Scarino.
© 2013 Anthony J. Liddicoat and Angela Scarino. Published 2013 by Blackwell Publishing Ltd.

These kinds of questions evidence deeply held and often unquestioned assumptions about both the nature of language and language learning on the one hand, and the assessment process on the other. They give rise to further questions, for example: Is traditional, summative assessment the only form of assessment that is of value? Is objectivity the only quality that is needed in assessment? In addition to conceptual issues, are there larger constraining forces at play in establishing what is and is not permissible in language assessment?

In this chapter we contextualize assessment and language learning in relation to:

- the tension between traditional and alternate assessment paradigms;
- the institutional character of assessment;
- an understanding of the process of assessment.

We then consider four processes within an understanding of assessment as an assessment cycle – conceptualizing, eliciting, judging, and validating, and identify features of an expanded view of assessment that is required to assess language learning as an intercultural endeavor. In so doing, we include examples from a research program in which teachers developed ways of assessing language learning within an intercultural perspective. We conclude the chapter by identifying and discussing complexities that need to be further addressed in this area.

Contextualizing Assessment and Language Learning

The tension between traditional and alternate assessment paradigms

It is important to consider assessment within the paradigm war (McNamara, 2003) because it highlights issues of the way in which the assessment process itself is framed, and therefore what is considered to be permissible or not in assessment. The fundamental purpose of assessment is to understand students' learning and to make considered judgments about their performance, understanding, and progress in learning. As such, there is an integral relationship between assessment and learning. In educational settings the relationship holds, not withstanding different purposes. The different purposes may be captured in three phrases, which have been adopted extensively by educational systems in current times: assessment *of* learning (which tends to be summative in purpose), assessment *for* learning, and assessment *as* learning (both of which tend to be formative in purpose).

Educational assessment is situated in a tension between two contrasting paradigms that provide an intellectual framework for understanding language assessment (see Shepard, 2000). The tension is between traditional assessment, which tends to be aligned with cognitive views of learning and psychometric testing, and alternate assessment, which tends to be aligned with sociocultural views of learning and a range of assessment practices that include, for example, performance assessment, classroom-based assessment, formative assessment, and dynamic assessment (see e.g. Birenbaum, 1996; Black and Wiliam, 1998; Fox, 2008; Gipps and Stobart, 2003; Lantolf and Poehner, 2008).

The traditional paradigm focuses on testing "content" through "objective" procedures, normally as single events. Student performances are then referenced either to the performance of other students or to a predetermined standard. It is a psychometrically oriented perspective that addresses the "measurement" of learning (i.e. assessment of learning). Assessment within an alternate paradigm, while variously understood (Fox, 2008), seeks to expand on the traditional conception of assessment. Its focus is on finding appropriate ways of demonstrating what it is that students know. The alternate paradigm allows for formative assessment (assessment for learning) as well as summative (assessment of learning), recognizing the power of assessment to form or shape learning (see Black and Jones, 2006). It allows for diverse evidence from diverse learners and valuing the product of learning as well as the process (Birenbaum, 1996; Gipps, 1999; Teasdale and Leung, 2000). It also recognizes that assessment is a dynamic, ongoing process of coming to understand students' performance over time, thus it frequently involves a collection of performances over time to provide evidence of growth and learning.

As Moss, Girard, and Hanniford (2006) explain, the difference between the contrasting paradigms is philosophical. The contrast is between, on the one hand, a naturalist view of social science that seeks to study social phenomena in the same way that the natural sciences study natural phenomena, and, on the other hand, an interpretive approach to social science that views social phenomena as different from natural phenomena. The major difference is that the aim of the interpretive view is "to understand what people mean and intend by what they say and do and to locate those understandings within the historical, cultural, institutional, and immediate situational contexts that shape them" (see also Haertel *et al.*, 2008). Assessing language learning within an intercultural perspective is more fruitfully conceptualized within an alternate assessment paradigm and an interpretive approach to social science.

Moss (1996) has argued for the need to expand conceptions of assessment to include voices from interpretive research traditions, to draw upon sociocultural theories of learning, and to complement traditional assessment by considering a hermeneutic perspective. From sociocultural theories of learning, she derives a view of learning, and therefore assessment, at any point in time and over time, that is contextualized in the interaction between learners and their environments, which include conceptual tools, physical tools, and other people (Moss, 2008; Moss, Girard, and Hanniford, 2006). As discussed in Chapter 3, learners bring to their learning their life-worlds, their home cultures and languages, and the trajectory of experiences, interests, motivations, and values developed from them. Now we highlight that, equally, learners bring all of this to assessment. Thus from a sociocultural approach, assessment, like learning, focuses on experience and meaning-making related to that experience in the context of language and culture and their positioning. As Gee explains:

A sociocultural approach places a premium on learners' experiences, social participation, use of mediating devices (tools and technologies) and position within various activity systems or communities of practice. The word "culture" has taken on a wide variety of different meanings in different disciplines. Nonetheless, it is clear that, as part and parcel of our early socialization in life, we each learn ways of being in the world, of acting, and interacting, thinking and valuing, and using language, objects and tools that critically shape our early sense of self. A situated, sociocultural perspective amounts to an argument that students learning new academic "cultures" at school (new ways of acting, interacting, valuing and using language, objects and tools) and, as in the case of acquiring any new culture, the acquisition of these new cultures interacts formidably with learners' initial cultures. (2008, p. 100)

Gee highlights the new culture of learning at school, which extends the culture of home and peers. This is arguably all the more intense when learning includes entering into and "moving between" multiple (or at least two) linguistic and cultural systems and interpreting and reflecting on the process of "moving between" in relation to self and other. Assessment of language learning within an intercultural perspective needs to capture this sociocultural and interpretive nature of learning. Although framed in slightly different terms, researchers working within this alternate assessment paradigm highlight a common set of features of assessment. Gipps (1999) highlights some of the implications of sociocultural theories of learning for the practice of assessment. For instance, there is a requirement to assess process as well as product; the conception of assessment must be dynamic rather than static; and attention must be paid to the social and cultural context of both learning and assessment. Assessment is interactive and mediated, that is, scaffolded through talk and other mediational tools and technologies. Shepard (2006) draws on sociocultural theories to develop formative assessment or assessment for learning, emphasizing that assessment can be formal and taken at particular points in time, or informal, where assessment is integrated into processes of teaching and learning. Delandshere (2002) sees assessment as a process of inquiry that focuses less on assessment activities *per se*, and more on the evidence of meaning-making that emerges from the learning environment. Within the alternate paradigm, then, there is a recognition of: "(1) the centrality of the classroom (teaching practice and learning process); (2) the active role played by students/learners in assessment processes ... (3) a heightened view of process; and (4) outcomes characterized by summaries of learner competencies which are detailed, descriptive and informative" (Fox, 2008, p. 102).

Within such a view of assessment there is a particularly important role for formative assessment or assessment for learning. Black *et al.* (2002) describe assessment for learning as any assessment for which the first priority is to serve the purpose of promoting learning, rather than certification or accountability. They specify that an assessment activity can be of value in learning only if it provides information that can be used as feedback by teachers and peers to modify the teaching and learning activities in which they are participating. It can be described as formative only if it indeed "forms" or "shapes" learning. Formative assessment is more than a rehearsal for summative assessment; it is used to change what students do in terms of their action and their understanding. The research of Black *et al.* (2002) and Wiliam *et al.* (2004) has shown that systematic formative assessment can actually change students' achievements and success. This is particularly important because standardized summative assessments do not provide the necessary information about students' achievements and, indeed, processes of thinking and reflecting to assess language learning within an intercultural perspective.

Moss (1996, 2008) and Moss, Girard, and Hanniford (2006) consider hermeneutics to be a useful theoretical resource for expanding assessment. As discussed in Chapter 3, particularly in relation to the philosophical hermeneutics of Gadamer (2004), hermeneutics focuses on the process of coming to understand "the bringing of understanding into language" (Moss *et al.*, 2006, p. 130). This process of interpreting towards understanding has implications for both eliciting and judging language learning, for, at a fundamental level, elicitation in assessment involves gathering, observing, and analyzing evidence, and judging relies on interpreting this evidence, that is, making inferences so that conclusions can be reached in order to make decisions.

Because assessment is fundamentally linked to learning, just as in Chapter 3 we argued for an expanded view or learning, here we argue for an expanded view of assessment, which recognizes the role of interpretation by both the assessed and the assessor (see also Scarino, 2010). Before considering what it is that assessing language learning within an intercultural perspective might entail, we consider the institutional character of assessment as a force that often constrains the possibilities of assessment and then we outline how we understand the process of assessment itself.

The institutional character of assessment

A further dimension of the contextualization of assessment relates to the institutional setting in which any particular assessment system and process resides. For example, in the context of K-12 language learning, language learning is defined by national or state curriculum frameworks. (See, for example, the national frameworks of K-12 Standards of the USA, the National Curriculum of England and Wales, the *Common European Framework of Reference*, or the South Australian Curriculum Standards and Accountability Framework.) These frameworks, which vary in their degree of prescription, set the systemic policy requirements for assessment. They describe at a highly generalized level what students need to know (the nature and scope of learning) and what is an appropriate standard (the level of achievement expected). Through a set of descriptive categories, they frame the learning that is valued by the educational system and a system of levels that describe, in particular ways, outcomes or standards of performance. The *Common European Framework of Reference* (Council of Europe, 2001) is a framework that is gaining momentum well beyond Europe and so can be seen as an international framework (Rong, 2009). It is being used as a framework for referencing language learning and assessment in diverse languages, in diverse state and national educational contexts, and in relation to the learning of students of diverse ages and diverse language backgrounds, who are learning in diverse program contexts and conditions. It is used for diverse purposes ranging from diagnosis to national reporting (Morrow, 2004). Alderson (2005) presents a detailed discussion of diagnosis in this context. Like all frameworks, its definitional categories and architecture of levels provide the language for assessing and reporting standards of language learning, but because of its international reach it has become a dominant influence on teaching, learning, and assessment in many contexts around the world. The implications of this influence are discussed in detail by McNamara and Roever (2006). At the same time all these frameworks have significant limits that need to be recognized. They potentially constrain the way in which constructs are described. This is because they necessarily generalize from particular contexts of learners, policy, and program settings, and even languages themselves. The higher the degree of generalization (such as the *Common European Framework of Reference*, which is in fact a "scale of scales"), the less likely it is that the framework will relate to the local practices of teaching, learning, and assessment in any particular context. And yet, teachers are often obliged to adopt the frameworks simply because they are members of particular educational system communities and they are required by policy to do so. This can become a cause of tension. Teachers may *adapt* frameworks to fit their local context and thereby may compromise curriculum and assessment policy; not to do so, however, may compromise learners and learning (Brindley, 2001; Scarino, 2000, 2008; Shohamy, 2008).

Understanding the Process of Assessment

As depicted in Figure 8.1, assessment can be depicted as a cyclical process of four interrelated macroprocesses (Liddicoat and Scarino, 2010; Scarino, 2009; Scarino and Liddicoat, 2009): conceptualizing (what to assess and its representation), eliciting (how to gather evidence), judging (how to appraise), and validating (how to justify and assure the quality of the assessment process itself). These macroprocesses are mutually informing rather than linear. Conceptualizing language learning for the purposes of assessment guides the eliciting process. The judging process then incorporates a consideration of what it is important to assess (conceptualizing), giving due attention to whether the ways of eliciting have, in fact, canvassed the language use and learning that is of interest. Validating is the process of quality assurance in which the whole cycle is reconsidered and inferences are warranted; the quality of assessment cannot just be assumed, it needs to be demonstrated.

The value of the cycle resides in its ecological conception of assessment and the fact that it holds for all forms of assessment – "for," "of," and "as" learning. Within this ecological view of assessment, the starting point for assessment is not the procedures and related technical analyses performed, but the *conceptualization* of what is to be assessed, namely, the construct. The construct in languages education is what we mean by language learning itself, and specifically here, what we mean by language learning within an intercultural perspective. The notion of "construct" also reminds us that this is in fact a construction, a theorization. It is in this sense that any assessment is fundamentally a conceptual matter at least as much as it is a technical one. The way we understand the construct influences elicitation, how we construe evidence, the inferences and judgments we make, and how we justify them. In other words, the assessment cycle invites a shift in the consideration of assessment from a stand-alone instrument, or procedure, or structured activity to the totality of formal and informal inferences and judgments made. All four interrelated processes in the assessment cycle are deeply interpretive at every turn.

Assessing learning within an intercultural perspective presents challenges that are both theoretical and practical, not the least because assessment is, in fact, interpretive and therefore unable to yield the certainty that teachers and other stakeholders in the assessment process have come to expect. Furthermore, the expanded view of language, culture, and learning

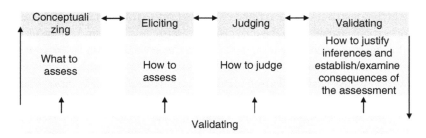

Figure 8.1   The assessment cycle. *Source*: Scarino, A. and Liddicoat, A. J. (2009) *Language Teaching and Learning: A Guide*, Melbourne, Curriculum Corporation, p. 71.

within an intercultural perspective demands new ways of thinking about assessment. We discuss these challenges in relation to each macroprocess of the assessment cycle.

Conceptualizing

Conceptualizing what to assess in relation to students' language learning within an intercultural perspective necessitates consideration of the ways in which the construct of "communicative competence" has been modeled, both in efforts to assess intercultural language learning (Byram, 2008) and in language testing more generally (Bachman, 2007; Chalhoub-Deville, 2003; Shohamy, 2007b).

Risager (2007) describes two approaches to modeling "intercultural competence"; one has its origin in anthropology and sees the intercultural as linked to but separate from communicative competence, and the other has its origin in linguistics and sees cultural/ intercultural competence within linguistic competence. Of the anthropologically based models, the most elaborated is that of Byram and Zarate (1994) and Bryam (1997), which is based on clusters of knowledge, skills, and attitudes called *savoirs* (see Chapter 4 for a detailed discussion). Although this model maps various dimensions, it does not deal with the relationship between these *savoirs* and communication. Further, the modeling does not make explicit its view of knowledge as embodied in the knower. Byram (1997) also developed a model of "intercultural communicative competence" that includes linguistic competence, sociolinguistic competence, and discourse competence (typical components of models of communicative competence developed by Canale and Swain (1981) and van Ek (1986), and discussed below), as well as intercultural competence. Byram describes intercultural competence as attitudes, knowledge, skills of interpreting and relating, skills of discovering and interacting, and critical cultural awareness/political education. A difficulty inherent in all such modeling is the relationship between these components. Risager (2007) extends the modeling by adding two further important dimensions; namely, languacultural competencies and resources, and transnational cooperation. She maintains that these additions foreground the plurilingual nature of communication. Nevertheless, the issue of the interrelationship among components remains. Sercu (2004) also extends the construct to include a "metacognitive dimension" that is intended to capture planning, monitoring, and students' evaluation of learning. The monitoring of learning processes that Sercu describes, however, focuses on learning processes in general and not specifically on the interplay of language and culture in both communication and learning, in variable contexts in diversity. It does not fully capture the dynamic process of negotiating meaning across cultures and connecting one's own intrapersonal/intracultural and interpersonal/intercultural experiences.

There is a long line of models that have their origin in linguistics (Bachman, 2007; Bachman and Palmer, 1996; Canale and Swain, 1981; van Ek, 1986). The Bachman and Palmer (1996) model remains the most comprehensive model available. It is fundamentally a psycholinguistic model that treats interaction as a process that occurs in the mind of the individual as learner, and not as a social process of construction of meaning in context (Chalhoub-Deville, 2003; McNamara, 1996, 2001; McNamara and Roever, 2006). It also treats language ability monolingually and not across languages and cultures.

Kramsch (1986), one of the most important researchers in language learning within an intercultural perspective, has contributed in a distinctive way to discussions about the construct. She expanded the notion of "communicative competence" by introducing the term "interactional competence" to render the socially interactive nature of communication and to capture the nature of communication across languages and cultures. She emphasizes the "sphere of intersubjectivity," that is, the interaction between the subjective life-worlds of the interactants, as a requirement for successful communication. She also emphasizes the importance of "metalanguage skills," which for her include the ability to reflect on the processes of communication and to see oneself from an outsider's point of view. Most recently, Kramsch has expanded the construct of interactional competence to include a focus on the phenomenology of meaning-making, which she calls "symbolic competence," and which she describes as follows:

> Language learners are not just communicators and problem-solvers, but whole persons with hearts, bodies, and minds, with memories, fantasies, loyalties, identities. Symbolic forms are not just items of vocabulary or communication strategies, but embodied experiences, emotional resonances, and moral imaginings. We could call the competence… symbolic competence. Symbolic competence does not do away with the ability to express, interpret and negotiate meanings in dialogue with others, but enriches and embeds it into the ability to produce and exchange symbolic goods in the complex global context in which we live today. (2006, p. 251)

This description extends the construct to an understanding that goes beyond communication and learning languages as social practices, to include the interpretation and negotiation of symbolic systems.

Thus the conceptualization of the construct in assessing language learning within an intercultural perspective includes the experience of interpreting and constructing meaning in communicative interaction in the contexts of diverse situations – interactional competence – *and* the capability of analyzing the process of meaning-making itself in the context of diverse cultures – symbolic competence. The relationship between the experiential and analytic dimensions remains a complex issue for both elicitation and judgment (Scarino, 2009), but it is minimized at least to some extent when assessment is implemented within a long-term perspective, as discussed below.

Having discussed the conceptualization of the construct of "communicative competence" and its expansion for the purposes of assessing language learning within an intercultural perspective, it is necessary to operationalize the construct for the purposes of assessment (Papademetre and Scarino, forthcoming). This can be summarized as the need to capture each of the following:

- observation, description, analysis, and interpretation of phenomena shared when communicating and interacting;
- active engagement with the interpretation of self (intraculturality) and "other" (interculturality) in diverse contexts of social exchange;
- understanding the ways in which language and culture come into play in interpreting, creating, and exchanging meaning, and the recognition and integration into communication

of an understanding of the self (and others) as already situated in one's own language and culture when communicating with others;

- understanding that interpretation can occur only through the evolving frame of reference developed by each individual; learning a new language becomes a part of this process.

What is being assessed is the learners' meaning-making in communication and learning to communicate in diversity. This occurs in the context of the learners' personal, interpretive frameworks and how they interpret themselves and others and others' interpretations of them. It is language use that matters to the learners themselves, that invites them to make sense of concepts, themselves, others, and their world. In practice, the substance of assessment may include focuses on students' analysis and reflection of their:

- performance – interaction (in speaking or writing) in critical moments where they consider: How will I be perceived?
- concepts and conceptualization – exploration of personal, cultural, intercultural experiences through texts (print, visual, etc.) and how these concepts operate in different social and cultural contexts;
- language – exploration from diverse perspectives of naming, greetings, forms of address, politeness, and so on.

Regardless of the focus of assessment, learners perform their knowledge or learning and their analysis and reflection on the role of language and culture in communication and in learning to communicate. When assessing performance, the focus is on the learners' participation in and management of the interaction; openness to the expectations of the other; the exchange itself; responding to others; and the processes of interpreting, comparing, connecting, taking multiple perspectives into account, relating, valuing, and applying. When assessing analysis and reflection, the focus is on the capability to manage variability, processes of noticing, interpreting contexts, roles, relationships, processes, choices, diverse perspectives, change and, ultimately, critical awareness about the process of communication as the interpretation, creation, and exchange of meaning.

This expanded conceptualization of what is to be assessed has significant implications for eliciting, judging, and validating.

Eliciting

In eliciting students' learning it is necessary to capture the multidimensional nature of language learning within an intercultural perspective. At a most general level, we include *active-receptive tasks* and *active-productive tasks* (Scarino and Liddicoat, 2009). Active-receptive tasks are designed to actively engage students in listening and reading. The focus in assessment procedures of this kind is on (i) understanding interactions, texts and attitudes (observing, noticing, comparing, interpreting) and (ii) meta-awareness. To achieve active engagement, texts should be selected that are meaningful to the learners themselves and questions should be developed that encourage understanding and responding to meaningful content by observing, noticing, comparing the choice of words, tone, meanings, biases, implications, and so on. It is this latter kind of reflection that directly elicits the intercultural dimensions of interaction for meaningful communication. In spoken or written active-productive tasks, the focus is on experiences that are meaningful to the learner (and worthy of his/her investment) and that also require intercultural negotiation. This entails the development of scenarios with careful attention to the positioning of the learner, and related questions to elicit meta-awareness.

It is not sufficient to develop only such active-receptive and active-productive procedures (Liddicoat and Scarino, 2010). Although they yield useful snapshots of performance, developing an intercultural perspective is a long-term process of cumulative experiences and reflection. It is therefore necessary to develop assessment procedures that can be continued over a period of time. Examples of such procedures include ongoing observations, portfolios of spoken and written work, logs that record intercultural observations and experiences, journals, and extended projects, all of which should be strengthened by reflective analyses, cumulative commentaries, summations, explanations, and elaborations. These kinds of procedures resonate with the principles of dynamic assessment that focus on the development of learner's abilities (Lantolf and Poehner, 2010). As described in Liddicoat and Scarino (2010), all procedures need to include questions that encourage learners to decenter, that is, to stand back from the experiences of communicating and reflect on their personal meaning-making. They need to encourage meta-awareness of the interplay of language and culture, across their home language and the language being learned. As Kramsch (2006, p. 251) states, "today it is not sufficient for learners to know how to communicate meanings; they have to understand the practice of meaning making itself." Procedures need to invite students to analyze, explain, and elaborate on this meta-awareness. In developing assessment procedures, it is necessary to consider the positioning of the student as both participant and analyzer in the interaction. Finally, the procedures need to elicit students' understanding of different perspectives, as an ethical concern. In these ways processes for eliciting language learning can be expanded from the: "conventional instrument-based understanding of assessment to incorporate all of the evidence-based evaluations and judgments that occur in interaction ... these may include formal assessments ... as well as informal assessments, both tacit and explicit, that routinely occur in classroom interaction" (Moss, 2008, p. 223).

Within such an expanded view of eliciting, the aim is not necessarily to define, *a priori*, what we are looking for, but to better understand the nature and process of learning that is occurring. As Delandshere explains, "if our purpose is to understand and support learning and knowing and to make inferences about these phenomena, then it seems that the idea of inquiry-open, critical, dialogic – rather than assessment as currently understood, would be more helpful" (2002, p. 1475).

When understood in this way, assessment is, in fact, a process of inquiry, akin to the research process. Eliciting learners' language learning focuses on inquiry into the *meanings* that learners make of, or accord to, phenomena and experiences, and as such is an interpretive process. It includes: what learners know and are able to enact, how they figure things out, what they mean when they act or interact, how they actually use language and culture, how they participate in activities, what positions they enact in relation to each other and the learning material, and finally, what identities they are developing. It may include moment-to-moment interaction and reflection tasks, students' own written work, conversations that probe students' meanings, surveys, interviews, and other kinds of self-report and summaries of actions.

An example.   The example discussed below illustrates some of the features of assessment of language learning within an intercultural orientation. It comes from a study in which teachers designed and taught units of work, including assessment procedures intended to elicit language learning within an intercultural perspective (Moore, 2006). They also participated in ongoing debriefing discussions about the processes. The example comes from a teacher of French at Year 5 (primary school) level, working with her class on a unit in which they were comparing canteens and lunch at school in Australia with the French "cantine." The teacher had introduced the theme by initiating a comparison between the learners' own school canteen and a canteen in France. She began by inviting learners to write down their initial thoughts, so that she could return to their original conceptions at the end of the unit. Among other things, they then looked at different texts; they formulated questions they would ask of school students in France; and they viewed and compared and discussed diverse lunch menus. The teacher gathered evidence about learners' formulation of questions, composing and performing short role-plays, and reading and understanding texts, as it emerged from the various interactions that were part of this unit of work and as appropriate to the level of learning for her students, in the context of their particular program. She also gathered evidence by recording particular interactions between groups of students and by inviting learners to reflect on their experience of working on this particular unit.

An important resource used by the teacher was an e-mail written by two French children who had visited the school in Australia and had written back, commenting on the experience from their point of view (Box 8.1). This source text provides an example of authentic language of French children who had themselves visited the learners' school in Australia and hence had a real connection with the learners. In this e-mail letter, the French children

---

Box 8.1   E-mail from French children on la cantine

Bonjour

Nous nous appelons Lucien, Noëlle et Loïc. On a 10, 9, et 6 ans. Nous avons visité votre école à Adelaïde l'année dernière lors de notre tour du monde. Nous faisons un reportage sur votre pause de midi et la nôtre à la cantine.

Votre pause de midi
Vous n'allez pas dans une cantine.

Nous avons été surpris car vous mangez très vite en 5 minutes votre petit pique-nique froid alors que nous c'est tout autre chose.

Notre cantine

Nous, c'est un restaurant self-service. On appelle ça «le Self». On prend un plateau et ensuite on a le droit de choisir entre deux entrées et entre trois desserts: le plat principale est obligatoire.

Les règles de la cantine sont:

Obligation de prendre une entrée.

Obligation de prendre un laitage (produit fait de lait: fromage ou yaourt)

Obligation de prendre le plat principale. On peut quand même demander d'en avoir un tout petit peu si on n'aime pas ou beaucoup si c'est super bon.

On a le droit de choisir sa place à table mais il ne faut pas crier.

Respecter les «dames» de service: dire merci, s'il vous plaît, etc.

Ne pas rendre son plateau à moitié plein car on doit manger le tout.

On n'a pas le droit de sortir avant les autres sans autorisation du directeur, des maîtres ou des maîtresses.

Nous mangeons en moyenne dans une demi-heure.

A noter que pour Loïc en maternelle, pour beaucoup d'école ce n'est pas un «self» mais un restaurant. Les élevés vont s'asseoir à une table puis on les sert avec une entrée, un plat et un dessert. Il y a à peu près les mêmes règles et le même temps pour manger.

Ensuite, on va jouer… On s'arrête à 11h30 et on reprend à 1h30 l'après-midi. Cela permet à ceux qui rentrent manger chez eux d'avoir le temps.

Source: Moore (2006)

re-consider that experience, adding detailed information about their own context. This rich source affords opportunities for intercultural comparison. As such, it illustrates the need for careful selection of resources and tools that will develop learners' language and permit its assessment.

The learners were asked to read the letter in groups and to decipher meaning, as much as possible in interaction with others. The teacher gathered evidence of learning by recording the interactions of some groups. An extract is presented below:

1   The transcript that follows is part of the discussion between six learners. The group is working out a section of the letter from the Previtali children about their school canteen rules.

	Tyson:	I don't know four words in this whole thing!
5	**Hannah**:	What does this mean? *Viande*
	Bec:	It's a food or something …
	Tyson:	Do you know what *principal* is?
	Several:	Principal!
	Caitlin:	Yeah, but how do you know principal means principal?
10	Tyson:	It's obvious.
	Caitlin:	Even though it may have the same spelling, how do you know it means like principal, the head of the school?

Another learner: (to Tyson)		You're not thinking right.
Tyson:		I don't know any more words then.
15		Bread ... orange ... apple ...
Reece:		*Règles*. Here we go. *Règle* means rule (using dictionary). Obviously *règles* means rules.

Teacher comes to see how they are going ...

Teacher:		Reece tell me about *règles* being rules
20	Reece:	I'm not sure on *obligations*
Teacher:		*Obligations* means what you have to do. So, what is the first thing you have to have?
Reece:		You have to have one entrée.
Teacher:		Yes.

25 Then with guidance from the teacher they work out that students have to have an entrée,
a dairy product (cheese or yoghurt). They then figure out that *plat principal* is a main meal,
and that they have a little if they don't like it and lots if they do.
The group continues without the teacher.

30	Reece:	*Respecter...* I think it means respect the servers.
Caitlin:		But that's English. That might not actually mean anything to do with respecting. It may, but it may not. Reece, you don't know what everything means.
Reece:		You have to have one ... um ... You have to have one dairy
35		thing. You have to have *le plat principal*,
Bec:		The main meal.
Reece:		Yeah, the main meal.
Caitlin:		We already know.
Josh:		What's *le plat principal*?
40	Bec:	That's the main meal
Others confirm.		
Reece:		And then it says you can have a small one or a big one, depending on if you like it or not. And it's like respect ... respect the people who work there, respect the servers ... and
45		say please.
Hannah:		Have manners.
Reece:		Yeah, yeah manners, that's what it means.
Hannah:		I'm not highlighting anything. I've highlighted one sentence.
Reece:		I'm not highlighting words, I'm highlighting sentences. If you
50		know one word you can basically figure out the rest.

| Caitlin: | Yeah, but I just tend not to … because it confuses me if I don't know a word. |
| Reece: | I'm highlighting because I can read this, right? (Moore, 2006) |

This was one of many ways in which the teacher elicited evidence of learning. For example, she can see that Tyson is working at the word level in trying to decipher meaning (lines 4, 7, 10). Caitlin is aware that cognates may not necessarily mean the same across the two languages (lines 9, 11–12). She continues to problematize meaning (lines 30–32). Reece has developed some dictionary skills (lines 16–17); he is able to draw a connection between "respecter" and "respect" and reinterpret respect as "to say please" (lines 41–43). Hannah is able to abstract from "say please" to the more general concept of good manners (line 44). Reece has also learned the reading strategy of deciphering meaning at the sentence level through a focus on key words (lines 47–48). Caitlin, though able to problematize meaning, is not ready to incorporate Reece's strategy into her repertoire (lines 49–50). These kind of data from interactions among peers reveals a great deal of information for the assessment of individual learner's capabilities. This kind of interaction could lead to a reflection on processes of translation, as "moving between" languages and on words and their meanings, across languages. These processes are ideas about communication within an intercultural perspective that are appropriate to Year 5 children learning French in a limited exposure program.

At the end of the unit the teacher elicited learners' reflections on the initial comparison by asking the students to reflect on where they would prefer to spend their lunchtime and to explain their reasons. Two of the responses are presented in Box 8.2. These two texts, written by two different students, represent their reflection as part of formative assessment as appropriate to their level of learning. The first text reveals the way in which the learner is referencing her experience of Germany and her experience of her home culture of meals in imagining her experience of lunchtime in a French *cantine*. The reflection reveals the nature and extent of comparison that she is able to make. In the second, the learner's reflection indicates an interest in experiencing difference, connected to her conception of home. As a single episode, these reflections reveal perceptions at a moment in time. For the teacher, they provide a source of insight into the learners' developing comparative perspective *vis-à-vis* French culture and their distinctive ways of drawing connections in their language and culture learning.

The way in which the learners' responses incorporate their own understandings, values, and positioning represents an additional layer of information for the teacher. Having gathered evidence in a range of ways over a period of time, the teacher was able to develop a profile of the learning of the diverse members of her class.

This example as a whole provides evidence gathered in different ways that are appropriate to learning at a primary level. It includes evidence of interaction (as the learners interact to decipher the meaning of a text) as well as participation in and reflection on processes of learning language and culture. These sources of evidence supplement evidence of oral and written interactions in French.

> ### Box 8.2   Students' responses to reflection task
>
> 3.   Where would you like to spend your lunchtime? Explain your reasons.
>
>   (1)   I would, to be honest, prefer to spend my lunchtime in France. That's because they eat a hot meal for lunch and I am used to that from Germany because they have a cafeteria with hot meals, as well. And to eat a real big meal for lunch is better than just a cold sandwich. It will help children to concentrate better when they're actually full of food and lunch is the most important meal of the day, so it should be rich. And the students in French schools all eat together in a big hall and there wouldn't be so many food scraps around the school. And food should be eaten properly at a table to avoid tummy problems. I think cafeterias are very nice and they should be everywhere.
>
>   (2)   I would like to spend a couple of days in France just for a change. I would be interested to know what it would be like over there but I would not like to live over there as my home is here and always will be.
>
> *Source*: Moore (2006)

Judging and validating

Judging and validating performance is interrelated with the conceptualization of language learning and the processes used to elicit this learning. Just as we have discussed the way in which conceptualizations of the construct and ways of eliciting evidence of learning have expanded, so too it becomes necessary to expand our understanding of evidence of learning. Within a traditional view of assessment, the focus is generally only on looking for features captured in the prespecified statements of criteria and standards, without also allowing space for particular qualities to emerge from learners' work itself. The prespecification is an integral part of establishing objectivity as the desired characteristic of traditional assessment. In the process of judging within an alternate view of assessment, it becomes necessary to reconsider the tools that are normally used, namely, criteria and standards (Scarino, 2005a, 2005b). James and Brown (2005, p. 19) argue for new ways that do justice to the "dynamic, shifting and sometimes original or unique" learning. They propose "perhaps drawing on ethnographic and peer-review approaches in science, appreciation and connoisseurship in the arts, and advocacy, testimony and judgment in law." These approaches represent alternate ways of identifying qualities as evidence of learning.

Within alternate approaches, judging is inherently social and cultural, and includes a process of interpretation and seeking to make sense of the learning (Scarino, 2005b). Criteria become provisional considerations that can be fine-tuned, expanded, and elaborated in the experience of considering actual student performance. At this point it is also necessary to reconsider the conceptualization of the construct and the implications of this conceptualization for identifying criteria. In language learning within an intercultural

Table 8.1 Framework for developing criteria for active-receptive assessment tasks

For receptive tasks (listening and reading)	
Nature and scope of the interaction	*Level of complexity/ sophistication*

Understanding of theme/concept from social life in texts, tasks, experiences
Recognition of diverse assumptions/perspectives
Response to different perspectives:
   noticing   deciding
   explaining   comparing
   connecting   relating
   applying   valuing
   abstracting
   questioning/challenging
Understanding the process of interpretation/understanding themselves as interpreters/
ability to reflect:
   questioning assumptions (own and others)/conceptions
   managing variability (understanding how language use is enmeshed with
     variable contexts of culture)	

Source: Scarino, A. and Liddicoat, A. J. (2009) *Language Teaching and Learning: A Guide*, Melbourne, Curriculum Corporation.

perspective, the focus is not only on knowledge and skill but also on "embodied experience, meaning, language, culture, participation, positioning and identities enacted" (Moss, 2008, p. 238). In this expanded view it becomes necessary to recognize the judgment process as interpretive and to consider the kinds of evidence that will be needed to support interpretations and decisions, recognizing that this entails considering how we understand evidence in general and in any particular assessment episode.

Tables 8.1, 8.2, 8.3, taken from Scarino and Liddicoat (2009, pp. 75–76) are intended to provide a framework for developing provisional criteria for judging performance, both in instances of active-receptive and active-productive interactions and within a long-term perspective. As a framework they allow for the inclusion of features related to evidence that is related to the particular context of learning.

These tables provide a framework for developing active-receptive and active-productive assessment tasks. The framework for developing criteria for active-receptive tasks (listening and reading) is structured in such a way as to require that: (i) the source material provided incorporate diverse assumptions and perspectives, thereby providing material for comparison across languages and cultures and making observations about linguistic and cultural positioning; (ii) responses capture evidence of different ways of interacting with the source material and different ways of processing, analyzing, and using it; there is a strong emphasis on comparison; and (iii) responses capture evidence of reflection and understanding of the processes of interpretation and self-understanding as an interpreter. Similarly, the framework for developing criteria for active-productive tasks requires that: (i) the source experience be one that captures a "critical moment"; the critical moment should involve the learners' direct experience of intercultural

Table 8.2 Framework for developing criteria for active-productive assessment tasks

For productive tasks (speaking and writing)	
Nature and scope of the interaction	*Level of complexity/ sophistication*
Spoken or written in "critical moments" (i.e. moments where students' responses matter to their identity)	
Managing the interaction:	
giving a personal perspective / personal information	
responding to other(s)	
openness to the perspectives or expectations of others:	
noticing comparing	
deciding explaining	
connecting relating	
valuing applying	
abstracting questioning	
Understanding the process of interpretation / understanding themselves as interpreters / ability to reflect:	
interpreting contexts, roles, relationships	
managing variability: understanding how language use is enmeshed with variable contexts of culture	

Source: Scarino, A. and Liddicoat, A. J. (2009) *Language Teaching and Learning: A Guide*, Melbourne, Curriculum Corporation.

Table 8.3 Framework for developing criteria to capture long-term development

Within a long-term perspective	
Cumulative questions to be addressed while building up a long-term picture of learning	*Level of complexity/ sophistication*
What connections can the student draw within and across themes, topics and concepts?	
What connections can the student draw between his/her responses/comments and those of others?	
How has the student come up with these connections?	
Does the student's engagement with these questions and his/her own/others' responses to them provide variable ways of understanding social life-worlds in the language and culture being learned and any other languages and cultures? How?	

Source: Scarino, A. and Liddicoat, A. J. (2009) *Language Teaching and Learning: A Guide*. Melbourne: Curriculum Corporation.

engagement and comparison; (ii) the action capture evidence of the formulation of a personal perspective, response to another, and the consideration of diverse perspectives; and (iii) the action capture evidence of reflection and understanding of the processes of interpretation and self-understanding as communicator. Table 8.3 provides a framework for developing criteria to capture the long-term development of connections in language learning within an intercultural perspective and reflection on the linguistic and cultural construction of knowledge, practices, and experiences.

An initial conceptualization of criteria does not preclude, at any point, consideration of evidence that emerges from the performances of particular individuals. The column labeled "level of complexity/sophistication" in Tables 8.1 and 8.2 is a reminder that the evidence will differ in nature and scope as well as in complexity (e.g. nature and extent of elaboration, qualification, explanation).

The frameworks capture, albeit in a highly generalized way, the dual processes of action and reflection on the role of language and culture in interpreting and creating meaning of phenomena, self and others, across languages and cultures. The cumulative evidence gathered over the long term is particularly important in the context of language learning within an intercultural perspective because of its experiential and developmental character. Here the emphasis is on making connections across and reflecting on concepts and processes.

Validation is the process of warranting the interpretations or inferences made about student performance and learning, and examining the consequences of the interpretations, inferences, and conclusions reached (Messick, 1989b). In explicating Messick's validity framework, and in particular recognizing the need to address the social and cultural character of the meanings assigned to test scores, McNamara and Roever (2006, p. 14) set out the following key questions for validation:

- What reasoning and empirical evidence support the claims we wish to make about candidates based on their test performance? Are these interpretations meaningful, useful, and fair in the particular context?
- What social and cultural values and assumptions underlie test constructs and hence the sense we make of scores? What happens in our education system and the larger social context when we use tests?

These questions expand the traditional approaches to validation substantially. They do so by acknowledging that our conceptions of what it is that is being assessed are aspects of desired learning that have been prioritized by assessors and that they ultimately reflect social and cultural values. They also highlight the fact that assessments do exert influence in different ways for different learners in different contexts and that this influence needs to be examined. It is through critical consideration of existing frameworks and by asking critical questions that the assessment process as a whole is both expanded and becomes accountable with respect to the process of learning itself.

The need for experimentation

That assessment of language learning within an intercultural orientation is complex and challenging must be acknowledged. A personal expression of some aspects of this challenge comes from a teacher of Chinese who describes the struggles she experienced while

Box 8.3 Teacher's reflection on assessing interculturality

One of the struggles that I think I really had for myself in it, was when it came to, because I had, sort of structured the task, were very structured, which I worried a little bit had guided them in some way to responding. But I sort of started off with getting them to think about what values they held in a woman by writing or presenting a speech about a woman that they admired. It was really good to see quite a few of them write about their mum or sister, rather than some big celebrity or something. So that was really good. But that got them to think about themselves and what they valued.

Then we looked at the Chinese text and looked at more Chinese society and then the final task, which I think helped them to bring it together, was the English component where they reflected on what it means to be a woman in China today and then the Chinese blog (in Chinese) which allowed them to really write on whatever aspect they wanted, what it means to be a woman in today's world, sort of a more global perspective.

And one of the things I found was for the less capable language students, the struggle I had with the English reflection was that they were able to say some of the most amazing things. But when it came to the Chinese, they could make a statement, but they couldn't really expand or explore that further, and I was then assessing them, sort of having to make that decision, well, do I then look at their English component to see how they have developed that idea? And while I can see what they might be wanting to say in Chinese because they haven't got that in there because of their language, do I still credit them for that because, you know, I can see where they are going? But I don't want to penalise them twice for language use but also then penalise them because they haven't said enough, even though that's purely because of their language has limitations, so that was sort of something that I found. I was worried if I was making a subjective view on where I thought they were going when it might not of actually be where they were going. So that was a really big challenge for me.

But I think that most students, one of the things, that did impress me was on the level of language that they actually achieved, like it was quite amazing, some of the things, some of the sentences, some of the things they were saying in language. I was like wow, I haven't taught them this! And they were making up their own sentences and really because they obviously had something they wanted to say. So that was really good, cos' I found their language just went up a notch, which was fantastic ....

Basically, well, as far as what I had put in my criteria, ... it was hard putting marks to it, I think if I had written a descriptor on this is you know, is where the student has come, this is what they've done really well, I think it would have been easier, but having to attach a mark so they can get their marks in Year 11 was really hard. But I just sort of put... the student's response clearly articulates the similarities and differences between her own values on female identity and the values of others, as evident in her own community and those expressed in the texts studied; that was the sort of Chinese perspective, and they had to refer to texts within their writing, and that was important. And the meaning of those connections within the student's own ideas is clearly expressed, so how, you know, maybe how the texts have, how they can sort of use that to come to their own understanding.

Source: Foster (2007)

experimenting with assessing language learning within an intercultural perspective (Foster, 2007). The text is a transcription of her reflection during a debriefing session where she describes to fellow teachers her experience of assessing her students' learning in a unit of work relating to women in China. It captures the complexity as well as the desire and value of experimentation.

The value of the exercise was that she succeeded in inviting students to "think about themselves." It was also a topic that was meaningful to an upper secondary group of students in an all-girls school; it mattered to the learners and afforded opportunities for comparison in general (i.e. women in the world) and personally. The topic stretched the students but the teacher notes that the language level achieved was higher than she expected. Finally, she appreciates that the students had come "to their own understanding." This teacher faced a challenge to her own cultural choices and concerns about her role in "guiding" students' thinking. Another challenge relates to her realization that students' reflection in English can be much deeper than in Chinese, which raises questions about how to reconcile this for the purposes of assessment. She is also concerned about subjectivity in marking, a challenge that relates to the tension in assessment paradigms discussed at the beginning of this chapter. A further challenge for the teacher was assigning marks to the work and her sense that a profile description would do more justice to capturing student learning.

In the absence of an integrated theory of language that is focused on meaning and meaning-making and the role of language and culture in meaning-making of ideas, phenomena, self, and other, the challenge remains to connect language and culture in learning and to assess that learning. What is needed is more research in language assessment along sociocultural and interpretive lines, and much experimentation in diverse contexts to explore possibilities. The examples provided here and in the larger study from which they are derived are promising.

9

Programming and Planning

Programs and Programming in a Traditional Perspective

Programming and planning for intercultural language learning presents a fundamental tension between traditional and more recent views of curricula and programs. Programming and planning have traditionally focused on objectives, content, activities, and outcomes, and the effort to map these in some coherent way across a defined program duration. Inevitably, promoting content as the focus of programming and planning has led to the standardization of curricula and programs: the selection, ordering, and standardization of content expressed as knowledge and skills, and statements of predicted outcomes. This standardization prestructures both what will happen in the teaching and learning process and teachers' interpretations and understanding of teaching and learning. If the goal becomes only to cover the content, there is little space for attending to the people involved: namely their relationships, connections, diversity, individuality, and meaning-making. What has been neglected in a focus on content is a consideration of how the learning program was actually experienced by the participants, primarily the teachers and students, and in particular how teachers and students interact (Bullough, 2006; Mayes, 2005). As has already been argued in Chapter 3, meaning-making in interaction is a process in which participants necessarily draw upon their whole cultural make-up, and it is this focus that learning programs for intercultural language learning need to incorporate. The traditional view of programming is derived from a view of learning as a process of accumulating items of factual knowledge, which are tightly sequenced and hierarchically organized (Shepard, 2000). These items are to be taught explicitly by teachers and are received, internalized, and stored incrementally in the minds of individual students.

Traditional programming did not ignore students; it was recognized that the needs and interests of the students should be taken into account (Nunan, 1988). This led to the needs analysis process becoming the precursor of programming (West, 1994). However, two

Intercultural Language Teaching and Learning, First Edition. Anthony J. Liddicoat and Angela Scarino.

problems arise with using needs analysis as a basis for planning learning. The first stems from the terms or categories by which learners' needs are identified. These normally have been understood in terms of the categories of the program itself, for example, the themes and topics of interest to learners and the grammatical items needed to accomplish a task. This means that the categories were preestablished and determined a framework for identifying learners' needs; these categories established what counted as a need and preshaped what could be included as content. The second problem with the analysis of students' needs arises because the program tended to fix the description of the learners' needs when, in fact, these are constantly changing. Needs were identified for types of students rather than for individuals or groups. Needs tended to be seen as changing when contexts changed rather than when learners changed.

Developing programs for language learning within an intercultural perspective presents a challenge to these traditional views. This is because the content of language and culture and the needs analysis of the learners represent only a part of what is involved in learning to communicate interculturally in a particular language and culture at any particular time and over time. The essential feature of intercultural language learning is its focus on the interpretation, the making and the exchange of meanings in interactions among teachers and students, processes that are central to both communication and learning. These processes are not amenable to being listed as an inventory of items, and therefore cannot be presented as one in a program. Given the complexity of the understanding of content in an intercultural perspective on intercultural language teaching and learning, a first consideration in understanding planning is to consider how content can be understood.

Conceptualizing Content for Language Teaching and Learning

The conceptualizations of language, culture, and learning discussed earlier in this book entail a review of what constitutes the content of language teaching and learning, and therefore of assessment. The argument has been made that teaching language from an intercultural perspective requires an expanded view of basic concepts such as *language*, *culture*, and *learning*. In the case of content, there is also a need for an expanded view. This section will examine how content has been understood and how that understanding is expanded in intercultural language teaching and learning.

Structural understandings of content

Content for language programs typically has been understood as linguistic content; however, what is meant by linguistic content has changed according to language teaching approaches. Most traditionally the content of language programs has been understood in terms of grammatical structures and vocabulary (Wilkins, 1972). The content has been organized and chosen according to a structural analysis of language, that is, a grammatical view of language that focuses on how words are organized into sentences and how sentence structures relate to each other (Richards, 1981). Learners have been introduced to language structures in a graded way, from the simplest structures to the most complex. Vocabulary was graded in terms of frequency, familiarity, simplicity, or other frameworks and organized in a similar fashion to grammar. The content was considered to be covered when the learner had mastered the defined set of structures and vocabulary for a particular course or program. Content was often taught and assessed using activities based around the required grammar and vocabulary, and activities and texts were chosen because of the ways they exemplified these requirements. This could mean that students were exposed to and required to produce language that was not communicatively useful, but which foregrounded the language focus of the teaching and learning (Wilkins, 1972).

In structurally oriented language programs culture is usually an incidental aspect of the content. It may provide content for tasks, such as reading passages, but its role is often very limited. In many cases, cultural information, often in the form of literary studies or area studies, may be used as language practice for more advanced students, but it may be disconnected from language teaching and learning.

Communicative understandings of content

In communicative language teaching (CLT) the content of language learning was contexted in situations of use, so that the focus was placed less on the language as independent subject matter and more on language as a communicative tool for learners (Wilkins, 1972). The focus on language structures largely remained; for example, Richards (1981) states that content is linguistic content, although the details of language content were also determined in terms of meaning. Grammar and vocabulary were still organizers of content as the structures of language were considered fundamental to the understanding and articulation of meanings. This content was organized differently, with an emphasis on matching content more closely with the perceived communicative uses that learners would require in the language (Littlewood, 1981). This means that instead of grading language from the structurally simple to the structurally complex, content was organized in terms of those structures that would most enhance the learners' communicative repertoires. Littlewood (1981) argues that the emphasis on communicative use would mean that content could be organized in terms of structures that learners may need to use productively and those which they may need to use only receptively. This means that different structures might need to be learned in different ways and that the idea of mastery of structures is not the same for all structures.

In CLT the aim was to teach structures in the context of a communicative function or need, and attention was given to locating the learning of grammar and vocabulary within communicative contexts. Communicative contexts have been understood in a number of ways.

Functional–structural. A functional–structural view of content uses the idea of communicative functions as a way of organizing language structures for learning. In a structural–functional approach to language teaching and learning, content is understood in terms of linguistic activities such as: introducing oneself, asking for directions, making requests, describing people, talking about hobbies or pastimes, giving reasons, etc. Grammatical structures are embedded in such activities and taught in a communicative context through these.

Vocabulary is chosen to support the particular function being taught. In developing content for teaching purposes a functional–structural approach begins with simple structures and progresses through to more complex structures. This means that teachers may recycle functions in their teaching so that more complex structures can be integrated into the same function.

Functional–situational. Functional–situational views of content retain a view of linguistic content based on structures and vocabulary; however, the linguistic content does not provide the basis for organizing the content. Instead, the situations in which learners are likely to use the language provide the organizing principle for the content, which is largely understood in terms of the functions that language users need to be able to use in particular situations (Wilkins, 1972). In such an approach, language of very different levels of complexity may be grouped together on the basis of its relevance to the function rather than being graded and introduced in terms of complexity. Functional–situational views of content do not therefore assume a progression through language structures. This means that situations can be considered as independent modules that can be taught in any sequence and the idea of developmental progression through the content may be lost.

Notional. Notional views of content are based on the concepts that learners are expected to be able to express, such as time, cause, argument, and emotions. The content focuses on possible communications that language learners will need to comprehend and produce (Wilkins, 1972). Some notions may be connected closely to particular language structures or vocabulary; for example, time links closely with the grammatical feature, tense, and with time adverbials such as "today," "tomorrow," "early," "late," "before," "after." Other notions, such as argument or expressing emotions, do not. The content is determined not by features of language but by what students of the language will need to be able to do with the language they are learning. Other aspects of language use, such as structures or functions, will be determined by the required notions – those aspects of language which are highly likely to be needed for expressing a particular notion are included as content in teaching the notion. Notions are not sequentially related to each other, rather, the priority is determined by learners' needs, although some notions may presuppose or relate to others, for example, argument may require the expression of cause. This means that the sequencing of notions may be relatively variable.

Topic-based. Another way of organizing content for language learning is by topics about which learners will be expected to communicate, for example, leisure, sport, housing, and schooling. Each topic provides a basis for selecting language structures, functions, and vocabulary and for designing various language activities (Bourke, 2006). Topic-based views of content do not assume a progression through language structures – any topic may potentially use similar or different structures, as the link between topic and structure is very loose. Topics can therefore be considered as independent modules that can be taught in any sequence, so that any developmental progression is understood independently from topic.

In reality, CLT has often blended these various ways of understanding content. For example, a teacher who organizes content by topic may select a particular topic as the basic organizing principle and then embed within the topic a number of language functions.

Underlying all of these views of content are language structures and vocabulary, that is, content is linguistic content. They differ primarily in how they organize this content. In some formulations, views of content have moved away from a progressive, developmental perspective to focus on meanings alone as the primary organizer of content. Such meaning-based approaches mean that sequencing becomes a matter not of developing content but of cycling through topics, notions, or functions in order to cover as wide a range of communicative situations as possible. This represents a problem in organizing progression in language learning, as topics, notions, or functions have not been understood in a developmental way. Littlewood (1981) has argued that content understood in these terms is really only suitable for learners who have acquired the basic structures of language and therefore can begin to develop their communicative potential further; however, functional approaches to content have been adopted at all levels of language learning.

Culture is not a primary part of content in CLT and may or may not be a feature of language programs. Where culture is included it is largely there as a support for the linguistic content. It may provide aspects of a topic in a topic-based view of content or it may be something that determines a particular choice of functions, for example, "bargaining." Cultural information may be viewed as content for tasks rather than for programs; for example, a reading passage may deal with cultural information or a writing project may research a cultural topic. In this way culture becomes incidental content rather than the focus of the language program itself. Another way in which culture may be included in CLT programs is as an alternate to content – information that may be used to interest or motivate students but which may be only tangentially linked to the linguistic content. Culture then becomes, in effect, time off from the "real" content of language learning.

Content-based language teaching

Content-based language teaching is essentially derived from communicative language teaching. In content-based approaches to language teaching, content is understood in a way that separates language learning from content. Content is understood as nonlanguage content (mathematics, science, history, etc.) with which language learning will be in some way brought into relation (Mohan, 2001; Mohan and Huang, 2002). It is therefore an extension of the view that language structures do not provide the means of organizing learning content and that some other organizer is necessary. Content-based language teaching provides an academic focus for communicative language use in school contexts and is an attempt to make the focus of language education authentic within school contexts.

In content-based teaching the nonlanguage content becomes the organizing principle for language learning. Students are exposed to the language forms and functions they need to be able to acquire and express the subject matter of a particular discipline, and the discipline determines what language will be acquired and when. Progression is therefore understood in relation to development in the acquisition and expression of the nonlanguage content, for example, in the complexity of texts or ideas understood and communicated in the language.

Content-based language teaching includes culture only to the extent that culture is considered to be relevant to the nonlanguage content. This means that it may be excluded entirely from the teaching of language through mathematics or science or it may become an object for study in some form in subjects such as art or social studies.

Concept-based understandings of content

Concept-based views of content focus on ideas, beliefs, and issues. Language programs following such views use the concepts and the relationships between concepts as the organizing dimension for content. Concept-based approaches to curriculum begin with those higher level abstract ideas that are relevant to a particular curriculum domain and that serve to develop learners' understanding of that domain. These ideas then become a starting point for developing questions and experiences that provide learners with opportunities to link broad concepts to particular instances of the concept (McCoy and Ketterlin-Geller, 2004). The emphasis is placed on thinking processes that enable the learner to draw connections between events, information, or interactions and the broader concepts that organize the curriculum.

Content for intercultural language teaching and learning

The content for intercultural language teaching and learning is multiple. It includes:

- language structures and vocabulary
- aspects of culture
- communicative functions
- concepts
- interactions.

Language structures and vocabulary are important elements of any language learning and they need to be held in focus in any language learning program. However, language structures and vocabulary are not separated from other aspects of language. Language structures and vocabulary are used by speakers for particular purposes and to achieve particular goals. In addition, they are instantiations of ideas, concepts, and values. That is, language structures and vocabulary are learned not only for their own sake, but for what they can show about language, culture, and their relationship.

Similarly, language functions are an important part of language use. In teaching functions from an intercultural perspective, it is not simply the function that is important but rather what the performance of a function represents about the context in which it is performed. That is, functions are culturally contexted ways of acting and the same function may be realized in different ways in different cultural contexts and at different levels of complexity. These differences in realizing language functions have two important implications for intercultural language teaching and learning:

- Language functions embody cultural understandings about how human interaction works in a particular culture and throw into relief different understandings of interactions in different cultural contexts.
- Any situation that involves a presentation of self through language may be evaluated positively or negatively by other language users. Learning to communicate in new cultural contexts brings into relationship different possibilities for the presentation of self, with consequences for understanding one's own identity and that of one's interlocutors.

The discussion of language structures and functions above highlights the conceptual nature of content in intercultural language learning. From the conceptual perspective, language learning is seen as a process of investigation of ideas and issues that arise as languages and cultures are brought into contact through the act of learning. According to Scarino and Liddicoat (2009), in intercultural language teaching and learning, conceptual learning means students coming to:

- understand language, culture, and their interrelationship and be able to discuss and describe them;
- understand how context affects the way language is used to construct, interpret, and communicate meanings;
- engage in reasoning and problem-solving on language- and culture-related issues;
- pose questions about, and find personal responses to, linguistic and cultural diversity;
- transfer their learning from the context in which they learned it to other contexts.

This view of language learning as conceptual means that concepts need to be one of the organizers of content – that the language program needs to foreground these concepts and ensure that they are presented through language learning in a sustained and integrated way.

Intercultural perspectives on languages teaching and learning highlight the importance of interactions as instantiations of the integration of language and content. These may be interactions between teachers and students, between students, and between students and others (including the voices of others as they are encountered through texts, video, digital technologies, etc.). Interactions need to bring opportunities to students to explore their own ideas, interpretations, and reactions as they encounter the ideas, interpretations, and reactions of others. Learning from interaction involves:

using language as a starting point for interaction to generate ideas, interpretations and responses

seeking opinions and the reasoning behind these

probing responses to elaborate deeper and more complex understandings

drawing out, analysing and building on personal experiences

eliciting variability in contributions, and engaging with the diversity found as a resource for further interaction

engaging in open dialogues between participants in which all have opportunities to explore
    their own perceptions and understandings
developing language abilities to meet interactional needs rather than limiting interactional
    opportunities to current language capabilities. (Scarino and Liddicoat, 2009)

When preparing the content of language teaching and learning for the constellation of
language structures and vocabulary, communicative functions, concepts, and interactions
described above, the positioning of the learner must be taken into account. At each point,
the learner is positioned in relation to language and culture in two important ways, as
performer and as analyzer. As performers, learners are required to produce language as
communication that is mindful of the cultural embeddedness of their understandings of
communicative performance and which accommodates to and interacts with the multiple
possibilities influencing those performances. As analyzers, they need to be able to articulate
their own understandings and interpretations of what occurs in any communicative
performance and how those interpretations and understandings are themselves culturally
embedded. In understanding content for the purposes of assessment, the multiple levels of
content need to be borne in mind. Assessment needs to span the full range of possibilities,
both of areas of focus (structure, function, concept, interaction) and of positions (performer,
analyzer, insider, and outsider).

Planning for Complexity

Planning for language learning is a process that captures the developmental nature of
language learning and various approaches have been adopted to address the idea of
development. Development has been considered in different ways at different points of time,
but has often been understood as the development of linguistic complexity, either in the form
of linguistic structures to be learned or in the form of communicative tasks to be performed.
Complexity of linguistic structures usually has been considered in terms of language-internal
features, such as the perceived difficulty of a structure or its frequency of use. Understanding
complexity of communicative tasks, however, is more complex as it encompasses not only
the complexity of language but also nonlanguage features. Skehan (1996, 1998), for example,
identifies three processes that contribute to the complexity of language learning tasks: complexity of the linguistic system, or the complexity and variety of linguistic forms; cognitive
complexity, which includes the dimensions of familiarity with topic and / or forms and cognitive processing demands; and the communicative stress of the conditions under which the
task is performed. Robinson (2001) has argued that the cognitive factors in complexity involve
resource-directing and resource-depleting processes. Resource-directing factors include
things like the number of elements in the task, the amount of contextual support given, and
the reasoning demands made on the speaker. Resource-depleting factors are those which
make demands on attention and working memory and include time available, the demands
the task makes, and whether or not the student has prior knowledge to bring to bear on the
task. Skehan (1996, 1998) and Robinson (2001) represent complexity in terms of difficulty and
regard a task as complex when it is more difficult to perform. Within the context of planning

language learning, planning for complexity would mean sequencing tasks in a progression from lesser to greater linguistic complexity and/or cognitive demand on the learner. This view of complexity therefore includes complexity of language and cognitive load, but does not consider complexity in terms of cultural difference, intercultural perspective, the social demands of interactivity, or interpretation.

When understanding language learning from an intercultural perspective, however, such understandings of complexity are incomplete, as they represent only the complexity found in the language task and do not include the complexity of interpretation. It is therefore important to consider what complexity may mean in the context of the expanded view of language, culture, and learning that we have adopted. In our view, complexity relates to the ability to draw distinctions from experiences and to establish connections and relationships among observations and ideas – that is, to levels of sophistication in processes of analysis, synthesis, and interpretation.

Views of complexity based primarily on language as the organizer of complexity typically produce ways of understanding complexity that involve a movement from knowledge or use of small parts of the language system to larger parts of the system – that is, a progression from part to whole. Viewing progress in language learning as progression from part to whole is problematic when referenced to making and interpreting meaning, as it does not consider the inherent completeness of the process of interpretation. That is, an act of interpretation is in effect a complete, holistic, integrative act, not a partial act, and it does not develop in complexity through a juxtaposition of multiple acts of interpretation. A simple interpretation is no less an interpretation than a complex interpretation. The difference lies in the nature, extent, and elaboration of the interpretation or the sophistication with which an interpretation is expressed, asserted, or defended. This means that the development of complexity is an elaboration of a holistic process rather than one of parts leading towards a whole. In qualitative development of interpretations, a number of processes can be identified:

- Elaborating – the ability to provide more developed, intricate, or refined interpretations of experiences of language, culture, and their relationship.
- Explaining – the ability to provide accounts of one's own interpretations and to communicate these to others.
- Exemplifying – the ability to relate interpretations to specific instances of experience of language and culture.
- Relating – the ability to bring different interpretations into relationship with each other. This may involve the bringing together of one's own interpretations made at different times or in relationship to different experiences of language and culture, or the bringing together of interpretations of the same experiences by others.
- Reformulating – the ability to modify interpretations based on new information or ideas obtained from experiences of language and culture or from interactions with others about experiences. Reformulation requires understanding interpretation as a historical process that evolves over time and relates to changes in context and experience.

These processes imply that the processes of development are not linear but recursive (Liddicoat, 2002) and that language programs require recursion. To develop complexity, learners need to be able to return to interpretations and to work further with them. This implies that language programs need to plan for recursion by encompassing connectedness between experiences and interactions, and relationships of thinking and interpretation over time. The discussion so far has assumed that language learning is a conceptual activity in which language, culture, and their relationship provide an entry point for abstract thinking and that the conceptual levels provide the point of engagement for a recursive process of learning.

Planning for Conceptual Learning

Intercultural language teaching and learning is a conceptually oriented way of understanding the languages curriculum. Planning for teaching and learning therefore emphasizes the conceptual underpinnings and development of learning and concepts as the starting point for developing programs. Conceptual learning involves deep learning and seeks to engage learners in advanced, abstract thinking. In language learning, this means thinking about language, culture, and their relationship and using this as a way of developing knowledge. If it is to be successful, conceptual learning needs to be planned. Moreover, it needs a long-term consistent focus that is developed through the process of planning.

This means that, in planning, concepts are used to organize the sequence of learning and to provide a framework for integrating aspects of language, culture, and their relationship. From this perspective, learning is seen as a progression in the development and expression of concepts, and learning development is seen in terms of increasing complexity expressed about and through language. This contrasts with more traditional approaches to planning and programming, which have seen language itself as the driving element of the program and sequencing in terms of relationships between grammatical features. In this kind of conceptual learning students come to understand language, culture, and their interrelationship and to be able to discuss and describe them, rather than acquiring language structures as preconditions for some future use of the language. Students also grow to understand how language in context constructs, interprets, and communicates meanings, and engage in reasoning and problem-solving about language- and culture-related issues.

Concepts in intercultural language teaching and learning are not necessarily specifically linguistic, rather they orient to broader points of intersection between language, culture, and learning, which allows the relationship between languages and cultures to be explored. A concept therefore may represent a level of abstraction beyond language. Such concepts may be expressed as questions. For example: How does culture shape communication? How does culture influence the ways we understand language in use? Or they may be expressed as themes for investigation, for example, the nature and role of cultural identities, and ways of understanding or using space. These concepts are broad and can be broken down into smaller components that permit a more focused exploration of the concept. For example, the concept "ways of understanding and using space" mentioned above might be addressed through particular related domains of knowledge, such as the following.

- Ideas of personal space: private space and shared space in homes; how living space is organized and what this says about ways of life; whether people have private space (e.g. their own room) or whether they live in shared space; whether or not private space is made available to others (e.g. guests' access to the house); leisure activities at home; etc.
- Ideas of public space: what public spaces are available; how much public space is available; what are the expectations and obligations for using public space; leisure activities in public spaces; etc.
- Ideas of space in specific locations, for example, schools: what are the expectations about space at school and the ways it is used (e.g. classrooms, sporting areas, space for leisure); how much of each sort of space is available and what does this indicate about how people use space; how space is organized at school; etc.
- Ideas of proximity and distance: what is considered geographically close or distant; how this affects travel; what is considered to be a long way to travel; when, why, and how often do people travel a long way; what is seen as being local; etc.

A conceptually driven program with an intercultural focus begins with a concept or concepts relating to the intercultural learning that students will take away from their language learning experience, either short term or long term, and uses the concepts to organize other aspects of the program (see Figure 9.1). This model implies multiple levels of interconnection that work both vertically and horizontally. The vertical connections lead from the concept through to the specificities of content and allow all of the dimensions of learning that are planned to cohere around a common focus. The horizontal connections are developmental sequences through which learning develops in complexity and sophistication.

Planning for conceptual learning needs to foreground the concepts being dealt with in the program (Perkins and Unger, 1999). Figure 9.1 shows the concept as an overarching organizational feature that leads to the identification of topics, that is, specific foci or contexts through which the concept is explored. Each overarching concept is addressed through different domains of knowledge about the concept, which become the locus for decision-making about other levels of detail in organizing language. Concepts are sequentially related to each other in long-term planning so that each concept can grow out of consideration of a prior concept and develop towards some next concept. Concepts are articulated through domains of knowledge. Domains of knowledge are selected areas of content through which aspects of a concept can be investigated. For example, the concept "ways of understanding and using space" could be explored through possible topics such as:

- personal space and shared space
- living space/housing
- leisure activities
- natural and built environment
- work places/schools
- proximity and distance.

Thus domains of knowledge are derived from the concept and the concept ensures the interrelationship of a series of topics during the course of a language program. The

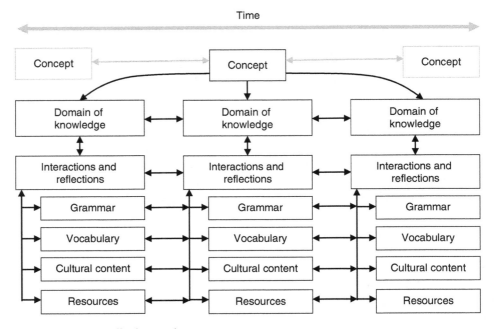

Figure 9.1   Conceptually driven planning.

domains of knowledge selected for a language program are interrelated because they are derived from the same topics; however, attention needs to be given to the relationship between the concept and the domains and between the domains themselves. The domains of knowledge as particular instantiations of a concept are interrelated and their sequencing is developmental. It is important to identify how the domain of knowledge develops or extends students' understanding of the concept and of the language and culture in the ways they think about the concept. It is also important to articulate the specific ways in which each domain relates to other domains, how a current domains draws on the learning that was developed in previous domains, and how it in turn prepares the way for further learning in other domains. Each domain is not simply a part of the overarching whole but also a microcosm in which learning happens and which can then be extended and elaborated through explorations of new domains.

These domains provide ways of determining which interactions and reflections will constitute the processes through which learning will occur. The choice of interactions and reflections reflects decisions about what experiences will be afforded to the students to enable them to develop their conceptual understanding. This means designing experiences that allow the concept to be explored through their situated engagement with the target language and culture. One of the key elements of providing deeper learning in the language classroom is focusing on interactions where one frame of reference meets another as planned classroom practice, such as between teacher and student, student and student, student and text, teacher and text. Such interactions provide learning experiences that invite learners to consider language, culture, and their relationship and draw their attention to, and encourage processes of, noticing, comparison, and reflection. These interactions provide experiences for students and teachers, and opportunities to reflect on and analyze how these experiences provide deeper and decentered development of knowledge and understanding for the learner. In interactions and reflections, students and teachers participate as performers and analyzers of the languages and cultures present in the interaction. The learning experiences provided by interactions can be represented in a program as key questions that encourage a process of inquiry and dialogue and draw explicit connections between learners' own language(s) and culture(s) and experience and the concepts addressed in the resources provided.

The selection of interactions and reflections also needs to attend to the ways in which they will develop the students' linguistic knowledge and contribute to expanding their target language repertoire. Interactions and reflections require particular learning about language and culture, including language forms (grammar, vocabulary, text types) and input in the form of texts and resources and cultural content that will be needed to explore the concept in its particular context. At this point the conceptual organization of the program intersects with other sequences of learning that also need to be addressed, especially in the sequence of language development, to ensure that the program develops the linguistic resources of students in sustained ways.

Developing an interculturally oriented language program requires particular consideration to ways of representing connections across the program as a whole. These connections need to be made at the local, short-term level and at the long-term level (Scarino, 1995). Connections can and should be made at a number of different levels and in different ways (Scarino and Liddicoat, 2009):

- *Global-level connections* are connections between the overarching concepts and the topic or theme through which the concept is investigated. They organize and shape the overall experience of learners as they progress through their language learning.
- *Local-level connections* are connections between particular episodes of learning (units of work, lessons) and overarching concepts that relate each topic or theme to some larger learning. They are also the links between the individual episodes themselves as each builds on prior learning and provides a basis for new learning.
- *Personal connections* are connections that students will be able to make with the material presented by their learning experiences. They include issues such as how learners will come to see global and local connections, how learners will display the connections they make, and what space is available for making additional personal connections. Personal connections are also the unexpected connections students may draw between their personal experiences and the current learning experience. Although these cannot be planned in advance, planning needs to allow opportunities for such connections to be developed and explored when they occur. At the same time, personal connections need to be integrated into an overall scope and sequence of learning in ways that reaffirm the connections and develop desired learnings.

At all of these levels, and at any time, connections can also be made between languages and literacy, and between languages and all other areas of the curriculum.

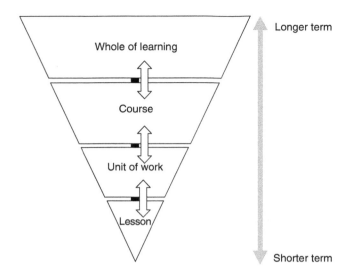

Figure 9.2   Levels of planning. Adapted from Scarino, A. and Liddicoat, A. J. (2009) *Language Teaching and Learning: A Guide*, Melbourne, Curriculum Corporation.

Long-Term and Short-Term Planning

Complex content for language learning, such as that discussed above, requires a process of planning at a number of levels that mutually influence and inform each other (Scarino, 1995). These levels can be understood as an inverted pyramid moving from the most general level of planning to the most specific (see Figure 9.2).

At the broadest level of planning there is the level of the students' entire learning experience over a number of years, from their entry into language learning to their exit from it. This is a view of planning at the most general level, which seeks to give shape to the process of learning for a cohort of students and to articulate how this cumulative experience of language learning coheres and develops. This level of planning has often been ignored or considered only in very general terms. The next level involves planning for particular stages of learners' progress through their learning – a year, a semester, or in some cases a shorter time – in which the learners follow a particular program of learning. Course-level planning provides a structure for planning units of work to ensure that the ways in which they are put together develop learning progressively over the course of the year. Such plans establish a coherent, connected focus of learning with an emphasis on the development of learning over time (Kohler, 2003). Below this is the planning of units of work – a series of lessons with a common focus. At the lowest level is the lesson plan, which articulates what will be covered at a particular time. It is at the lower levels of this diagram that most focus has been given in teachers' planning. Ideally, planning takes place at all of these levels to ensure that students' experiences of language learning are developmental and coherent. In reality, longer term planning may rely on external sources such as textbooks, syllabuses, or curriculum frameworks. Although such documents have a role in supporting the various levels of planning, they are not in themselves plans of programs for particular learners, as we have argued above. The short-term or long-term use of any external plan requires adaptation to the purposes, needs, and interests of teachers and students.

Planning whole of learning

Whole-of-learning planning is typically done by governmental or other curriculum agencies that map over time what will be achieved in an extended sequence of learning in the form of a curriculum or syllabus. Such documents usually have focused on objectives, content, activities, and outcomes and map these across defined spans of time. These documents allocate to education authorities the role of long-term planning and separate it from the work of teachers themselves. This has meant that teachers have not been seen as the sources of the thinking that gives coherence to their overall programs and to the learning experiences of their students over the course of their learning. Rather, teachers' planning has been seen as a process of implementing an overall framework conceived by others. If language learning is considered as a way of engaging with the meaning-making of individuals, such forms of planning alone do not suffice as plans for the whole of learning because they are inevitably standardized for generic types of learners rather than to local contexts and particular learners. There is therefore a need for teachers themselves, when working from an intercultural perspective, to consider the forms that the whole of their students' learning will take.

A whole-of-learning plan is the longest term plan and the one that is by nature the most indeterminate, as many experiences, interactions, and developments over time influence how the plan will unfold. It is therefore a plan that deals primarily with general levels of learning and which requires further elaboration when it is implemented in the classroom. Such a plan can be seen in Table 9.1. This plan is designed for a group of learners in a small rural school that covers 11 years of education, from Prep(aratory) to Year 10. The overall structure has a unifying concept that shapes language learning in a coherent way across the whole period of learning. The teacher frames her teaching in terms of an exploration of group membership:

> I have designed a long-term plan that focuses on one dimension of intercultural learning – groups within cultures and how language creates, sustains, and refines groups within a social context. The enduring understandings for students are that they have membership of groups and that they move between them. … I have mapped a Prep to Year 10 long-term plan for intercultural learning that aims to develop a sophisticated understanding of subcultural groups by students over several years of schooling. (Bignell, 2007, p. 10)

This overarching idea is not framed in terms of language forms and structures but in terms of larger concepts, which provide a framework in which language, culture, and learning can be brought together. The organizing principle is not language *per se*, but rather the deeper learning that engagement with language affords. Moreover, the ultimate goal is not the acquisition of some amount of language, understood structurally, but rather is related to the transformative role that learning an additional language can provide for these students.

Such a program obviously needs elaboration before it can be translated into learning experiences for particular learners and there is much that is relevant for language

Table 9.1   Whole-of-learning plan

Year group	Intercultural learning focus	Learning Experience	Enduring understanding
Prep–Year1	Membership of groups Movement between groups	Introducing yourself Introducing others Groups in my classroom	Students have membership of multiple groups, e.g. gender, school classes Students move between groups Language can be gender-based (inclusive and exclusive)
Year 2–3	Variability within groups	Family celebrations such as birthdays or Easter	A family is a group Language shows shared membership (last names/ surnames) Family groups often celebrate the same activities but not all family groups do so in the same way
Year 4–5	Place and identity Stereotypes and groups	Students create a brochure/homepage for visiting Japanese tourists to the area.	How place influences personal identity. Is anyone typical? Are stereotypes useful? How can I represent my culture to another cultural group?
Year 6–8	How subcultural groups contribute to national identity	What evidence of other cultural groups can be seen in our Australian way of life? Is a quilt a suitable metaphor to describe Australia's culture? Is this the same for Japan? Interview Japanese visitors to find out how they see Australian culture.	Elements of many subcultures contribute to our national Australian identity Is this true for other countries/ nations?
Year 9–10	Is youth culture a global culture?	Explore youth culture through multimedia, e.g. magazines, websites, music videos, fashion with a focus on Australia and Japan. Am I really so different from you? What makes us the same?	Language reflects culture How a shared language is used to include and exclude people from groups How group culture can transcend physical and political boundaries How does youth culture play out on a world stage and what does it mean for the individual

Source: Bignell, J. (2007) Phase 1 teacher participant example: Japanese Years Prep–10: Programme for Years Prep–1: "We are one, but we are many." Accessed February 5, 2008, from Commonwealth of Australia from http://www.iltlp.unisa.edu.au/doclibexamples/iltlp_example_japanese_prep_yr1.pdf

learning that is not included in such a plan. Elaboration is required when a whole-of-learning program is developed at lower levels. This is presupposed in Table 9.1 by the division of the plan into year levels, which indicate where course-level planning will be focused.

Planning a course

Planning at the course level aims to develop a program for learning over a more limited period of time during which a particular teacher and a particular group of students will work together. It aims to develop a component of the whole-of-learning plan and to elaborate this as part of a broader sequence of learning. An example of an interculturally oriented course plan can be seen in Table 9.2, which presents a program designed for Year 9 learners of Chinese. Table 9.2 presents an overarching conceptual frame for the year's work – establishing relationships – and then maps this over a number of contexts in which the concept will be investigated. It further elaborates four subconcepts (key cultural and intercultural concepts) that will be used to investigate the overarching concept in each context. This gives a matrix of twenty main areas of focus, which will be investigated by the learners. The plan then maps the language that students will learn while investigating these concepts. This section of the plan resembles a more conventional mapping of content and covers the range of language forms and structures that typically would be expected in a language program. The significant feature of this program is that the language is not the driving force of the plan, but is integrated into a conceptual framing of intercultural language learning. At the same time, conventional forms of language learning are thoroughly embedded within the concept-driven framework through the key language concepts.

The program plans a coherent series of learning experiences across the course of a year, in which language is organized in a way that allows learners to explore cultural and intercultural issues at a conceptual level. Within the course of the year, students will move through a series of topics, each of which has its own language focus. The topics are not independent, rather they are collectively shaped by the concepts that organize the program. The level of detail here is more specific than in the whole-of-learning program discussed above, but some aspects of the plan need further elaboration before they can be implemented in the classroom. The five contexts listed here imply a series of units of work, which will be the next level of development in a shorter term plan.

Planning a unit of work

The long-term plan is further elaborated by a group of lessons that can be developed and related to each other. For many teachers, this planning takes the form of a unit of work, which may span a few weeks or a whole term. The unit gives a focus to a series of lessons through a topic or theme that shapes choices about vocabulary, grammar, content, skills, strategies, and communicative activities. Units of work are a way of ensuring that a series of lessons have a common thread and they construct connections among lessons in terms of the overall content and focus of attention. Units of work themselves need to be framed in a broader context of teaching and learning.

Table 9.2 Course plan: cultural and intercultural concepts

	Year 9	Technology and communication	The human environment	Leisure	Education	The natural environment
				Establishing relationships		
Key cultural and intercultural concepts	Social organization	Emergence of the individual	The changing nature of the community over time and space	The individual and the community	The state, the community and the school	Individual choices and their impact
	Interpersonal relationships	Developing relationships in the modern context	Personal space and its impact on housing	Influence of others on choices	Choices and aspirations Parental influence and guidance	The natural environment and its impact on lifestyles
	Values systems	Friendship choices and the values which influence them Interpreting others' actions	Preservation versus modernization (e.g. should we keep traditional housing?)	Local traditions, global influences The importance of health and fitness in daily life	National values reflected in education	Making choices and reflecting on their implied values
	Change	The use of technology in daily life (e.g. mobile phones, email chat rooms)	Housing traditions over time and regions Becoming global citizens Futures	Impact of technology on changing leisure choices	Work/study options for the future	Variations in climate The future
Key language concepts	Related vocabulary	Review of personal data (e.g. naming, age, place of residence, year level)	House types; house rooms Location words	Leisure and sport activities Stative verbs showing how something is done (e.g. 快,慢,好) Optative verbs (e.g. 会,可以,能)	School subjects and facilities Uniform Occupations Conjunctions	Weather and climate Holiday activities

Grammar concepts	Questioning Ordering of place and time from biggest to smallest	Describing relative location using: sentence order (SPAO) conjunctions (because, therefore…) comparison similarity(一样) difference (比) verbs expressing opinions using 喜欢	Complement of time Complement of degree Adverbs of frequency (常常, 平常,不少) Sentence order: STAO Use of optative verbs (can, possibility, etc.)	Adverbs of time (before, during, after) Sentence order STPAO Use of conjunctions (however, although, not only… but also…)	Use of stative verbs with adverbs of degree (很,不,非常, 真,比较, etc.)
Communicative functions	Exchanging personal details Sending emails Chatting codes	Expressing opinions using 喜欢 Responding to real estate advertisements	Making a suggestion Discussing abilities Exchanging personal information	Expressing opinions using 觉得 Justifying opinions	Making choices dependent on weather conditions
Text types	Conversation Advertising Forms (online and printed) Email Websites Chat rooms	House plans Real estate advertisements (Internet and printed) Letters	Conversation Letters Forms Websites (penfriends, Olympics) SMS	School timetables and plans School websites Letters	Weather reports (printed, online, TV) Diary entries Conversations Letters
Characters	Using Chinese language word processing packages to discover the relationship between pronunciation and characters Discuss internal components of characters (familiar and unfamiliar) and discover relationship between the characters' internal components and meaning Creation of compound words using characters' original, individual meanings How modern concepts (e.g. email) are conveyed using pre-existing characters				

Source: Andrews, S. (2007) Phase 1 teacher participant example: Chinese Year 9: "Establishing relationships." Accessed February 5, 2008, from Commonwealth of Australia from http://www.iltlp.unisa.edu.au/doclibexamples/iltlp_example_chinese_yr9.doc

An example of a unit of work plan can be seen in Box 9.1. This plan shows a unit of work developed from the course discussed in Table 9.2 and shows how the unit of work "Technology and Communication" is fleshed out into a more detailed description of the experiences afforded to students over a series of lessons. The planning at this level specifies interactions and learning tasks that provide a range of different entry points to the program's key conceptual learnings. It identifies a series of tasks for the students to perform, focus questions to direct their attention in the task, vocabulary that will be needed for the task, and in some cases a follow-up task that works through the learning. This level of planning also locates assessment tasks and required resources at points in the unit of work. The planning for a unit of work is much more elaborated than at the course level and focuses much more on what students will do to develop their learning.

Box 9.1   Unit of work plan

Technology and Communication
Key Learning Interactions
Learning Tasks

- In small groups, hold a discussion in English reflecting on the role communication plays in developing relationships with friends, family, and others, both locally and overseas (if appropriate), and how this communication varies.

  Focus questions:
  汉语: How do you communicate with your friends and family?
  汉语: Create a list of the different ways in which you communicate with others. How has this changed over time for you, your parents, and grandparents? Can you imagine how this will change in the future?
  Key vocabulary: communication (e.g. 沟通, 说话, 写信, 打电话, 发传真, 上网, 发电子邮件, 聊天儿, 进聊天室)

- Listen to Chinese conversations involving the exchange of personal information and identify information about phone numbers.

  Focus questions:
  汉语: How are phone numbers presented in Chinese?
  汉语: How does this compare to the way they are presented in Australia?
  汉语: When would it be appropriate for you to hold such a conversation, and with whom?
  Key vocabulary: 电话号码, 多少
  Task: 汉语: Hold a conversation with a partner in which you exchange your phone numbers (land-line).

- Listen to a phone conversation and identify key phrases.

  Focus questions:
  汉语: How do you answer the phone in English?
  汉语: What about your parents and your friends?
  汉语: How was the phone answered in this conversation? What do you think this may mean?
  Task: Hold a phone conversation with a partner.

- View a number of Chinese addresses and make connections about how they are constructed linguistically.
    Focus question:
    汉语: Compare this with how addresses are written in Australia (issue of ordering largest to smallest).
    Key vocabulary: 街, 路, 号
- Using Chinese mobile phone advertisements (e.g. Chinese e-bay) locate the characters for mobile phone (手机)
    Focus questions:
    Consider the reasons for the popularity of the mobile phone in China. How are they similar or different to Australia?
    汉语: What do these characters mean individually and why have they been used to create the compound for mobile phone?
    汉语: How is it different from the word for telephone? Why do you think this was necessary?
    汉语: How would you ask a Chinese person for his/her mobile phone number?
    汉语: How would you reply if asked?
    Task: Hold a conversation with a partner in which you exchange your mobile phone numbers.
- Look at a series of Chinese advertisements (taken from e.g. magazines, papers, and Internet) and identify keywords and characters relating to phone numbers, addresses, and email addresses.
    Focus questions:
    汉语: Where have you seen these characters before?
    汉语: What do they mean individually? Can you guess what they mean when put together? Compare their presentation with Australian advertising material.
    Task: Present your own details in this way.

Key Assessment Task
Imagine you are meeting a Chinese student at a school in China. Use Chinese to hold a conversation in which you introduce yourself, exchange other relevant personal information, and relevant contact details.
   OR
Prepare a series of conversations in Chinese reflecting your understanding of the way contact details are represented in China. Consider the context in which these conversations take place, and the relevance of the information you are exchanging.

Learning Tasks
Analyse and compare a variety of Chinese and Australian types of identification (e.g. drivers' licences, VISAs, passports, ID cards).
   Focus questions:
   汉语: What information is provided? Do the cards provide the same information?

汉语: What Chinese characters do you recognise and what do they mean? Can you work out the meaning of the other characters? What do these texts tell you about the information that is seen as being important for each of these situations?

Task: Complete a number of printed forms for different purposes (e.g. VISA application, magazine subscription, email application) providing the required details.

Using the Internet and your knowledge of English language websites, access www.yahoo.com.cn to explore creating a Chinese email address.

Focus questions:

汉语: Looking at the web page, what do you notice?

汉语: What can you recognise?

汉语: What are the similarities between the Chinese page and the Australian page? What keywords can you locate and what do you think they mean? Check your meanings.

In small groups, consider the impact the development of email has had on communication across the world. How prevalent do you think its use is in China and why? Do you foresee any problems with its use in China? In Australia? Across cultures?

Key vocabulary: important terms taken from web pages

Task: Complete a form applying for an email address. Use the Chinese Microsoft word processing package to send each other and your teacher emails in Chinese. Create a word list reflecting the new vocab you have learned.

Extension Task

Explore www.yahoo.com.cn and locate the chat rooms. Consider the impact the use of chat rooms has on the formation of your relationships with others.

Task: See if you can access an appropriate chat room and hold a conversation in Chinese. Create a word list reflecting the new vocabulary you have learned.

Focus questions: Why did you select that chat room? Why did you choose that person to talk to? What factors influenced your choices? Why do you think that person chose to respond to you or communicate with you?

Key Assessment Task

Create a folio of "printouts" reflecting the interactions you had exploring www.yahoo.com.cn, including your word lists, printouts of the online forms you have completed, printouts of your email inbox, emails you have sent, and any online interactions you had in Chinese chat rooms (e.g. greetings, enquiries of others and their responses). Include annotations on these pages describing and reflecting on your understanding of the vocabulary and the tasks. Complete a self-assessment evaluation of your learning. Discuss the role technology plays in formulating your relationships with others.

Resources

Ni Hao 2, Units 6 and 7

Ni Hao 4, Unit 2

Copies of VISAs, passports, drivers' licences, ID cards in Chinese and English

VISA application form, magazine subscription application, printout of email application.

Internet, printer and access to Chinese websites, including www.yahoo.com.cn and ebay

Source: Andrews (2007, pp. 8–10)

Planning a lesson

Lesson planning focuses on a single episode within a larger program of learning. Lesson planning has been recognized as an important way of ensuring that a lesson is focused and achieves its objectives (Farrell, 2002; Woodward, 2001). Such planning typically considers objectives, materials needed, class activities, and homework. The lesson plan is a way of taking a unit of work and mapping the activities onto specific lessons. The model of planning we are presenting breaks the program down into specific timetabled classes. It considers how the interactions and reflections developed for the unit of work will be delivered, given the local classroom conditions. It aims to determine how much of the unit of work can be accomplished during a particular span of time.

The Place of Context in Planning Programs

The view of planning and programming being put forward here is one which sees these activities as not simply the articulation of generalized course material, but as orienting to the particular individuals and groups involved in the process of teaching and learning. That is, a language program should be planned separately for the learning of individuals in particular settings. For this reason, planning is an activity for all teachers and cannot be replaced by a pre-prepared curriculum or textbook, as these too have to be adapted for a particular class. Planning with a focus on particular learners entails understanding the individual learners' contexts, the school setting, and social, cultural, and linguistic profiles of learners and their changing and developing nature. The process of language teaching and learning begins with people, who bring to the teaching and learning situation knowledge, values, and dispositions. It requires decisions and actions on the part of teachers as they respond to their particular learners and to the realities of their particular classroom and school context. It also requires decisions and actions on the part of learners, based on their evolving learning and understanding. In particular, it demands attention to the prior language and culture experiences of learners, both within the classroom and beyond, including the diversity of language and cultural knowledge learners bring to the language classroom. By reflecting closely on the context for intercultural language learning, teachers have the capacity to ensure that programs are developed that reflect particular learners and their linguistic and cultural identities, and their prior experiences with diverse languages and cultures.

Conclusion

In considering programming and planning in language learning, it is important to recognize that programs are no more than artifacts, or documented representations of learning priorities over time. Programs are not fixed nor do they constitute a complete representation of teaching and learning. Rather, programs are representations of intentions, and how their relationship to that will be enacted or realized in the classroom cannot be fully anticipated. This means that the planned program needs to be used flexibly to accommodate what learners and teachers need to do in the classroom to develop learning. The view we have developed here is that the program should encourage learning rather than simply cover predetermined content. Teaching and learning will always be characterized by the unpredicted and unpredictable, especially where learners' own meaning-making is a focus, and this is often the catalyst for deep learning. At times, students' interests, needs, and questions may lead teaching and learning away from the planned learning in order to pursue meanings and insights that emerge, and interculturally oriented language teaching and learning needs to have the potential to pursue such opportunities. The planned program therefore should not be considered a rigid framework, but rather a document that guides opportunities for learning.

In any planning there is an element of indeterminacy. The resulting program does not, and cannot, represent what actually will be done. This does not, however, mean that the program will be abandoned. Instead, the plan itself remains the focus point for learning and a way to reconnect episodes of learning to a broader educational perspective. It is a resource to give learning shape, connections, and continuity. Long-term planning recognizes that in its enactment, interactions may develop different emphases in response to learners' constructions, questions, and statements of understanding. The program that results from long-term planning should be understood as a flexible frame that is intended for elaboration in practice: that is, planning is an open process that is responsive to the unfolding of the enacted curriculum. A program that focuses on learners as being individual, diverse, and always developing, and on the importance of interaction for interpreting and making meaning, is necessarily dialogic. In this context, while teachers, who know their learners well, can anticipate a great deal about the interactions that will occur (their purpose, key questions that will stimulate reaction, noticing and comparing that lead to learning, resources to challenge thinking), they also understand that any interaction cannot be fully specified in advance. There will always be a degree of unpredictability, because it is not possible to anticipate fully how particular individuals (whether students or teachers) will interpret particular contexts.

10

Evaluating Language Programs

In Chapters 2, 3, and 4 we have considered an expanded view of language, culture, and learning and their interrelationship, which we see as necessary in teaching and learning languages within an intercultural perspective. In Chapters 5–9 we have described the way in which this expanded view influences the ecology of language teaching and learning: the tasks, interactions, and experiences, as microcosms of language learning; the resources selected, adapted, developed, and used; the technologies that mediate language learning; the nature and means for assessing and judging language learning; and how all these aspects are brought together in theorizing and planning programs of work – all within an intercultural perspective. To these aspects we now add the process of evaluating, which is the critical process that ensures the overall dynamism of the overall program, within an intercultural perspective in the ecology. Evaluation requires continuous informal, and at times formal, reflection on the functioning and quality of the language-learning program as a whole.

The ecological metaphor is used here to highlight the interrelationship of all aspects and the inevitable influence of a change in any one aspect over all other aspects in the ecology (see Kramsch (2002) and van Lier (2002) for further discussion of ecological perspectives). It also highlights the notion presented in Chapter 1, of intercultural language learning as a stance, an overall perspective that permeates language teaching and learning as a whole, rather than just the methods employed. The stance that teachers and learners bring to the act of theorizing, conceptualizing, teaching, and learning languages comes from their own enculturation into primary and subsequent languages and cultures, their own situatedness in time and space, their own experiences and reflections on these experiences, and their beliefs, desires, motivations, commitments, and ethical values. These are part of their own dynamic framework of knowledge and understanding and their identities as teachers and learners (Scarino and Liddicoat, 2009). This stance also permeates the process of evaluation.

In this chapter we consider evaluation as an integral aspect of the ecology of language teaching and learning. It is the aspect that ensures the system remains open to ongoing improvement and renewal (Clark, 1987). First, we discuss the nature and purpose of

Intercultural Language Teaching and Learning, First Edition. Anthony J. Liddicoat and Angela Scarino.
© 2013 Anthony J. Liddicoat and Angela Scarino. Published 2013 by Blackwell Publishing Ltd.

program evaluation; we then consider paradigms that shape the evaluation process and the process of evaluation itself. In so doing, we discuss how the view of language teaching and learning within an intercultural perspective shapes the frame of reference for evaluating language programs and the processes involved. We then consider the relationship between evaluation and teacher professional learning. We conclude the chapter and the book by highlighting language teaching and learning as action and interpretive understanding across languages and cultures.

Nature and Purpose of Program Evaluation

Evaluation is a process of systematic inquiry into the functioning and quality of the language program as a whole and of each of the aspects. In contrast to the process of assessment, it focuses on programs, not individuals. Its major purpose is to support ongoing improvement in the quality of the language program and, fundamentally, students' language learning. This description recognizes that evaluation is first and foremost a systematic process of inquiry that continues over time; there is no sense in which the effective functioning and quality of the program can be established once and for all. Inquiry implies a process of finding things out through gathering evidence, analyzing data, drawing conclusions, and acting upon the findings. Although improvement is the goal for both educational systems and teachers, the purpose of a particular program evaluation may be oriented more towards administration or instruction (Cohen, 1994) depending on the specific purposes of those involved. Administrative purposes relate to matters such as selection for access to language or general educational programs, placement, decisions about progression through levels in sequences of courses, or indeed resourcing. Instructional purposes relate to matters such as student achievement, approaches used, student involvement, the use of contemporary resources and technologies, and so on.

An evaluation can be formative or summative, internal or external, informal or formal, depending on the requirements of those responsible for the program and the various participants in the program. Formative evaluation involves regular, ongoing reflection on the overall operation of the program, to inform its ongoing development. It also tends to be internal and informal. It is generally conducted by a teacher or a group of teachers to ensure that the program is achieving its goals, particularly with respect to students' language learning. With formative evaluation, the agent for the evaluation and for recommending improvement is the teacher(s). Summative evaluation generally occurs at the end of a cycle of program implementation and development. Its scope may include the program as a whole or any one of its interrelated aspects. It tends to be external and formal, and is often commissioned by the educational system or other authority. With summative evaluation, the agent for evaluation and for recommending improvement is the authority responsible for improvements, which are then to be implemented by teachers.

Any process of evaluation will require a frame of reference for establishing quality. This is a complex matter for two reasons: first, it is difficult to define what is actually meant by quality, and second, agreement as to what constitutes quality is difficult to achieve. This is because perceptions as to what constitutes quality are likely to be different for different participants in the educational process (students, teachers, parents, employers, government, academic researchers) and because these perceptions derive from different perspectives or ideological points of view about language teaching and learning (Clark, Scarino, and Brownell, 1994). Thus, for any program, there are likely to be multiple perceptions and expressions of quality, depending on the participants. Notwithstanding these complexities, however, because the process of evaluation requires a frame of reference for quality, understandings of quality in language teaching and learning need to be articulated. The value of program evaluation often resides in the very fact that it requires participants to articulate assumptions and perspectives that are often held tacitly. These understandings of quality then become a frame of reference for considering the ways in which and the extent to which the program, teaching, learning, and assessment are, in fact, effective and of appropriate quality. They also inform the decision-making or action that result from the process of evaluation.

Taken together, the chapters of this book can be read as an articulation of quality in language teaching and learning within an intercultural perspective, as we understand it. The evaluation of a language program, in our terms, needs to address the theoretical perspectives on language, culture, learning, and their relationship that the program embraces, and how these perspectives are then evidenced in each aspect of the program and in the processes of teaching and learning. From each of the chapters of this book, it is possible to derive a set of criteria or features that constitute quality for the purposes of evaluating language programs within an intercultural perspective.

Key questions that an evaluation needs to address include:

- What is the purpose of the evaluation? Why is the evaluation being conducted?
- What is the focus and scope of the evaluation?
- Whose perspectives are to be included?
- What assumptions and understandings do these perspectives bring?
- What is the theoretical base that informs the program (specifically, the view of language, culture, and learning, and their interrelationship)?
- What assumptions about the nature of "quality" are being made?
- What kinds of evidence, and how much, are needed to evaluate the program and why?
- How will the evidence be gathered and analyzed?
- How confident can participants be about the conclusions?

The most sustained work on program evaluation in applied linguistics has been undertaken by Lynch (1990, 1996, 2003). Two aspects of his contribution are particularly relevant to the key evaluation questions outlined above: his consideration of paradigms that shape program evaluation and the process of evaluation that he describes through the context-adaptive model (CAM).

Paradigms that Shape Program Evaluation

The paradigm debate, discussed in Chapter 8 as families of theories related to assessment, also applies to the process of evaluation. Lynch (1996) describes the paradigm debate in education and psychology as a debate between advocates of positivistic, quantitative research methodology on the one hand and advocates of naturalistic, qualitative research methodology on the other (Lynch, 1996). This debate is relevant to evaluation because it helps to identify the assumptions held by participants in the process, that is, the lenses through which they understand evaluation in all its processes.

Although reducing the paradigm debate to a dichotomy (positivistic–naturalistic) constitutes an oversimplification of complex discussions on both sides (see Lincoln and Guba, 2000 and Schwandt, 2000) for a full discussion), it is worth characterizing the two paradigms in relation to the assumptions they make about "what we are trying to know, and how we can pursue that knowledge" (Lynch, 2003, p. 3). Within the positivist paradigm, knowing is independent of the knowers (the evaluators) and their attempts to know it, for "in order to capture the reality as it 'really is', we need to be objective and approach it from the perspective of the distanced observer" (Lynch, 2003, p. 3). On the other hand, within a naturalistic paradigm, knowing is understood as dependent on the knowers (the evaluators) and their attempt to know it. Within this paradigm, knowledge is understood as a social construction and "must be understood subjectively (and intersubjectively) through interaction of participants in the research process" (Lynch, 2003, p. 3).

This distinction between paradigms gives rise to different approaches to evaluation. The approaches that align with the positivist research paradigm are experimental and quasi-experimental designs that focus primarily on outcomes (e.g. test results), with the results of one group matched against a comparison (or "control") group. The approaches that align with the naturalistic (i.e. interpretivist) research paradigm are nonexperimental, with the design evolving as part of describing and interpreting the program. As Lynch notes, however, the differences in assumptions between paradigms extend beyond methodology:

> The approaches to evaluation that use the positivist paradigm see the programme as an objective reality that exists externally to the evaluator and evaluation. With a disinterested stance by the evaluator in relation to the programme, and with a distinction between facts and values in relation to the programme, this objective reality can be captured, or at least reasonably approximated in the data-gathering and analyses. The approaches that are … interpretivist … see the programme as a socially interpreted and constructed reality, one that the evaluator must directly engage with in order to understand. Furthermore, this understanding will be one of many possible understandings, all of them "interested" … and value-laden. (2003, p. 7)

The paradigm, which provides the theoretical context in which the evaluation is set, shapes the purposes, nature, and scope as well as the process of evaluation as a whole, namely, the ways of gathering, interpreting, analyzing, and warranting evidence.

Within the dialogic perspective on language teaching and learning described in this book, we highlight the value of participatory processes of evaluation. These necessarily include multiple perspectives and interpretations, of both insiders and outsiders to the program. The combination of insiders and outsiders is useful as it includes those who know the program best, as well as others who can bring an external perspective. Value derives from individual and collective reflection on the nature, scope, processes, and outcomes of teaching and learning language in the context of a particular language program. This reflection includes articulating assumptions (both theoretical/conceptual and practical) that participants bring to the evaluation process, and recognizing the diverse frameworks of knowledge, understanding, values, desires, and motivations that shape participants' practices, interpretations, and judgments. It also uses dialogue as the basis for reaching an understanding of diverse perspectives about the program, which may or may not be fully reconciled in this process of evaluation. Dialogue makes it necessary to express perspectives and rationales, making them available for interpretation by others. If nothing else, it at least achieves a shift in participants' understanding of the different perspectives and in their understanding of themselves in the encounter (Moss, 2008). It is in this way that we see evaluation as inter-interpretive at every point.

The Process of Evaluation

Lynch's (1990, 1996, 2003) CAM for evaluation is particularly useful because it recognizes the complexities in evaluation, ensures systematicity, and is friendly to the diverse stakeholders as participants in the particular context. It accords central importance to context and the need to ensure that evaluation is undertaken in a way that fits the particular context of the particular program and evaluation. Lynch's CAM is a "flexible, adaptive heuristic – a starting point for inquiry into language education programs that will constantly reshape and redefine itself depending on the context of the program and the evaluation" (1996, p. 3). The model sets out a series of steps that allow for adaptability. The adaptability emerges from a process of working backwards and forwards through the steps in a way that is progressively modifiable, that is, it allows for constant adjustment along the way.

The salience that CAM gives to context can be usefully compared to Brown's concept of "testing-context analysis," which he has developed as part of ensuring "defensible and stakeholder-friendly testing" (2008, p. 276). In his conception of "context," in addition to focusing on language needs, Brown includes needs that are extralinguistic, such as political, social, and economic. We extend this conception to evaluation. Testing-context analysis involves "the systematic collection and analysis of all information necessary for defining defensible testing procedures" (Brown, 2008, p. 278). Following Brown, the analysis of the testing context, and in our sense, the evaluation context, includes the need to *defend* to the relevant participants or stakeholders the process, the interpretation of the results and findings, and conclusions reached. This process of defence is required to ensure validity. Validity, in its contemporary sense, is not a property of the test or evaluation process itself, but relates to the *defensibility of the inferences made* when a test or evaluation process is used in a particular setting, with particular people, for particular purposes (after Messick, 1989a, 1989b). According to Messick, the defensibility argument needs to be made on the basis of evidence that supports the interpretation of meanings and ensures that the interpretation is relevant and useful to the particular purpose in the particular context, and that it takes into account values implications and social consequences, intended or unintended. For Messick, it is these considerations, taken together, that need to be taken into account in validation. Brown sees these issues of relevance, utility, values implications, and social consequences as being "unavoidably central" (2008, p. 280) to curriculum development and integral to his testing-context analysis. The same applies to evaluation within the ecological view of language teaching and learning that we have described. Furthermore, the

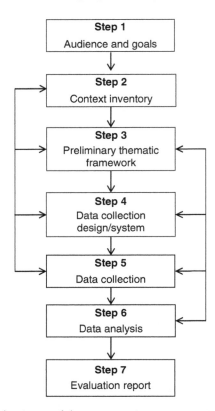

Figure 10.1   The context-adaptive model. *Source*: Lynch, B. K. (1990) A Context-Adaptive Model for Program Evaluation, *TESOL Quarterly*, 24 (1): 25.

consideration of values implications and social consequences carries with it a consideration of ethical implications in the interpretations made in the assessment or evaluation. We consider that the ethical implications are particularly intense in the intercultural context of communication, and indeed teaching, learning, assessment, and evaluation.

There is no doubt that Messick's (1989a, 1989b) integrated conception of validity, adopted by Brown (2008) in his attention to test-context analysis, is challenging, particularly in relation to formative and less formal contexts of evaluation. But it is exactly the interpretations made in all aspects of the ecology of teaching and learning that are the focus of teaching and learning within an intercultural orientation, and therefore we contend that this is a challenge that cannot be bypassed.

Lynch's (1990, 1996, 2003) CAM (Figure 10.1) provides a process for beginning to address the challenge of evaluation in this light. Although it formalizes the process of evaluation, the model can also be applied in less formal contexts of evaluation, where it gradually becomes the regular way in which participants think about their program.

The first step (*audience and goals*) involves identifying the multiple audiences (participants, "stakeholders"). This includes those responsible for the program, those interested in the program, and those who are participants in the program (students and teachers). Participants may be primary or secondary, depending on the context. According to Lynch, these audiences will have different goals or purposes for the evaluation, some related to administration and others related to teaching and learning purposes. These goals need to be articulated, including potential tensions across diverse perspectives.

The second step (*context inventory*) focuses on the details of the context. This includes time, group allocations, the availability of resources, program conditions, participants, program characteristics, theoretical, practical and philosophical influences, and socio-political and cultural aspects (see Lynch (1996, pp. 5–6) for a context inventory, and Lynch (2003, pp. 18–19) for sets of questions relevant to the context).

In step 3 (*preliminary thematic framework*) and as part of the development of the context inventory, themes relating to the evaluation goals will begin to emerge, including, for example, particular tensions, issues about levels of support available, relationships, and the status of the programs. This preliminary thematic framework will inform the design of the data collection.

At step 4 (*data collection design/system*), important decisions about the paradigm to be used for the design of the data collection come into play. These decisions about data collection also derive from the context and goals. Fundamentally (bearing in mind the scope: formative–summative, informal–formal, internal–external), the question to be addressed is: What type (nature and extent) of evidence will be needed to make a defensible argument? From the response to this question, data gathering processes can be developed to gather the necessary evidence. These may include various kinds of tests, surveys, questionnaires, observations, interview, portfolios, or diaries.

In step 5 (*data collection*), data are gathered according to the design for data collection. In step 6 (*analysis*), processes are established for undertaking the analysis. The nature of the analysis will depend on decisions about paradigms, previously informed by the audience, goals, and context. The nature and sufficiency of the evidence, the defensibility of the interpretations made, and the conclusions reached are complex and critical considerations at this point.

The final step (*evaluation report*) is the preparation of the evaluation report. The report must be useful to the audiences and responsive to the goals. There are important considerations here for how to successfully communicate the findings to diverse audiences.

The seven steps provide a means for ensuring that the evaluation is: carefully planned; systematic; conducted with sensitivity to audiences, goals, and context; based on evidence gathered from multiple sources; and interrelated in a way that addresses the fundamental goals of improvement in learning while respecting the qualities of defensibility and ethicality. What is also important is the decision-making that follows an evaluation. In this regard, Aoki, a Japanese-Canadian curriculum researcher, provides insight into reflection and action in curriculum evaluation: "Reflection by the evaluator and by participants allows new questions to emerge from the situation, which, in turn, leads to further reflective activity. Reflection, however, is not only oriented toward making conscious the unconscious by discovering underlying interests, assumptions and intentions, but it is also oriented toward action guided by the newly gained conscious, critical knowledge" (2005, p. 146).

Decisions are required that will lead to further action to ensure that necessary improvements are made, which over time and in their turn will also be subject to evaluation. In this way, the language program remains dynamic and evaluation becomes an ongoing part of an inquiry-based approach to teaching and learning and the overall stance that teachers and students develop as part of their experience of the language program. In this sense of inquiry, the process of evaluation is gradually integrated into the educational culture of teaching and learning that characterizes the particular language program.

The Principles for Teaching and Learning Languages and Implications for Evaluation

Having considered the process of evaluation, we now turn to a consideration of evaluation specifically within an intercultural perspective. The set of principles for teaching and learning languages that we proposed in Chapter 4 can be used as a framework for setting out some general implications for evaluation. In line with the concepts of stance and perspective as continuously forming and influencing the interpretations, judgments, and decisions of teachers, we frame the implications primarily for teachers as evaluators of their own programs in all aspects, as they gradually develop self-awareness as teachers. Table 10.1 sets out qualities to be captured in an evaluation of a program conducted within an intercultural perspective, and the corresponding features of the evaluation process itself that respect this perspective.

Though not exhaustive, the implications of the set of principles for program evaluation outlined above are intended to convey a flavor of the qualities sought in evaluation of a language program developed within an intercultural orientation, and some of the features of the process of evaluation itself. Specific evaluative questions within an intercultural perspective can be developed for any aspect of the program. The example below sets out questions that could be used to evaluate the goals, objectives, and outcomes of a language program developed within an intercultural perspective:

- Do the goals, objectives, and outcomes of my program focus on a range of opportunities for discovering the variability of meaning-making?
- Do they include a deliberate awareness of the language-and-culture-specific assumptions and biases inevitable in constructing knowledge?
- Do they include comparisons across languages and cultures in responding to sociocultural similarities and differences?
- Do they include learners' reflection on their own values and interpretive systems in evaluating "knowing" as social action?
- Do they cater for the development of an intercultural identity, that engenders intercultural sensitivity?
- Do they capture the scope of learning? What has been included or excluded, as requirements or expectations? (Papademetre and Scarino, forthcoming)

These kinds of questions can be used informally by teachers reflecting upon or evaluating their own program. They can equally be used as part of a formal evaluation. They focus on recognizing the way in which an intercultural perspective shapes both the frame of reference for the evaluation and the process of evaluation, as indeed any other perspective on language teaching and learning would do.

Table 10.1 Program evaluation for intercultural language teaching and learning

Principle for teaching and learning languages	Qualities of the program that reflect an intercultural perspective	Features of the evaluation process that respect an intercultural perspective
Active construction	Students' processes of interpretation and meaning-making in communicating in variable contexts, and their reflection on self and others in this process Students' experiences of language using and learning and their evolving understanding of the social, cultural, and linguistic construction of action and knowledge Language teaching and learning itself as an enculturating process	Includes various participants, including students as co-agents and contributors to the evaluation Evaluation process is actively constructed
Making connections	Development of students' capability to: connect the multidimensional knowledge in their learning connect their intrapersonal/intracultural and interpersonal/intercultural development recognize that their personal way of experiencing, interpreting, and understanding the world is enacted interactively and comparatively	Connects multiple sources of evidence relating to the various aspects of the evaluation Considers actions, values and consequences and their relationships
Social interaction	Experiences that develop personal understanding of how to: communicate across languages and cultures develop intercultural sensitivity in communication Interactions both inside and beyond the classroom The role of collective discussion, noticing, comparing and supporting multiple perspectives and values The development of learners' and teachers' understanding of the reciprocal relationship between one's own linguistic, cultural, and communication system and that of the target language	Incorporates multiple perspectives Incorporates dialogue in the evaluation process to allow diverse insights into the experience of the program to emerge and become available for discussion

(Continued on p. 176)

Table 10.1 (*Continued*)

Principle for teaching and learning languages	Qualities of the program that reflect an intercultural perspective	Features of the evaluation process that respect an intercultural perspective
Reflection	The development of students' capability to: decenter and reflect critically on their participation in and contribution to communication and on their language learning reflect when they compare and contrast interpret the variable aspects of communication and interaction within their own and across cultures Emphasis on ways in which enculturation affects how people see the world, communicate, and reflect on communication The teachers' reflective stance and self-awareness about teaching, learning, and their language program	Uses evaluation as a process of reflection on the development of students' language learning – as language users, as language learners and as people, and the reciprocal roles of teachers and learners in the process Utilizes reflection on the way individuals' interpretations and actions as learners and teachers are shaped by their own culturally constructed framework
Responsibility	The development of students': sense of responsibility and self-awareness as participants in communication and as learners within linguistic and cultural diversity understanding of ethical commitments in communicating and learning to communicate with others The responsibility of the teacher to continue to develop an intercultural stance	Recognizes the language teacher's responsibility: to the learners and the wider community for the development of the quality of the language program as a whole Recognizes the responsibility of other stakeholders in the program

Source: Lynch, Brian K. (1990) A Context-Adaptive Model for Program Evaluation, *TESOL Quarterly*, 24 (1): 23–42.

Evaluation and Teacher Professional Learning

Evaluation requires a commitment on the part of teachers and educational authorities to ongoing professional learning to ensure that teachers, as *a* (if not *the*) central resource in students' language learning, continue to resource themselves. Professional learning encompasses teachers' own experiences of and reflection on their continuing participation in the languages and cultures of interest to them, as practiced in contemporary times. It also includes continually developing their professional learning about and experimentation with the dynamic constructs of the field of language education. Crichton describes this as developing an investigative stance, which he describes as

> being alert to what is going on in the classroom, noticing developments and changes, attending to emergent needs, comparing achievements at one point in time with what has happened before and what might happen after, reflecting on teaching practice and assessment, evaluating activities and plans, developing and drawing on curriculums and the host of other activities that contribute to effective teaching practice. (2008, p. 32)

This investigative stance is integral to ways of working and thinking critically about teaching and learning languages within an intercultural perspective, in contexts of increasing linguistic and cultural diversity.

Conclusion

We have argued in this book for a reconceptualization of language, culture, and learning and their interrelationships as the key constructs that are integrated in language education and in the theories and processes that underlie it. Evaluation is the process that sustains this ecology as a living and evolving whole. The principles for intercultural learning we articulated in Chapter 4 provide a frame of reference for evaluation and underpin processes of language, culture, teaching, learning, assessment, resources, and planning as an engagement with interculturality in the context of language teaching and learning.

To conclude both this chapter and this book we consider language teaching and learning as requiring action and interpretive understanding across languages and cultures. Interpretive understanding is not a passive activity but an integral part of the lived experience of language teaching and learning. As Gadamer explains:

> Understanding, like action, always remains a risk and never leaves the room for the simple application of a general knowledge of rules to the statements or texts to be understood. Furthermore, where it is successful, understanding means a growth in inner awareness, which as a new experience enters into the texture of our own mental experience. Understanding is an adventure and, like any other adventure is dangerous. ... But ... [i]t is capable of contributing in a special way to the broadening of our human experiences, our self-knowledge, and our horizon, for everything understanding mediates is mediated along with ourselves. (1981, pp. 109–110)

The needs of the language learner as language user are not only those language capabilities which allow them to produce utterances in the target language but also to interpret them. This involves a shift towards seeing language as the integration of the linguistic system, social practice, and interpretation. People who communicate in an additional language cannot be unreflective communicators, but rather need to become intercultural mediators interpreting the world for themselves and for others. Such people need to see the power of language in human life and its potential to limit or expand horizons. Language and culture interact to shape perceptions and understandings of the world and language learning is an invitation to reconsider what and how we perceive and understand, and the role of language and culture in this. This reconsidering allows the possibility of becoming an active participant in linguistic and cultural diversity.

For us, active participation in linguistic and cultural diversity is both the starting point for and the goal of languages education. It is the perspective through which teachers understand and enact their practice and the end toward which learning contributes. If the goal of language learning is to communicate with people from diverse cultures this has important implications for the theory and practice of language teaching and learning. As we have argued, it involves an expanded view of language, culture, and learning and their relationships, which in turn necessitate an integrated, holistic, dynamic understanding of what is involved in teaching and learning languages. In particular, it involves a refocusing on languages as ways of making, communicating, and interpreting meaning and the learning of a language as an encounter with new ways of meaning.

Language teaching and learning lies at the intersection of languages and cultures as it is language learners who need to be the locus at which languages and cultures meet. It is through making sense of languages and cultures as meaning and acknowledging the diversity of meanings that people make and interpret that the language learner becomes open to the realities and richness of human diversity. In fact, we see diversity as the central feature of language education. Each learner will encounter languages and cultures in individual ways and each language teacher will bring a unique experience and understanding of the languages and cultures in their teaching context. We have attempted in this book to capture some of the implications of this diversity for theory and practice in language education and to articulate what it means to teach and learn languages from an intercultural perspective.

References

Abdallah-Pretceille, M. (2003) *Former et éduquer en contexte hétérogène*, Economica, Paris.

Abdullah, N. and Chandran, S. K. D. O. (2009) Cultural Elements in Malaysian English Language Textbooks, http://ddms.usim.edu.my/handle/123456789/713 (accessed January 31, 2010).

Adaskou, K., Britten, D., and Fahsi, B. (1990) Design decisions on the cultural content of a secondary English course for Morocco. *ELT Journal*, 44 (1): 3–10.

Al-Asmari, A. A. (2008) Integration of foreign culture into pre-service EFL teacher education: A case study of Saudi Arabia. University of Melbourne, Melbourne.

Alderson, C. J. (2005) *Diagnosing Foreign Language Proficiency: The Interface Between Learning and Assessment*, Continuum, London.

Alptekin, C. (2002) Towards intercultural communicative competence in ELT. *ELT Journal*, 56 (1): 57–64.

Andrews, S. (2007) Phase 1 Teacher Participant Example: Chinese Year 9: Establishing Relationships, http://www.iltlp.unisa.edu.au/doclibexamples/iltlp_example_chinese_yr9.doc (accessed October 31, 2012).

Anthony, E. M. (1963) Approach, method, and technique. *ELT journal*, 17 (2): 63–67.

Aoki, T. T. (2005) Interests, knowledge and evaluation: Alternative approaches to curriculum evaluation, in *Curriculum in a New Key. The Collected Works of Ted. T. Aoki* (eds W. F. Pinar and R. L. Irwin), Lawrence Erlbaum, Mahwah, NJ, pp. 137–150.

Arnold, E. (1991) Authenticity revisited: How real is real? *English for Specific Purposes*, 10 (3): 237–244.

Ashworth, P. (2004) Understanding as the transformation of what is already known. *Teaching in Higher Education*, 9 (2): 147–158.

Atkinson, D. (2002) Toward a sociocognitive approach to second language acquisition. *The Modern Language Journal*, 86: 525–545.

Bachman, L. F. (2007) What is the construct? The dialectic of abilities and contexts in defining constructs in language assessment, in *Language Testing Reconsidered* (eds J. Fox, M. Wesche, D. Bayliss, L. Cheng, C. E. Turner, and C. Doe), University of Ottowa Press, Ottowa, pp. 41–72.

Bachman, L. F. and Palmer, A. (1996) *Language Testing in Practice*, Oxford University Press, Oxford.

Intercultural Language Teaching and Learning, First Edition. Anthony J. Liddicoat and Angela Scarino.
© 2013 Anthony J. Liddicoat and Angela Scarino. Published 2013 by Blackwell Publishing Ltd.

Bakhtin, M. M. (1981) *The Dialogic Imagination: Four Essays* (trans. C. Emerson and M. Holquist), University of Texas Press, Austin, TX.

Bakhtin, M. M. (1984) *Problems of Dostoevsky's Poetics* (trans. C. Emerson), Manchester University Press, Manchester.

Barab, S. A., Hay, K. E., and Duffy, T. M. (1998) Grounded constructions and how technology can help. *Technology Trends*, 43 (2): 15–23.

Bateman, B. E. (2002) Promoting openness toward culture learning: Ethnographic interviews for students of Spanish. *Modern Language Journal*, 86 (3): 318–331.

Bauer, B., deBenedette, L., Furstenberg, G., Levet, S., and Waryn, S. (2006) Internet-mediated intercultural foreign language education: The Cultura Project, in *Internet-Mediated Intercultural Foreign Language Education* (eds J. A. Belz and S. L. Thorne), Heinle and Heinle, Boston, MA, pp. 31–62.

Bayart, J.-F. (2002) *The Illusion of Cultural Identity*, University of Chicago Press, Chicago, IL.

Beacco, J.-C. (2000) *Les dimensions culturelles des enseignements de langue*, Hachette, Paris.

Béal, C. (1990) It's all in the asking: A perspective on cross-cultural communication between native speakers of French and native speakers of Australian English in the workplace, in *Cross-cultural Communication in the Professions in Australia* (ed. A. Pauwels), Applied Linguistics Association of Australia, Melbourne, pp. 23–52.

Béal, C. (1992) Did you have a good weekend: Or why there is no such thing as a simple question in cross-cultural encounters. *Australian Review of Applied Linguistics*, 15 (1): 23–52.

Belz, J. A. (2002) Social dimensions of telecollaborative foreign language study. *Language Learning and Technology*, 6 (1): 60–81.

Belz, J. A. (2003) Linguistic perspectives on the development of intercultural competence in telecollaboration. *Language Learning and Technology*, 7 (2): 68–99.

Belz, J. A. (2005) Intercultural questioning, discovery and tension in internet-mediated language learning partnerships. *Language and Intercultural Communication*, 86 (3): 318–331.

Belz, J. A. and Kinginger, C. (2002) Cross-linguistic development of address form use in telecollaborative language learning: Two case studies. *Revue Canadienne des Langues Vivantes*, 59 (2): 189–214.

Bhabha, H. K. (1994) *The Location of Culture*, Routledge, New York.

Bignell, J. (2007) Phase 1 Teacher Participant Example: Japanese Years Prep–10: Programme for Years Prep–1: "We are one, but we are many" http://www.iltlp.unisa.edu.au/doclibexamples/iltlp_example_japanese_prep_yr1.pdf (accessed October 31, 2012).

Birenbaum, M. (1996) Assessment 2000. Towards a pluralistic approach to assessment, in *Alternatives in Assessment of Achievement, Learning Processes and Prior Knowledge* (eds M. Birenbaum and F. J. R. C. Dochy), Kluwer Academic, Boston, pp. 3–30.

Black, P. J., Harrison, C., Lee, C., Marshall, B., and Wiliam, D. (2002) *Working Inside the Black Box. Assessment for Learning in the Classroom*, NFER Nelson, London.

Black, P. J. and Jones, J. (2006) Formative assessment and the learning and teaching of MFL: Sharing the languages learning road map with learners. *Language Learning Journal*, 34 (1): 4–9.

Black, P. J. and Wiliam, D. (1998) Assessment and classroom learning. *Assessment in Education: Principles, Policy and Practice*, 5 (1): 7–74.

Block, D. (1996) "Not so fast!" Some thoughts on theory culling, relativism, accepted findings and the heart and soul of SLA. *Applied Linguistics*, 17: 65–83.

Bonk, C. J., Appelman, R., and Hay, K. E. (1996) Electronic conferencing tools for student apprenticeship and perspective taking. *Educational Technology*, 36 (5): 8–18.

Bonk, C. J. and King, K. S. (1998) *Electronic Collaborators: Learner-Centered Technologies for Literacy, Apprenticeship, and Discourse*, Mahwah, NJ: Lawrence Erlbaum.

Bourdieu, P. (1982) *Langage et pouvoir symbolique*, Arthème-Fayard, Paris.

Bourke, J. M. (2006) Designing a topic-based syllabus for young learners. *ELT Journal*, 60 (3): 279–286.

Breen, M. P. (1987) Contemporary paradigms in syllabus design, part I. *Language Teaching*, 20 (2): 81–91.

Brindley, G. (2001) Outcomes-based assessment in practice: Some examples and emerging insights. *Language Testing*, 18 (4): 393–408.

Brooks, N. (1975) The analysis of language and familiar cultures, in *The Cultural Revolution in Foreign Language Teaching* (ed. R. Lafayette), National Textbook, Lincolnwood, IL, pp. 19–31.

Brown, J. D. (2008) Testing-context analysis. Assessment is just another part of language. *Language Assessment Quarterly*, 54 (4): 275–312.

Brumfit, C. J. (1984) *Communicative Methodology in Language Teaching: The Roles of Fluency and Accuracy*, Cambridge University Press, Cambridge.

Bruner, J. (1996) *The Culture of Education*, Harvard University Press, Cambridge, MA.

Bullough, R. V. (2006) Developing interdisciplinary researchers: Whatever happened to the humanities in education? *Educational Researcher*, 35 (8): 3–10.

Bygate, M., Skehan, P., and Swain, M. (eds). (2001) *Research Pedagogic Tasks: Language Learning, Teaching and Testing*, Longman, London.

Byram, M. (1988) Foreign language education and cultural studies. *Language, Culture and Curriculum*, 1 (1): 15–31.

Byram, M. (1989a) *Cultural Studies in Foreign Language Education*, Multilingual Matters, Clevedon.

Byram, M. (1989b) A school visit to France: Ethnographic explorations. *British Journal of Language Teaching*, 27 (2): 99–103.

Byram, M. (1991) Teaching culture and language: An integrated model, in *Mediating Languages and Cultures* (eds D. Buttjes and M. Byram), Multilingual Matters, Clevedon, pp. 17–30.

Byram, M. (1997) *Teaching and Assessing Intercultural Communicative Competence*, Multilingual Matters, Clevedon.

Byram, M. (2002) On being "bicultural" and "intercultural", in *Intercultural Experience and Education* (eds G. Alred, M. Byram, and M. P. Fleming), Multilingual Matters, Clevedon, pp. 50–66.

Byram, M. (2008) *From Foreign Language Education to Education for Intercultural Citizenship*, Multilingual Matters, Clevedon.

Byram, M. and Feng, A. (2005) Teaching and researching intercultural competence, in *Handbook of Research in Second Language Teaching and Learning* (ed. E. Hinkel), Lawrence Erlbaum, Mahwah, NJ, pp. 911–930.

Byram, M., Gribkova, B., and Starkey, H. (2002) *Developing the Intercultural Dimension in Language Teaching. A Practical Introduction for Teachers*, Council of Europe, Strasbourg.

Byram, M. and Snow, D. (1997) *Crossing Frontiers. The School Study Visit Abroad*, Centre for Information on Language Teaching, London.

Byram, M. and Zarate, G. (1994) *Définitions, objectifs et évaluation de la compétence socio-culturelle*, Report for the Council of Europe, Strasbourg.

Byrnes, H., Maxim, H. H., and Norris, J. M. (2010) Realizing advanced L2 writing development in collegiate FL education: Curricular design, pedagogy, and assessment. *Modern Language Journal* 94 (Monograph Issue).

Canale, M. and Swain, M. (1981) Theoretical bases of communicative approaches to second language teaching and testing. *Applied Linguistics*, 1: 1–47.

Candlin, C. (1987) Towards task-based learning, in *Language Learning Tasks* (eds C. Candlin and D. Murphy), Prentice Hall, Eaglewood Cliffs, NJ, pp. 5–23.

Carel, S. (2001) Students as virtual ethnographers: Exploring the language culture connections, in *Developing Intercultural Competence in Practice* (eds M. Byram, A. Nichols, and D. Stevens), Multilingual Matters, Clevedon, pp. 146–161.

Carey, J. W. (1989) *Communication as Culture: Essays on Media and Society*, Routledge, New York and London.

Carney, N. (2007) Language study through blog exchanges, in *Proceedings of the 2nd International Wireless Ready Symposium Podcasting Education and Mobile Assisted Language Learning* (ed. M. Thomas), http://wirelessready.nucba.ac.jp/Carney.pdf (accessed April 9, 2010).

Carr, J. (1999) From "sympathetic" to "dialogic" imagination: Cultural study in the foreign language classroom, in *Striving for the Third Place: Intercultural Competence through Language Education* (eds J. Lo Bianco, A. J. Liddicoat, and C. Crozet), Language Australia, Melbourne, pp. 103–112.

Carroli, P., Hillman, R., and Maurer, L. (1999) Australian perspectives on (inter)national narratives in *Striving for the Third Place: Intercultural Competence through Language Education* (eds J. Lo Bianco, A. J. Liddicoat, and C. Crozet), Language Australia, Melbourne, pp. 155–166.

Chalhoub-Deville, M. (2003) Second language interaction: Current perspectives and future trends. *Language Testing*, 20 (4): 369–383.

Chomsky, N. (1959) Review of *Verbal Behaviour* by B.F. Skinner. *Language*, 35 (1): 26–58.

Chomsky, N. (1981) *Lectures on Government and Binding*, Foris, Dordrecht.

Clark, J. L. (1987) *Curriculum Renewal in School Foreign Language Learning*, Oxford University Press, Oxford.

Clark, J. L., Scarino, A., and Brownell, J. A. (1994) *Improving the Quality of Learning. A Framework for Target-Oriented Curriculum Renewal in Hong Kong*, Hong Kong Institute of Language in Education, Hong Kong.

Clarke, M. A. (1983) The scope of approach, the importance of method, and the nature of techniques, in *Georgetown University Round Table on Language and Linguistics* (eds J. E. Alatis, H. H. Stem, and P. Strevens), Georgetown University Press, Washington, DC, pp. 106–115.

Clarke, M. A. and Silberstein, S. (1988) Problems, prescriptions, and paradoxes in second language teaching. *TESOL Quarterly*, 22: 685–700.

Cochran-Smith, M. and Lytle, S. (1999) Relationships of knowledge and practice: Teacher learning in communities. *Review of Research in Education*, 24: 249–306.

Cohen, A. D. (1994) *Assessing Language Ability in the Classroom*, Heinle and Heinle, Boston, MA.

Coleman, J. A. (1997) Residence abroad within language study. *Language Teaching*, 30 (1): 1–20.

Coleman, J. A. (1998) Language learning and study abroad: The European perspective. *Frontiers: The Interdisciplinary Journal of Study Abroad*, 4 (1): 167–205.

Cook, G. (2010) *Translation in Language Teaching*, Oxford University Press, Oxford.

Corbett, J. (2003) *An Intercultural Approach to English Language Teaching*, Multilingual Matters, Clevedon.

Council of Europe. (2001) *Common European Framework of Reference for Languages*, University of Cambridge Press and Council of Europe, Cambridge.

Crawford-Lange, L. M. and Lange, D. L. (1984) Doing the unthinkable in the language classroom: A process for integrating langauge and culture, in *Teaching for Proficiency: The Organising Principle* (ed. T. V. Higgins), National Textbook, Lincolnwood, IL, pp. 139–177.

Crichton, J. (2008) Why an investigative stance matters in intercultural language teaching and learning: An orientation to classroom-based investigation. *Babel*, 43 (1): 31–33, 39.

Crozet, C. and Liddicoat, A. J. (1999) The challenge of intercultural language teaching: Engaging with culture in the classroom, in *Striving for the Third Place: Intercultural Competence through Language Education* (eds J. Lo Bianco, A. J. Liddicoat, and C. Crozet), Language Australia, Melbourne, pp. 113–126.

Curnow, T. J. (2009) Communication in introductory linguistics. *Australian Journal of Linguistics*, 29 (1): 27–44.

Damen, L. (1987) *Culture Learning: The Fifth Dimension in the Language Classroom*, Addison-Wesley, Reading, MA.

Daniels, M., Berglund, A., and Petre, M. (1999) Reflections on international projects in undergraduate CS education. *Computer Science Education*, 9 (3): 256–267.

Davies, A. (1991) *The Native Speaker in Applied Linguistics*, Edinburgh University Press, Edinburgh.

Davies, A. (2005) *A Glossary of Applied Linguistics*, Edinburgh University Press, Edinburgh.

Delandshere, G. (2002) Assessment as inquiry. *Teachers College Record*, 104 (7): 1461–1484.

Diller, K. C. (1975) Some new trends for applied linguistics and foreign language teaching in the United States. *TESOL Quarterly*, 9 (1): 65–73.

Duranti, A. (1997) *Linguistic Anthropology*, Cambridge University Press, Cambridge.

Eckert, P. and McConnell-Ginet, S. (1992) Think practically and look locally: Language and gender as community-based practice. *Annual Review of Anthropology*, 21: 461–490.

Eco, U. (2003) *Mouse or Rat? Translation as Negotiation*, Wiedenfeld and Nicolson, London.

Eisenchlas, S. (2009) Conceptualising "communication" in second language acquisition. *Australian Journal of Linguistics*, 29 (1): 45–58.

Elissondo, G. (2001) Representing Latino/a culture in Introductory textbooks. Paper presented at The National Association of African American Studies, National Association of Hispanic and Latino Studies, National Association of Native American Studies, and International Association of Asian Studies, Houston, TX.

Ellis, R. (2003) *Task-Based Language Learning and Teaching*, Oxford University Press, Oxford.

Ellis, R. (2010) Theoretical pluralism in SLA: Is there a way forward? In *Conceptualising "Learning" in Applied Linguistics* (eds P. Seedhouse, S. Walsh, and C. Jenks), Palgrave Macmillan, Basingstoke, pp. 23–51.

Elola, I. and Oskoz, A. (2008) Blogging: fostering intercultural competence development in foreign language and study abroad contexts. *Foreign Language Annals*, 41 (3): 454–477.

Fabos, B. and Young, M. D. (1999) Telecommunication in the classroom: Rhetoric versus reality. *Review of Educational Research*, 69 (3): 217–259.

Fanselow, J. F. (1987) *Breaking Rules*, Longman, New York.

Farrell, T. S. C. (2002) Lesson planning, in *Methodology in Language Teaching: An Anthology of Current Practice* (eds J. C. Richards and W. A. Renandya), Cambridge University Press, Cambridge, pp. 30–39.

Fasold, R. (1992) Qué es la lengua? *WINAK: Boletín Intercultural*, 7 (1–4): 61–68.

Firth, A. and Wagner, J. (1997) On discourse, communication and (some) fundamental concepts in SLA research. *The Modern Language Journal*, 81 (3): 285–300.

Fitch, W. T., Hauser, M. D., and Chomsky, N. (2005) The evolution of the language faculty: Clarifications and implications. *Cognition*, 97 (2): 179–210.

Fitzgerald, H. (2002) *How Different Are We? Spoken Discourse in Intercultural Communication*, Multilingual Matters, Clevedon.

Foster, M. (2007) Assessing the Intercultural in Language Learning, Unpublished Project Report, Research Centre for Languages and Cultures, University of South Australia.

Fox, J. (2008) Alternative assessment, in *Encyclopaedia of Language and Education*, 2nd edn (eds E. Shohamy and N. H. Hornberger), Vol. 7, *Language Testing and Assessment*, Springer and Business Media LLC, New York, pp. 97–109.

Freeman, D. and Richards, J. C. (1993) Conceptions of teaching and the education of second language teachers. *TESOL Quarterly*, 27 (2): 193–216.

Furstenberg, G. (2003) Reading between the cultural lines, in *Reading Between the Lines: Perspectives on Foreign Language Literacy* (ed. P. C. Patrikis), Yale University Press, New Haven, CT, pp. 74–98.

Furstenberg, G., Levet, S., English, K., and Maillet, K. (2001) Giving a virtual voice to the silent language of culture: the Culura project. *Language Learning and Technology*, 5 (1): 55–102.

Gadamer, H.-G. (1976) *Philosophical Hermeneutics* (trans. D. E. Linge), University of California Press. Berkeley, CA.

Gadamer, H.-G. (1981) *Reason in the Age of Science* (trans. F. G. Lawrence), MIT Press, Cambridge, MA.

Gadamer, H.-G. (2004) *Truth and Method*, 2nd edn (trans. J. Weinsheimer and D. G. Marshall), Continuum, New York.

Gallagher, S. (1992) *Hermeneutics and Education*, SUNY Press, Albany, NY.

Gee, J. P. (2008) A sociocultural perspective on opportunity to learn, in *Assessment, Equity and Opportunity to Learn* (eds P. A. Moss, D. C. Pullin, J. P. Gee, E. H. Haertel, and L. J. Young), Cambridge University Press, Cambridge, pp. 255–392.

Geertz, C. (1973) *The Interpretation of Cultures*, Basic Books, New York.

Geertz, C. (1983) *Local Knowledge*, Basic Books, New York.

Gipps, C. V. (1999) Sociocultural aspects of assessment. *Review of Research in Education*, 24: 355–392.

Gipps, C. V. and Stobart, G. (2003) Alternative assessment, in *International Handbook of Educational Evaluation: Practice* (eds T. Kellaghan and D. L. Stufflebeam), Kluwer, Dordrecht, pp. 549–575.

Gohard-Radenkovic, A., Lussier, D., Penz, H., and Zarate, G. (2004) La médiation culturelle en didactique des langues comme processus, in *La médiation culturelle et didactique des langues* (eds G. Zarate, A. Gohard-Radenkovic, D. Lussier, and H. Penz), Council of Europe Publishing, Strasbourg, pp. 225–238.

Gould-Drakeley, M. (2005) Intercultural Language Teaching and Learning in Practice Project. Unpublished Report, Research Centre for Languages and Cultures, University of South Australia.

Greenhow, C., Robelia, B., and Hughes, J. E. (2009) Web 2.0 and classroom research: What path should we take? *Educational Researcher*, 38 (4): 246–259.

Gumperz, J. J. (1982a) *Discourse Strategies*, Cambridge University Press, Cambridge.

Gumperz, J. J. (1982b) *Language and Social Identity*, Cambridge University Press, Cambridge.

Haertel, E. H., Moss, P. A., Pullin, D. C., and Gee, J. P. (2008) Introduction, in *Assessment Equity and Opportunity to Learn* (eds P. A. Moss, D. C. Pullin, J. P. Gee, E. H. Haertel, and L. J. Young), Cambridge University Press, New York, pp. 1–16.

Halliday, M. A. K. (1993) Towards a language-based theory of learning. *Linguistics and Education*, 5: 93–116.

Hammerley, H. (1991) *Fluency and Accuracy: Toward Balance in Language Teaching and Learning*, Multilingual Matters, Clevedon.

Hanna, B. E. and de Nooy, J. (2003) A funny thing happened on the way to the forum: Electronic discussion and foreign language learning. *Language Learning and Technology*, 7 (1): 71–85.

Hargreaves, D. (2005) *About Learning: Report to the Working Group*, Demos, London.

Harris, R. (2003) On redefining linguistics, in *Rethinking Linguistics* (eds H. G. Davis and T. J. Taylor), Routledge, London, pp. 17–68.

Haugh, M. and Liddicoat, A. J. (2009) Examining conceptualisations of communication. *Australian Journal of Linguistics*, 29 (1): 1–10.

Hauser, M. D., Chomsky, N., and Fitch, W. T. (2002) The faculty of language: What is it, who has it, and how does it evolve? *Science and Education*, 298: 1569–1579.

Heath, S. B. (1986) *Beyond Language: Social and Cultural Factors in Schooling Language Minority Students*, California State Department of Education, Sacramento, CA.

Holliday, A. (2010) *Intercultural Communication and Ideology*, Sage, London.

Holmes, J. and Meyerhoff, M. (1999) The community of practice: Theories and methodologies in language and gender research. *Language in Society*, 28: 173–183.

House, J. (2008) What is an "intercultural speaker"? in *Intercultural Language Use and Language Learning* (eds E. Alcón Soler and M. P. Safont Jordà), Springer-Verlag, pp. 7–21.

House, J. and Kasper, G. (2000) How to remain a non-native speaker, in *Kognitive Aspekte des Lehrens und Lernens von Fremdsprachen [Cognitive Aspects of Foreign Language Learning and Teaching], Festschrift für Willis J. Edmondson zum 60. Geburtstag* (ed. C. Riemer), Narr, Tübingen, pp. 101–118.

Hymes, D. H. (1974) *Foundations in Sociolinguistics: An Ethnographic Approach*, University of Pennsylvania Press, Pennsylvania.

Hymes, D. H. (1986) Models of interaction and social life, in *Directions in Sociolinguistics* (eds J. J. Gumperz and D. H. Hymes), Basil Blackwell, Oxford.

James, M. and Brown, S. (2005) Grasping the nettle: Preliminary analysis of some enduring issues surrounding the improvement of learning outcomes. *The Curriculum Journal*, 16 (1): 7–30.

Jayasuriya, K. (1990) *The Problematic of Culture and Identity in Cross-cultural Theorising.* Department of Social Work and Social Administration, University of Western Australia, Nedlands, WA.

Jurasek, R. (1995) Using ethnography to bridge the gap between study abroad and the on-campus language and culture curriculum, in *Redefining the Boundaries of Language Study* (ed. C. Kramsch), Heinle and Heinle, Boston, pp. 221–249.

Kalantzis, M. and Cope, B. (2008) *New Learning: Elements of a Science of Education*, Cambridge University Press, Melbourne.

Kasper, G. (1997) The role of pragmatics in language teacher education, in *Beyond Methods: Components of Second Language Teacher Education* (eds K. Bardovi-Harlig and B. Hartford), McGraw-Hill, New York, pp. 113–136.

Kasper, G. (2006) Speech acts in interaction: Towards discursive pragmatics, in *Pragmatics and Language Learning* (eds K. Bardovi-Harlig, C. Félix-Brasdefer, and A. Omar), University of Hawai'i Press, Honolulu, pp. 281–314.

Kerbrat-Orecchioni, C. (1993) Variations culturelles et universaux dans les systèmes conversationnels, in *Inter-actions: L'interaction, actualités de la recherche et enjeux didactiques* (ed. J.-F. Halté), Centre d'Analyse Syntaxique de l'Université de Metz, Metz. pp. 61–90.

Kern, R. and Liddicoat, A. J. (2008) De l'apprenant au locuteur/acteur, in *Précis de plurilinguisme et du pluriculturalisme* (eds G. Zarate, D. Lévy, and C. Kramsch), Éditions des archives contemporaines, Paris, pp. 27–65.

Kirkpatrick, A. (1991) Information sequencing in Mandarin letters of request. *Anthropological Linguistics*, 33 (2): 183–203.

Knutson, E. M. (2006) Cross-cultural awareness for second/foreign language learners. *Canadian Modern Language Review*, 62 (4): 591–610.

Kohler, M. (2003) Developing continuity through long-term programming. *Babel*, 38 (2): 9–16, 38.

Kohler, M. (2010) Moving between knowing and being: A case study of language teachers' mediation of the intercultural in practice. University of South Australia, Adelaide, SA.

Kohonen, V. (1992) Experiential language learning: Second language learning as cooperative learner education, in *Collaborative Language Learning and Teaching* (ed. D. Nunan), Cambridge University Press, Cambridge, pp. 14–39.

Kohonen, V. (2000) Student reflection in portfolio assessment: making language learning more visible. *Babylonia*, 1 (13–16).

Kramsch, C. (1986) From language proficiency to interactional competence. *Modern Language Journal*, 70 (4): 366–372.

Kramsch, C. (1987a) Foreign language textbook's construction of foreign reality. *Canadian Modern Language Review*, 44 (1): 95–199.

Kramsch, C. (1987b) Foreign language textbooks' construction of reality. *Canadian Modern Language Review*, 43: 95–119.

Kramsch, C. (1988) The cultural discourse of foreign language textbooks, in *Toward a New Integration of Language and Culture* (ed. A. J. Singerman), Northeast Conference on the Teaching of Foreign Languages, Middlebury, VT, pp. 63–88.

Kramsch, C. (1993a) *Context and Culture in Language Education*, Oxford University Press, Oxford.

Kramsch, C. (1993b) Language study as border study: Experiencing difference. *European Journal of Education*, 28 (3): 349–358.

Kramsch, C. (1994) Foreign languages for a global age. *ADFL Bulletin*, 25 (1): 5–12.

Kramsch, C. (1995a) The cultural component of language teaching. *Language, Culture and Curriculum*, 8 (1): 83–92.

Kramsch, C. (1995b) Introduction: Making meaning visible, in *Redefining the Boundaries of Language Study* (ed. C. Kramsch), Heinle and Heinle, Boston, pp. ix–xxxiii.

Kramsch, C. (ed.). (1995c) *Redefining the Boundaries of Language Study*, Heinle and Heinle, Boston.

Kramsch, C. (1998) Teaching along the cultural faultline, in *Culture as the Core: Interdisciplinary Perspectives on Culture Teaching and Learning in the Second Language Curriculum* (eds R. M. Paige, D. L. Lange, and Y. A. Yershova), CARLA, University of Minnesota, Minneapolis, pp. 15–32.

Kramsch, C. (1999) The privilege of the intercultural speaker, in *Language Learning in Intercultural Perspective: Approaches through Drama and Ethnography* (eds M. Byram and M. Fleming), Cambridge University Press, Cambridge, pp. 16–31.

Kramsch, C. (2002) Introduction: "How can we tell the dancer from the dance?", in *Language Acquisition and Language Socialisation* (ed. C. Kramsch), Continuum, London, pp. 1–30.

Kramsch, C. (2003) From practice to theory and back again, in *Context and Culture in Language Teaching and Learning* (eds M. Byram and P. Grundy), Multilingual Matters, Clevedon, pp. 4–17.

Kramsch, C. (2006) From communicative competence to symbolic competence. *Modern Language Journal*, 90 (2): 249–252.

Kramsch, C. (2008) Ecological perspectives on foreign language education. *Language Teaching*, 41 (3): 389–408.

Kramsch, C. (2009) *The Multilingual Subject*, Oxford University Press, Oxford.

Kramsch, C. and Nolden, T. (1994) Redefining literacy in a foreign language. *Die Unterrichtspraxis*, 27 (1): 28–35.

Kramsch, C. and Thorne, S. L. (2002) Foreign language learning as a global communicative practice, in *Globalization and Language Teaching* (eds D. Block and D. Cameron), Routledge, London, pp. 83–100.

Kramsch, C. and Whiteside, A. (2007) Three fundamental concepts in second language acquisition and their relevance in multilingual contexts. *Modern Language Journal*, 91: 907–922.

Kramsch, C. and Whiteside, A. (2008) Language ecology in multilingual settings. Towards a theory of symbolic competence. *Applied Linguistics*, 29 (4): 645–671.

Krashen, S. D. (1982) *Principles and Practice in Second Language Acquisition*, Prentice-Hall, Hemel Hempstead.

Kumaravadivelu, B. (1994) The postmethod condition: (E)merging strategies for second/foreign language teaching. *TESOL Quarterly*, 28 (1): 27–48.

Kumaravadivelu, B. (2003) *Beyond Methods: Macrostrategies for Language Teaching*, Yale University Press, New Haven, MA.

Lafayette, R. C. (1978) *Teaching Culture: Strategies and Techniques*, Harcourt Brace Jovanovich, Arlington, VA.

Lantolf, J. P. (1996) SLA theory building: Letting all the flowers bloom. *Language Learning*, 46: 713–749.

Lantolf, J. P. (2000) Second language learning as a mediated process. *Language Teaching*, 33: 79–96.

Lantolf, J. P. and Poehner, M. E. (2008) Dynamic assessment, in *Encyclopaedia of Language and Education*, 2nd edn (eds E. Shohamy and N. H. Hornberger), Vol. 7, *Language Testing and Assessment*, Springer and Business Media LLC, New York, pp. 273–284.

Lantolf, J. P. and Poehner, M. E. (2010) Dynamic assessment in the classroom: Vygotskian praxis for second language development. *Language Teaching Research*, 15 (1): 11–33.

Lantolf, J. P. and Thorne, S. L. (2006) *Sociocultural Theory and the Genesis of Second Language Development*, Oxford University Press, New York.

Larsen-Freeman, D. (2001) Grammar, in *The Cambridge Guide to Teaching English to Speakers of Other Languages* (eds R. Carter and D. Nunan), Cambridge University Press, Cambridge, pp. 34–41.

Larsen-Freeman, D. (2010) Having and doing. Learning from a complexity theory perspective, in *Conceptualising "Learning" in Applied Linguistics* (eds P. Seedhouse, S. Walsh, and C. Jenks), Palgrave Macmillan, Basingstoke, pp. 52–68.

Larsen-Freeman, D. and Cameron, L. (2008) *Complex Systems and Applied Linguistics*, Oxford University Press, Oxford.

Lave, J. and Wenger, E. (1991) *Situated Learning: Legitimate Peripheral Participation*, Cambridge University Press, Cambridge.

Levine, D. R. and Adelman, M. B. (2002) *Beyond Language: Cross-Cultural Communication*, Prentice Hall, Upper Saddle River, NJ.

Levy, M. (2007) Culture, culture learning and new technologies: Towards a pedagogical framework. *Language Learning and Technology*, 11 (2): 104–127.

Liaw, M. (2006) E-learning and the development of intercultural competence. *Language Learning and Technology*, 10 (3): 49–64.

Liddicoat, A. J. (1997a) Everyday speech as culture: Implications for language teaching, in *Teaching Languages, Teaching Cultures* (eds A. J. Liddicoat and C. Crozet), Applied Linguistics Association of Australia, Canberra, pp. 55–70.

Liddicoat, A. J. (1997b) Interaction, social structure and second language use: A response to Firth and Wagner. *Modern Language Journal*, 81 (3): 313–317.

Liddicoat, A. J. (2000) Everyday speech as culture: Implications for language teaching, in *Teaching Languages, Teaching Cultures* (eds A. J. Liddicoat and C. Crozet), Applied Linguistics Association of Australia, Canberra, pp. 51–64.

Liddicoat, A. J. (2002) Static and dynamic views of culture and intercultural language acquisition. *Babel*, 36 (3): 4–11, 37.

Liddicoat, A. J. (2004a) The conceptualisation of the cultural component of language teaching in Australian language-in-education policy. *Journal of Multilingual and Multicultural Development*, 25 (4): 297–317.

Liddicoat, A. J. (2004b) Language policy and methodology. *International Journal of English Studies*, 4 (1): 153–171.

Liddicoat, A. J. (2005a) Corpus planning: Syllabus and materials development, in *Handbook of Research in Second Language Teaching and Learning* (ed. E. Hinkel), Lawrence Erlbaum, Mahwah, NJ, pp. 993–1012.

Liddicoat, A. J. (2005b) Culture for language learning in Australian language-in-education policy. *Australian Review of Applied Linguistics*, 28 (2): 1–28.

Liddicoat, A. J. (2005c) Teaching languages for intercultural communication, in *An International Perspective on Language Policies, Practices and Proficiencies* (eds D. Cunningham and A. Hatoss), Editura Fundaţiei Academice Axis and Fédération Internationale des Professeurs de Langues Vivantes, Belgrave, pp. 201–214.

Liddicoat, A. J. (2007) Discourses of the self and other: *Nihonjinron* and the intercultural in Japanese language-in-education policy. *Journal of Multicultural Discourses*, 2 (1): 1–15.

Liddicoat, A. J. (2008) Pedagogical practice for integrating the intercultural in language teaching and learning. *Japanese Studies*, 28 (3): 277–290.

Liddicoat, A. J. (2009) Communication as culturally contexted practice: A view from intercultural communication. *Australian Journal of Linguistics*, 29 (1): 115–133.

Liddicoat, A. J., Crozet, C., and Lo Bianco, J. (1999) Striving for the third place: Consequences and implications, in *Striving for the Third Place: Intercultural Competence through Language Education* (eds J. Lo Bianco, A. J. Liddicoat, and C. Crozet), Language Australia, Melbourne, pp. 1–20.

Liddicoat, A. J. and Curnow, T. J. (2003) Language descriptions, in *Handbook of Applied Linguistics* (eds A. Davies and C. Elder), Blackwell, Oxford, pp. 25–53.

Liddicoat, A. J. and Kohler, M. (2012) Teaching Asian languages from an intercultural perspective: Building bridges for and with students of Indonesian, in *Bridging Transcultural Divides: Teaching Asian Languages and Cultures in a Globalising Academy* (eds X. Song and K. Cadman), University of Adelaide Press, Adelaide, SA, pp. 73–100.

Liddicoat, A. J., Papademetre, L., Scarino, A., and Kohler, M. (2003) *Report on Intercultural Language Learning*, Department of Education, Science and Training, Canberra.

Liddicoat, A. J. and Scarino, A. (2010) Eliciting the intercultural in foreign language education, in *Testing the Untestable in Foreign Language Education* (eds A. Paran and L. Sercu), Multilingual Matters, Clevedon, pp. 52–73.

Lincoln, Y. S. and Guba, E. G. (2000) Paradigmatic controversies, contradictions and emerging confluences, in *Handbook of Qualitative Research*, 2nd edn (eds N. K. Denzin and Y. S. Lincoln), Sage. Thousand Oaks, CA, pp. 163–188.

Littlejohn, A. P. (1998) The analysis of language teaching materials: Inside the Trojan Horse, in *Materials Development in Language Teaching* (ed. B. Tomlinson), Cambridge University Press, Cambridge, pp. 190–216.

Littlewood, W. (1981) *Communicative Language Teaching: An Introduction*, Cambridge University Press, Cambridge.

Littlewood, W. (2004) Second language learning, in *Handbook of Applied Linguistics* (eds A. Davies and C. Elder), Blackwell, Oxford, pp. 501–524.

Long, M. H. (1985) Input and second language acquisition theory, in *Input in Second Language Acquisition* (eds S. M. Gass and C. C. Madden), Newbury House, Rowley, MA, pp. 377–393.

Long, M. H. (1996) The role of linguistic environment in second language acquisition, in *Handbook of Second Language Acquisition* (eds W. C. Ritchie and T. K. Bhatia), Blackwell, Malden, MA, pp. 413–468.

Lui, Y. (2005) The contruction of culture knowledge in Chinese language textbooks, in *Struggles over Difference: Curriculum, Texts, and Pedagogy in the Asia Pacific* (eds Y. Nozaki, R. Openshaw, and A. Luke), SUNY Press, Albany, NY, pp. 99–114.

Lynch, B. K. (1990) A context-adaptive model for program evaluation. *TESOL Quarterly*, 24 (1): 23–42.

Lynch, B. K. (1996) *Language Program Evaluation: Theory and Practice*, Cambridge University Press, Cambridge.

Lynch, B. K. (2003) *Language Assessment and Programme Evaluation*, Edinburgh University Press, Edinburgh.

Magnan, S. S., Martin-Berg, L., Berg, W. J., and Ozello, Y. R. (2002) *Paroles*, 2nd edn, John Wiley & Sons, Inc., New York.

Makoni, S. and Pennycook, A. (2005) Disinventing and (re)constituting languages. *Critical Inquiry in Language Studies: An International Journal*, 2 (3): 137–156.

Malinowski, B. (1960) *A Scientific Theory of Culture and Other Essays*, 2nd edn, Oxford University Press, New York.

Maurer, L., Carroli, P., and Hillman, R. (2000) Teaching literature across cultures and across art-forms, in *Teaching Languages, Teaching Cultures* (eds A. J. Liddicoat and C. Crozet), Language Australia, Melbourne, pp. 89–104.

Mayes, C. (2005) *Teaching Mysteries: Foundations of Spiritual Pedagogy*, University Press of America, Lanham, MD.

McCoy, J. D. and Ketterlin-Geller, L. R. (2004) Rethinking instructional delivery for diverse student populations: Serving all learners with concept-based instruction. *Intervention in School and Clinic*, 40 (2): 88–95.

McGroarty, M. (1996) Language attitudes, motivation and standards, in *Sociolinguistics and Language Teaching* (eds S. L. McKay and N. H. Hornberger), Cambridge University Press, Cambridge, pp. 3–46.

McKay, S. L. (2004) Western culture and the teaching of English as an international language. *English Language Forum*, 42 (2): 10–15.

McNamara, T. (1996) *Measuring Second Language Performance*, Addison Wesley Longman, London.

McNamara, T. (2001) Language assessment as social practice: Challenges for research. *Language Testing Journal*, 18 (4): 333–349.

McNamara, T. (2003) Tearing us apart again. The paradigm war and the search for validity. *EUROSLA Yearbook*, 3: 229–238.

McNamara, T. and Roever, C. (2006) *Language Testing: The Social Dimension*, Blackwell. Oxford.

Messick, S. (1989a) Meaning and values in test validation. The science and ethics of assessment. *Educational Researcher*, 18 (2): 5–11.

Messick, S. (1989b) Validity, in *Educational Measurement*, 3rd edn (ed. R. L. Linn), Macmillan, New York, pp. 13–104).

Mohan, B. A. (2001) The second language as a medium of learning, in *English as a Second Language in the Mainstream: Teaching, Learning and Identity* (eds B. A. Mohan, C. Leung, and C. Davison), Longman, New York, pp. 107–126.

Mohan, B. A. and Huang, J. (2002) Assessing the integration of language and content in a Mandarin as a foreign language classroom. *Linguistics and Education*, 13 (3): 405–433.

Moore, C. (2006) Assessing the intercultural in language learning. Unpublished Project Report, Research Centre for Languages and Cultures, University of South Australia.

Morrow, K. (ed.). (2004) *Insights from the Common European Framework*, Oxford University Press, Oxford.

Moss, P. A. (1996) Enlarging the dialogue in educational measurement: Voices from interpretive research traditions. *Educational Reviewer*, 25 (1): 20–28, 43.

Moss, P. A. (2008) Sociocultural implications for assessment: Classroom assessment, in *Assessment, Equity and Opportunity to Learn* (eds P. A. Moss, D. C. Pullin, J. P. Gee, E. H. Haertel, and L. J. Young), Cambridge University Press, Cambridge, pp. 222–258.

Moss, P. A., Girard, B. J., and Hanniford, L. C. (2006) Validity in educational assessment. *Review of Research in Education*, 30 (1): 109–162.

Murphy-Lejeune, E. (2003) An experience of interculturality: Student travelers abroad, in *Intercultural Experience and Education* (eds G. Alred, M. Byram, and M. P. Fleming), Multilingual Matters, Clevedon, pp. 101–113.

Norton, B. (2000) *Identity and Language Learning: Gender, Ethnicity and Educational Change*, Longman, London.

Norton, B. and Toohey, K. (2002) Identity and language learning, in *The Oxford Handbook of Applied Linguistics* (ed. R. B. Kaplan), Oxford University Press, New York, pp. 113–123.

Nostrand, H. L. (1974) Empathy for a second culture: Motivations and techniques, in *Responding to New Realities* (ed. G. A. Jarvis), National Textbook, Skokie, IL, pp. 263–327.

Nunan, D. (1988) *The Learner-centred Curriculum*, Cambridge University Press, Cambridge.

Nunan, D. (2004) *Task-based Language Teaching*, Cambridge University Press, Cambridge.

O'Brien, A. and Alfano, C. L. (2009) Connecting students globally through video-conference pedagogy. *Journal of On-line Teaching*, 5 (4): 657–684, http://jolt.merlot.org/vol5no4/obrien_1209.pdf (accessed October 31, 2012).

O'Dowd, R. (2003) Understanding the "other side": Intercultural learning in a Spanish–English e-mail exchange. *Language Learning and Technology*, 7 (2): 118–144.

Odlin, T. (1994) Introduction, in *Perspectives of Pedagogical Grammar* (ed. T. Odlin), Cambridge University Press, Cambridge, pp. 1–22.

Oring, E. (1986) Folk narratives, in *Folk Groups and Folk Genres* (ed. E. Oring), Utah State University Press, Logan, UT, pp. 121–145.

Ortega, L. (2009) Acquisition, participation and in-betweenness as metaphors for L2 learning. Paper presented at the First Combined ALANZ/ALAA Conference (Applied Linguistics Association of New Zealand and Applied Linguistics Association of Australia).

Paavola, S., Lipponen, L., and Hakkarainen, K. (2004) Models of innovative knowledge and three metaphors of learning. *Review of Educational Research*, 74 (4): 557–576.

Paige, R. M., Jorstad, H., Siaya, L., Klein, F., and Colby, J. (1999) Culture learning in language education: A review of the literature, in *Culture as the Core: Integrating Culture into the Language Curriculum* (eds R. M. Paige, D. L. Lange and Y. A. Yeshova), University of Minnesota, Minneapolis, pp. 47–113.

Papademetre, L. and Scarino, A. (forthcoming) Reflections on practice: Given a set of principles for intercultural teaching and learning, what are the implications for languages pedagogy? *Australian Review of Applied Linguistics*.

Pauwels, A. (2000) Globalisation and the impact of teaching languages in Australia, in *Teaching Languages, Teaching Cultures* (eds A. J. Liddicoat and C. Crozet), Language Australia, Melbourne, pp. 19–26.

Pennycook, A. (1989) The concept of method, interested knowledge, and the politics of language teaching. *TESOL Quarterly*, 23: 589–618.

Perkins, D. and Unger, C. (1999) Teaching for understanding and learning, in *Instructional-Design Theories and Models: A New Paradigm of Instructional Theory* (ed. C. Reigeluth), Erlbaum, Mahwah, NJ, pp. 92–114.

Phipps, A. and Gonzales, M. (2004) *Modern Languages: Learning and Teaching in an Intercultural Field*, Sage, London.

Prabhu, N. S. (1984) Procedural syllabuses, in *Trends in Language Syllabus Design* (ed. T. E. Read), Singapore University Press/RELC, Singapore, pp. 272–280.

Prabhu, N. S. (1987) *Second Language Pedagogy*, Oxford University Press, Oxford.

Prabhu, N. S. (1990) There is no best method. Why? *TESOL Quarterly*, 24: 161–176.

Pulverness, A. (2003) Material for cultural awareness, in *Developing Materials for Language Teaching* (ed. B. Tomlinson), Continuum, London, pp. 426–438.

Reeves, T. C. (2003) Storm clouds on the digital education horizon. *Journal of Computing in Higher Education*, 15 (1): 3–26.

Richards, J. C. (1981) Method: Approach, design, procedure. *TESOL Quarterly* 16 (2): 153–168.

Richards, J. C. and Rodgers, T. S. (1986) *Approaches and Methods in Language Teaching*, Cambridge University Press, Cambridge.

Risager, K. (2007) *Language and Culture Pedagogy: From a National to Transnational Paradigm*, Multilingual Matters, Clevedon.

Rivers, W. M. (1981) *Teaching Foreign Language Skills*, 2nd edn, Chicago University Press, Chicago.

Roberts, C., Byram, M., Barro, A., Jordan, S., and Street, B. (2001) *Language Learners as Ethnographers*, Multilingual Matters, Clevedon.

Robinson, P. (2001) Task complexity, task difficulty and task production: Exploring interactions in a componential framework. *Applied Linguistics*, 22 (1): 27–57.

Robinson-Stuart, G. and Nocon, H. (1996) Second culture acquisition: Ethnography in the foreign language classroom. *Modern Language Journal*, 80 (4): 431–449.

Rogan, P. and Hoffman, F. (2003) *Katzensprung 1*, Heinemann, Melbourne.

Rong, F. (2009) Une étude méta-réflexive du Cadre européen commun de référence dans la perspective de son adaptation au contexte chinois. *Le français dans le monde: Recherches et applications*, 46: 88–97.

Sacks, H. (1975) Everyone has to lie, in *Sociocultural Dimensions of Language Use* (eds M. Sounches and B. G. Blount), Multilingual Matters, Clevedon, pp. 57–80.

Sacks, H. (1984) On doing "being ordinary", in *Structures of Social Interaction* (eds J. M. Atkinson and J. Heritage), Cambridge University Press, Cambridge, pp. 413–429.

Saussure, F. (1916) *Cours de linguistique générale*, Payot, Paris.

Saville-Troike, M. (1999) Extending "communicative" concepts in the second language curriculum: A sociolinguistic perspective, in *Culture as the Core: Interdisciplinary Perspectives on Culture Teaching and Learning in the Second Language Curriculum* (eds R. M. Paige, D. L. Lange, and Y. A. Yershova), CARLA, University of Minnesota, Minneapolis, pp. 1–14.

Scarino, A. (1995) Planning, describing and monitoring long-term progress in language learning. *Babel*, 30 (3): 4–13.

Scarino, A. (2000) Complexities in describing and using standards in language education in the school setting: Whose conceptions and values are at work? *Australian Review of Applied Linguistics*, 23 (2): 7–20.

Scarino, A. (2005a) Introspection and retrospection as windows on teacher knowledge, values, ethical dispositions, in *Second Language Teacher Education: International Perspectives* (ed. D. J. Tedick), Lawrence Erlbaum, New York.

Scarino, A. (2005b) Teacher judgments. Going beyond criteria for judging performance. *Babel*, 29 (3): 8–16, 38.

Scarino, A. (2008) The role of assessment in policy-making for languages education in Australian schools: A struggle for legitimacy and diversity. *Current Issues in Language Planning*, 9 (3): 344–362.

Scarino, A. (2009) Assessing intercultural capability in learning languages: Some issues and considerations. *Language Teaching*, 42 (1): 67–80.

Scarino, A. (2010) Assessing intercultural capability in learning languages: A renewed understanding of language, culture, learning and the nature of assessment. *The Modern Language Journal*, 94 (2): 324–329.

Scarino, A. and Liddicoat, A. J. (2009) *Language Teaching and Learning: A Guide*, Curriculum Corporation, Melbourne.

Scarino, A. and Papademetre, L. (forthcoming) Investigating cultural variability in the intercultural context of assessment of an Australian ESL syllabus in Malaysia: A case study.

Schmidt, G. and Jansen, L. M. (2004) Enhancing overseas study, in *Australian Perspectives on Internationalising Education* (eds A. J. Liddicoat, S. Eisenchlas, and S. Trevaskes), Language Australia, Melbourne, pp. 129–139.

Schmidt, R. (1990) The role of consciousness in second language learning. *Applied Linguistics*, 11 (1): 17–46.

Schmidt, R. (1993) Consciousness, learning and interlanguage pragmatics, in *Interlanguage Pragmatics* (eds G. Kasper and S. Blum-Kulka), Oxford University Press, New York, pp. 21–42.

Schwandt, T. A. (2000) Three epistemological stances for qualitative inquiry: Interpretation, hermeneutics, and social constructionism, in *Handbook of Qualitative Research*, 2nd edn (eds N. K. Denzin and Y. S. Lincoln), Sage, Thousand Oaks, CA, pp. 189–214.

Sedunary, M., Posterino, N., Kearns, S., and Tarascio-Spiller, M. (2007) *Ecco! Uno*, Heinemann, Melbourne.

Seedhouse, P., Walsh, S., and Jenks, C. (eds). (2010) *Conceptualising "Learning" in Applied Linguistics*, Palgrave Macmillan, Basingstoke.

Sercu, L. (2004) Assessing intercultural competence: A framework for systematic test development in foreign language education and beyond. *Intercultural Education*, 15 (1): 73–89.

Sercu, L. (2008) La formation de l'acteur/locuteur: Enseignement comme aide ou entrave, in *Précis de plurilinguisme et du pluriculturalisme* (eds G. Zarate, D. Lévy, and C. Kramsch), Éditions des archives contemporaines, Paris, pp. 55–58.

Sewell, W. H., Jr. (1999) The concept(s) of culture, in *Beyond the Cultural Turn* (eds V. E. Bonnell and L. Hunt), University of California Press, Berkeley, CA, pp. 35–61.

Sfard, A. (1998) On two metaphors for learning and the dangers of choosing just one. *Educational Researcher*, 27: 4–13.

Shen, F. (1989) The classroom and the wider culture: Identity as a key to learning English composition. *College Composition and Communication*, 40 (4): 459–466.

Shepard, L. A. (2000) The role of assessment in a learning culture. *Educational Researcher*, 29 (7): 4–14.

Shepard, L. A. (2006) Classroom assessment, in *Educational Measurement*, 4th edn (ed. R. L. Brenman), American Council on Education/Praeger Publishers, Westport, CT, pp. 623–464.

Shohamy, E. (2007a) *Language Policy: Hidden Agendas and New Approaches*, Routledge, London and New York.

Shohamy, E. (2007b) Tests as power tools. Looking back. Looking forward, in *Language Testing Reconsidered* (eds J. Fox, M. Wesche, D. Bayliss, L. Cheng, C. E. Turner, and C. Doe), University of Ottowa Press, Ottowa, pp. 141–152.

Shohamy, E. (2008) Language policy and language assessment: The relationship. *Current Issues in Language Planning*, 9 (3): 363–373.

Shopen, G. (1993) Semantics as a resource for teaching critical literacy. *Australian Review of Applied Linguistics*, 16 (1): 1–18.

Skehan, P. (1996) A framework for the implementation of task-based instruction. *Applied Linguistics*, 17 (1): 38–62.

Skehan, P. (1998) *A Cognitive Approach to Language Learning*, Oxford University Press, Oxford.

Skehan, P. (2003) Task-based instruction. *Language Teaching*, 36 (1): 1–14.

Sobolewski, P. (2009) Use of ethnographic interviews as a resource for developing intercultural understanding. *Babel*, 43 (2): 28–33.

Stern, H. H. (1983) *Fundamental Considerations in Language Teaching*, Oxford University Press, Oxford.

Svalberg, A. M.-L. (2007) Language awareness and language learning. *Language Teaching*, 40: 287–308.

Swain, M. (1995) Three functions of output in second language learning, in *Principles and Practice in Applied Linguistics* (eds G. Cook and B. Seidlhofer), Oxford University Press, Oxford, pp. 234–250.

Swain, M. (2006) Languaging, agency and collaboration in advanced second language proficiency, in *Advanced Language Learning: The Contribution of Halliday and Vygotsky* (ed. H. Byrnes), Continuum, London, pp. 95–108.

Swain, M. and Deters, P. (2007) "New" mainstream SLA theory: Expanded and enriched. *Modern Language Journal*, 91: 820–836.

Swidler, A. (1986) Culture in action: Symbols and strategies. *American Sociological Review*, 51 (2): 273–286.

Tajfel, H. and Turner, J. C. (1986) The social identity theory of intergroup behaviour, in *The Social Psychology of Intergroup Relations* (eds W. G. Austin and S. Worchel), Nelson-Hall, Chicago, MI, pp. 220–237.

Teasdale, A. and Leung, C. (2000) Teacher assessment and psychometric theory: A case of paradigm crossing? *Language Testing*, 17 (2): 163–184.

Thomas, J. (1983) Cross-cultural pragmatic failure. *Applied Linguistics*, 4 (2): 91–112.

Thomas, J. (1984) Cross cultural discourse as unequal encounter: Towards a pragmatic analysis. *Applied Linguistics*, 5 (3): 226–235.

Toyoda, E. and Harrison, R. (2002) Categorization of text chat communication between learners and native speakers of Japanese. *Language Learning and Technology*, 6 (1): 82–99.

Tudini, V. (2007) Negotiating and intercultural learning in Italian native speaker chat rooms. *Modern Language Journal*, 91 (4): 575–601.

Van Ek, J. A. (1986) *Objectives for Modern Language Learning*, Council of Europe, Strasbourg.

Van Lier, L. (1994) Forks and hope: Pursuing understanding in different ways. *Applied Linguistics*, 15: 328–347.

Van Lier, L. (2000) From input to affordance: Social-interactive learning from an ecological perspective, in *Sociocultural Theory and Second Language Learning* (ed. J. P. Lantolf), Oxford University Press, Oxford, pp. 245–259.

Van Lier, L. (2002) An ecological-semiotic perspective on language and linguistics, in *Language Acquisition and Language Socialization. Ecological Perspectives* (ed. C. Kramsch), Continuum, London, pp. 140–164.

Van Lier, L. (2004) *The Ecology and Semiotics of Language Learning. A Sociocultural Perspective*, Kluwer, Boston.

Vatrapu, R. K. (2008) Cultural considerations in computer supported collaborative learning. *Research and Practice in Technology Enhanced Learning*, 3 (2): 59–201.

Venuti, L. (2006) *The Translator's Invisibility: A History of Translation*, Routledge, London.

Vygotsky, L. S. (1978) *Mind in Society. The Development of Higher Psychological Processes* (trans. M. Cole), Harvard University Press, Cambridge, MA.

Warschauer, M. (1998) Online learning in sociocultural context. *Anthropology and Education Quarterly*, 29 (1): 68–88.

West, R. (1994) Needs analysis in language teaching. *Language Teaching*, 27 (1): 1–19.

White, L. (2003) *Second Language Acquisition and Universal Grammar*, Cambridge University Press, Cambridge.

Widdowson, H. G. (1983) *Learning Purpose and Language Use*, Oxford University Press, Oxford.

Widdowson, H. G. (1994) The ownership of English. *TESOL Quarterly*, 28 (2): 377–388.

Widdowson, H. G. (1998) Context, community and authentic language. *TESOL Quarterly*, 32 (4): 705–716.

Wierzbicka, A. (1979) Ethno-syntax and the philosophy of grammar. *Studies in Language*, 3: 313–383.

Wierzbicka, A. (1985) Different cultures, different languages, different speech acts. *Journal of Pragmatics*, 9: 145–178.

Wierzbicka, A. (1986) Does language reflect culture? Evidence from Australian English. *Language in Society*, 15: 349–373.

Wierzbicka, A. (1991) *Cross-Cultural Pragmatics: The Semantics of Human Interaction*, Mouton de Gruyter, Berlin.

Wiliam, D., Lee, C., Harrison, C., and Black, P. J. (2004) Teachers developing assessment for learning: Impact on student achievement. *Assessment in Education. Principles, Policy and Practice*, 11 (1): 49–65.

Wilkins, D. A. (1972) Grammatical, situational and notional syllabuses. *AILA Proceedings, 1972*, Julius Gross Verlag, Heidelberg, pp. 254–265.

Willis, J. (1996) *A Framework for Task-Based Learning*, Longman, London.

Windschitl, M. (1998) The WWW and classroom research: What path should we take? *Educational Researcher*, 37 (1): 28–33.

Wittgenstein, L. (1953) *Philosophische Untersuchungen*, Blackwell, Oxford.

Woodward, T. (2001) *Planning Lessons and Courses: Designing Sequences of Work for the Language Classroom*, Cambridge University Press, Cambridge.

Yoshino, K. (1992) *Cultural Nationalism in Contemporary Japan: A Sociological Enquiry*, Routledge, London and New York.

Zarate, G. (1983) Objectiver le rapport culture maternelle/culture étrangère. *Le français dans le monde*, 181: 34–39.

Zarate, G. (1986) *Enseigner une culture étrangère*, Hachette, Paris.

Zarate, G. (1993) *Représentations de l'étranger et didactique des langues*, Didier, Paris.

Zemiro, J. and Chamberlain, A. (2004) *Tapis volant 2*, 2nd edn, Thomson Nelson, South Melbourne.

Index

Tables are indicated in **bold**, figures in *italic*, and boxes in ***bold and italic***.

Intercultural Language Teaching and Learning, First Edition. Anthony J. Liddicoat and Angela Scarino.
© 2013 Anthony J. Liddicoat and Angela Scarino. Published 2013 by Blackwell Publishing Ltd.